Clear and Effective
Legal Writing

Clear and Effective Legal Writing

Veda R. Charrow
AMERICAN INSTITUTES FOR RESEARCH

Myra K. Erhardt
AMERICAN INSTITUTES FOR RESEARCH

LITTLE, BROWN AND COMPANY
Boston and Toronto

Library of Congress Catalog Card No. 84-80740
ISBN 0-316-13771-5

Eighth Printing

The contents of this book were developed under grant
No. GOO-80-04754 from the Fund for the Improvement
of Post-secondary Education, Education Department.
However, these contents do not necessarily represent the
policy of that agency, and you should not assume
endorsement by the Federal Government.

BB

Published simultaneously in Canada by Little, Brown &
Company (Canada) Limited

Printed in the United States of America

The following people were contributors to the project that resulted in this book.

Consultants

Larry A. Bakken
Hamline University School of Law

Daniel O. Bernstine
University of Wisconsin Law School

Robert P. Charrow
Member, Washington, D.C. and California Bar

Andrew J. King
University of Maryland School of Law

Sallyanne Payton
University of Michigan Law School

Jane Peterson
Dallas Community College District

Janice C. Redish
American Institutes for Research

Chris Williams
University of Maryland School of Law

Richard C. Wydick
University of California at Davis School of Law

Advisors

Norman Brand
Member, ABA Committee on Legal Writing

Michael H. Cardozo
Member, ABA Committee on Legal Writing

Fred J. Emery
Chairman, ABA Committee on Federal Register Reports and Paperwork

To our children, Elizabeth Charrow and Michael Erhardt

Summary of Contents

Table of Contents

Part III

Part IV

Preface

From 1980 to 1983, the Document Design Center at the American Institutes for Research was awarded a grant, funded by the Fund for the Improvement of Post-secondary Education, to conduct a project to develop and evaluate a course in clear and effective legal writing. The project was an outgrowth of the Document Design Center's studies of legal and bureaucratic writing and projects to help lawyers write clear documents. Besides ourselves — a linguist and a lawyer-writer — the project also involved seven law professors and two writing and language specialists who served as consultants, and an advisory board of three lawyers with experience in clear legal writing.

For lawyers and nonlawyers alike, legal language and legal writing can often be impersonal, ambiguous, confusing, and difficult to understand. Most lawyers believe that their legal writing problems began in law school, where legal writing courses, if they existed, did not teach them how to write clearly and effectively. We wanted to apply our experience and knowledge to discovering why this happens and what can be done about it.

To find out how to make law students and their professors aware of the deficiencies in legal writing, and to help us discover how best to improve law students' writing, we analyzed legal writing texts, law school textbooks and casebooks, and law students' writing samples. We also investigated legal writing teachers' problems in teaching first-year legal writing courses.

With the help of our consultants and advisors, we developed and field tested a course in legal writing. The end product of that course is this book. Clear and Effective Legal Writing follows a conceptually sound model for clear writing, using examples and exercises — many of them taken from students' papers — that are legally oriented. It also takes into account the special constraints that the law and legal situations impose on writing. We hope that it will have a strong impact on the way legal writing is taught, helping to make legal writing clearer and easier for writers and readers alike.

Veda Charrow
Myra Erhardt

December 1984

Acknowledgments

Although we did the majority of the work and the writing for Clear and Effective Legal Writing, it was in many ways a collaborative effort. We would like to thank the following people:

Our consultants and advisors, whose support, advice, and suggestions were invaluable.

Jane Peterson, who performed above and beyond her duty as a consultant, and wrote the Appendix, which is an excellent mini-course in English.

Nancy Campbell, at Little, Brown and Co., for her expertise and hard work in producing Chapter 8 on graphic techniques.

Anthony L. Colasurdo for his memo on the Delaware Automobile Guest Statute.

Professor Lawrence Tribe for his Supreme Court brief, *Larkin v. Grendel's Den.*

Henryk Hiller for his moot court brief, *National Audubon Society v. Clark.*

The support staff at the Document Design Center and especially Sally Dillow, who prepared and proofread the final draft of the manuscript.

And special thanks to Dana Wilson, who did such a fine job of editing our manuscript.

Clear and Effective
Legal Writing

I

1

Introduction

What Is Legal Writing?

The aim of all writing is to communicate. However, when you write legal documents, you will have special concerns: You may be writing for a highly specialized audience and you may have to accommodate the idiosyncracies and constraints of legal writing. Although you may write about many subjects, your subject matter will almost always be affected by the legal aspects or the legal ramifications of whatever subject you are addressing.

Even though legal writing is specialized, effective writing and effective legal writing share the same characteristics: Both require clarity, logical organization, precision, and conciseness. Effective legal writing successfully communicates not only the facts and the law involved in a particular situation, but also your point of view and conclusions as an advocate. In order to communicate clearly and effectively, you need to understand the unique language of the law, you need to sharpen your writing skills, and you need to carefully plan each document that you write.

Much of the work that law students and lawyers do requires good writing skills. Because this is so, the legal writing course you take in law school is an important one. No matter how accomplished writers become, they can always refine their writing so that it is clearer, more precise, better organized, and more concise. As a law student, you will want to learn how to adapt your present writing style to the requirements and peculiarities of legal documents, as well as to continue to develop your writing skills. In this book we strive to provide you with specific techniques and strategies for accomplishing these goals.

B A Systematic Approach to Writing

This book is designed to help you develop your own writing style in a careful and systematic way. It presents legal writing as a step-by-step process that can help you build writing skills and avoid the pitfalls that can destroy clarity and credibility.

It is valuable to begin any writing task by articulating the steps you plan to take. Carefully thinking through each step will help you construct a complete, well-formed document. It is also worthwhile to place the steps in a workable order, even though you may have to be flexible in the way you carry out various parts of the writing process. As you write, you may end up moving the steps around or even omitting some of them.

A suggested writing plan, based on the chapters of this book, appears on page 5. Whether you use this plan, modify it, or create your own, it is important that you have a writing plan and that you are comfortable with it.

1. Pre-writing Stage

Before you begin to write any legal document, there are several steps that you need to go through. You should clearly identify your purposes and keep them in mind. You must understand your audience — what it knows, what it wants to know, how it will react. You must be aware of any constraints that circumstances, rules, or customs place on the form or content of your document. And you must arrange what you know into a logical sequence. Only then do you begin to apply your writing skills — writing and rewriting to create a document that does what you want it to.

Begin by asking yourself what is the *purpose* of the document — what is it supposed to accomplish? How much material should you include in the document in order to accomplish your purpose? Will there be conflicting messages in the document because you have several purposes but have not thoroughly thought out how to balance them? Are you confused about whether you are trying to persuade or merely inform? The more you work out these conflicts *before* you write, the easier the writing task will be.

Next ask yourself who will use the document. A single document may have more than one *audience:* judges, other attorneys, your client, other private citizens. These diverse audiences may have varying degrees of sophistication and varying needs. Finding the proper amount of information and the right level of sophistication to serve these different audiences is not a

FIGURE 1-1

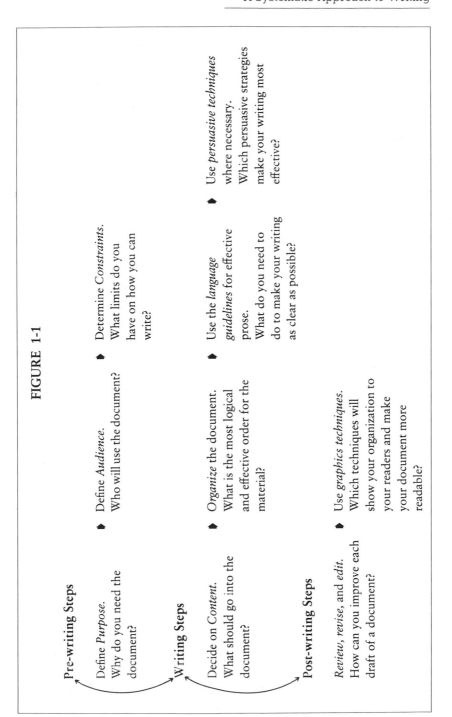

Pre-writing Steps

Define *Purpose*.
Why do you need the document?

▲ Define *Audience*.
Who will use the document?

▲ Determine *Constraints*.
What limits do you have on how you can write?

Writing Steps

▲ *Organize* the document.
What is the most logical and effective order for the material?

Decide on *Content*.
What should go into the document?

▲ Use the *language guidelines* for effective prose.
What do you need to do to make your writing as clear as possible?

▲ Use *persuasive techniques* where necessary.
Which persuasive strategies make your writing most effective?

Post-writing Steps

▲ Use *graphics techniques*.
Which techniques will show your organization to your readers and make your document more readable?

Review, revise, and *edit*.
How can you improve each draft of a document?

simple task. Documents should not be so difficult that they seem obscure to some readers nor so simple that they seem patronizing to others. Keep in mind that even highly sophisticated audiences will appreciate a well-organized, clearly written document.

There are usually *constraints* on what you can do when you write a legal document; you should understand your constraints before you begin to write. Time is a major limitation that attorneys must consider, no matter what legal task they are performing. Practicing attorneys have to juggle the affairs of many clients and still meet court and filing deadlines. In law school, too, you will have deadlines, and you must tailor your writing plans to meet them.

There are often other constraints to deal with, such as format, paper size, mailing requirements, and reproduction needs. Many times these are dictated by courts or by a law firm or agency.

2. Writing Stage

Next you must *organize* your material. Ask yourself what kind of document you are writing: Is it a basic expository document or a more complex document that will require you to present the pros and cons of a particular subject or issue? Once you identify which kind of document you will be producing, you can set up an outline that will help accomplish the ultimate purpose of the document.

After you have organized the document and worked out an outline, then you begin the actual writing. As you write, you use techniques of sentence structure and style to produce clear and readable prose. If the purpose of the document is to persuade, there are specific strategies you can use that will make your document more effective. These include using a logical structure to present your reasoning and carefully choosing vocabulary, grammatical structure, and a discourse structure that will make your arguments more forceful.

3. Post-writing Stage

At this stage, you have a full draft of a document in your hands. This does not mean the job is finished. One draft of a document is rarely enough, especially in legal writing. After you finish a first draft, read through the document critically. This is the time to edit and revise: Check both content and form to make sure that your document is complete, correct, and presented in the best possible way. In the final draft, you will also want to check for typographical errors.

Finally, you will need to give some thought to the best ways of physically presenting the document. There are graphics techniques that you can use to help you make your points more effectively and make the document more pleasing to read.

C Some Comments on the Way This Book Is Written

We've tried to organize this book to be as useful as possible to law students. In Chapter 2 we give some background to explain why legal writing is the way it is and how it got to be that way. Understanding the development of legal language can help you to judge the merits of particular legal constructions and usages. The subsequent chapters parallel the writing plan presented on page 5, moving through the writing process step by step.

We have also chosen to use a writing style that we feel will make the book most useful: The style is intentionally direct and conversational because we felt that this style was the best for communicating our ideas and techniques. This does not mean that the ideas and techniques themselves are simple. You will probably find that many of the exercises are challenging, and you may need to reread portions of the book in order to complete them.

2
Legal
Writing
Distinguished

A Traditional Legal Writing

1. Characteristics of Traditional Legal Writing

Traditional legal writing has many unique characteristics. Some of them have value and reflect the complexity of legal concepts and the nuances of the legal process. Other characteristics, however, are not necessary and survive only because of habit. These include overly long, complicated sentences, intrusive phrases and clauses, redundant phrases, poorly organized sentences and paragraphs, and a host of similar problems that we will discuss in Chapter 5. Legal language also contains unusual and archaic words, phrases, and sentence structures that became part of legal language as the law evolved over the centuries. Often these constructions are so rigid and overused that neither lawyers nor lay people understand them.

a. *Poor Writing*

Some legal writing is simply poor writing. Examples of poor writing can be found in all types of legal writing, even in the opinions of judges. For instance, read the following passage from a court opinion that is often excerpted in contracts casebooks:

> If, on the other hand, the evidence shall disclose that springs such as defendant contracted for were not purchasable in the open market, or were of designs specially adapted for defendant's vehicles and obtainable only by special order to some manufacturer, so that they were not obtainable by such diligence as above defined, and that, by plaintiff's failure to deliver at the time agreed, defendant was prevented from producing from its factory the number of vehicles which, but for the plaintiff's delay in delivering, that factory would, with reasonable cer-

tainty, have produced, and that defendant, with reasonable certainty, would have been able to sell all of such output during the then current season, in such case it is clear the defendant would have lost the difference between the cost of manufacture and the net selling price of the vehicles it was so prevented from manufacturing and selling.

Kelley, Maus & Co. v. LaCrosse Carriage Co., 120 Wis. 84, 91, 97 N.W. 674, 676 (1903).

There is nothing legally complex in this passage — it is just poorly written. When you come across passages such as this in your casebooks, you will probably find yourself mentally "translating" them by untangling the parts of the passage, sorting out all of the information in a sentence, and rearranging the parts into a simpler and more familiar order. You may have some trouble doing this on occasion, because it will be hard to tell which clauses relate to each other and how all of the information fits together.

b. *Archaic Constructions*

Archaic and obsolete constructions also appear in all types of legal documents. For example, you may come across the kind of language that appears in this short excerpt from a form release:

Greetings:
Know ye that I, John Smith of Columbus Ohio, for and in consideration of $3,000 dollars, to me in hand paid by Jane Jones, do by these presents for myself, my heirs and assigns, remise, release, and forever discharge Jane Jones . . .

These constructions may give you pause, until you become accustomed to them. You should not, however, become so accustomed to seeing them that *you* use them, unless they are absolutely necessary.

2. Why Legal Writing Is the Way It Is

Legal writing does not have to have the characteristics in the examples above in order to have legal effect. It retains those characteristics because certain aspects of legal language have evolved separately from the rest of the English language and because through the centuries lawyers have continued to use archaic and poorly written documents as models.

Legal language, like the rest of the English language, has various functions — to explain, elicit information, and persuade, among other things. There are various ways of using different features of language — ways of organizing text, various sentence structures, and vocabulary — that fulfill those functions. Thus, there are typical ways of organizing legal documents to make them more or less persuasive. There are a variety of sentence structures that can be used to make legal documents more or less explanatory. Vocabulary can be used to impress or simply to communicate. But, to many people, the term "legal language" conjures up only jargon, terms of art, and "boilerplate" — the words, phrases, or larger structures whose meanings have been "stabilized" through legal interpretation and that appear to embody the power of the law. This aspect of legal language is what makes it exotic and special and different from other professional jargons as well as from ordinary English. It is also the aspect that is most often criticized by lawyers and nonlawyers alike. This part of legal language is quite distinct from standard English: Its development, which has spanned centuries, has differed in several important ways from the development of ordinary English.[1] These differences stem from historical, sociological, political, and jurisprudential processes; each has helped make legal language a unique variety of English.

3. Foundations of Legal Writing

a. *Historical Factors*

During the period that English common law was evolving, the English language went through a number of linguistic changes. Those changes were not always reflected in legal language. Legal language had its own processes of change and growth, so that its development paralleled but did not always mirror that of the rest of the English language.

Ordinarily, languages change over time through ordinary use — words develop new meanings and old meanings are lost; terms that become archaic drop out of the language; grammatical constructions shift to reflect changes in the status of competing dialects (*ain't* versus *isn't* and *aren't*, for example). Legal terms also change through use. But legal language has developed a number of its forms and meanings through a different process — a legal-historical process. An example of this is the legal meaning of *fresh,* as in *fresh fish.* The lay person will probably understand fresh fish to mean fish that has been recently caught. But the legal definition of fresh fish, which has been set by regulations, is fish that has never been frozen, no matter when it was caught. It is the courts, legislatures, and government agencies that decide the

---

1. There is an excellent discussion of the evolution of legal language in D. Mellinkoff, *The Language of the Law* (1978).

meaning of many legal terms, rather than ordinary usage and historical change.

The meaning of the legal term *negligence* developed through litigation. The term has been refined through a history of appellate court decisions, so that it now has a very specialized meaning in the law. In ordinary usage, *negligence* is synonymous with *carelessness,* but the legal meaning, honed by more than a century of litigation, is much narrower. In California, negligence is

> the doing of something which a reasonably prudent person would not do, or the failure to do something which a reasonably prudent person would do, under a given set of circumstances.

Most legal meanings, like meanings of words in ordinary usage, do have a certain flexibility; there is a range of meanings for a given word. But in the law the range in meaning is a result of different judicial, statutory, or regulatory interpretations or formal negotiations, not of ordinary linguistic processes.

Our legal system is derived from the legal system of England. Legal proceedings and legal writing in England were first done entirely in Latin, then in a mixture of French, Latin, and English, and finally in English alone. This complicated evolution has left us with some unusual clause and phrase structures and a good deal of terminology that is a combination of Latin, French, and archaic English. These archaic constructions and words have survived for a number of reasons. When ordinary English changes, older words are replaced with newer ones, and the meaning of the older words either changes or the words drop out of use. In legal language, on the other hand, older words are not always replaced; rather, new words are simply added to the previously used terms. This creates strings of synonymous words.

As the use of French and Latin was giving way to English in the courts, the English word was often added to the French or Latin word. The lawyers of the time probably feared that in translating French or Latin into English some of the highly specialized meanings of the legal vocabulary would be lost. To avoid this, French or Latin terms were often retained and used *with* the English term to represent a concept. Even though the original problem of multiple languages of the law no longer exists, the following multiple terms are still in active use:

> cease and desist
> null and void
> remise, release, and forever discharge

> good and sufficient
> rest, residue, and remainder
> false and untrue
> acknowledge and confess
> give, devise and bequeath

A number of legal concepts were never translated into English, but have remained in Latin:

> prima facie
> res judicata
> mens rea
> nolo contendere
> habeas corpus

or French:

> in lieu of
> lien
> easement
> tort
> oyez

Also, some archaic English has never been updated:

> witnesseth
> wherein
> aforesaid
> heretofore
> writ

Perhaps the most recognizable example of the use of archaic forms in legal language is the retention of *such, said,* and *which* as demonstrative adjectives or determiners, and *absent* as a preposition. For example, "*said* contract will continue to be in force, *absent* proof that the defendant defrauded the plaintiff."

The differences between legal language and the rest of the English language are not just at the level of words. Whole phrases and clauses exist that have no counterpart in everyday language:

> have you then and there this writ
> malice aforethought
> revoking all wills and codicils by me made
> fee simple (here, the adjective *follows* the noun)

These phrases and clauses, frozen in legal language, come from grammatical constructions that are no longer in general use.

The effect of the independent development of legal language is nicely summed up in the discussion of the word *may* in Black's Law Dictionary. Unlike in ordinary usage, in legal language *may* can carry mandatory meaning. Black's Law Dictionary explains that courts frequently "construe 'may' as 'shall' or 'must' to the end that justice may not be the slave of grammar."[2] Unfortunately, when grammar becomes the slave of justice, the result is often incomprehensible, poorly written documents.

b. *Sociological Factors*

Legal language is the primary tool of the legal professional. Unlike physicians who have instruments and procedures, engineers who have blueprints and computers, and scientists who have microscopes, test tubes, balances, and oscilloscopes, lawyers rely mainly on legal language. True, all professions have a body of thought and theory that is embodied in language, but for lawyers there is only one way of reaching and using this knowledge — through legal language.

In addition, one very important function of legal language is a *performative* function, where the words constitute the act.[3] Legal language carries the force of the law. A person who has been pronounced guilty by a court *is* guilty (whether he or she really is). When a divorce is granted, two people who were previously married are un-married, by a set of written and spoken words. And, interestingly, in most jurisdictions, if a person has been missing for seven years, a court, on petition, can declare that person dead, even though he or she may (without the court's knowledge) be alive and well.

Naturally, it is not legal language by itself that has all this power. Society has granted to certain persons the authority to make decisions over life and property. But these decisions are effected by means of language, and only in law does language carry so much power.

This power of legal language and the fact that the law can only be communicated through it have helped create the ritualistic quality of some legal

2. Black's Law Dictionary 883 (5th ed. 1979).
3. J. Austin, *How to Do Things with Words* (1962).

discourse. The ritualistic quality, in turn, helps to enhance the power of the court. When you hear a uniformed bailiff crying "Oyez, oyez, oyez," demanding that "All rise," and requiring witnesses to state "the truth, so help you God," you are meant to be impressed by the power of the law. This ritualistic quality is not necessarily harmful. A society needs laws, and legal incantation may help persuade people to follow them. According to Professor David Mellinkoff:

> This was the early history of the language of the law — made rememberable by repetition, rhythm, rhyme, alliteration and an awestruck respect for the magic potency of certain words. Planned for that effect or willy-nilly, these features fastened upon the language of the law in a time of illiteracy when the very survival of law depended on mnemonic devices, and where the memory of man did not run — there was no law.[4]

But as Mellinkoff also states, "the necessity for repetition and the tricks of verse to insure the law's survival passed long ago."[5]

This view of language as carrying the power of the law appears to be one reason that lawyers resist even minor changes. For example, many lawyers would hesitate to substitute *stop* for *cease and desist* because they would worry that tampering with a time-honored term might somehow bring about the wrong legal result. There may be legal reasons (either because of precedent or statute) for retaining many terms, but there are few valid legal reasons for clinging to Latinisms (prima facie, supra); strings of synonyms (null and void; any and all; rest, residue and remainder); or archaic words and phrases (witnesseth, thereinabove, hereinbefore).

c. *Political Factors*

Some of the vagueness and ambiguity in legal documents is intentional. Laws are usually enacted as a result of discussion and compromise. The lawmaking process is not always a process of reconciling divergent views; often it is a process of carefully choosing language that everyone — even those with contradictory positions — can agree upon. Furthermore, many of the problems addressed in legislation are so complex that the legislature can provide only a vague framework, which must then be filled in by administrative agencies through the drafting of regulations.

Unfortunately, many of the political forces that cause a legislature to create a vague statute are still present when the regulation writers begin their

---

4. D. Mellinkoff, *The Language of the Law* 33 (1978).
5. Id. at 284.

job. In addition, many regulations are subject to comment by the public and lobbying by special interest groups. The result is often a compromise regulation, which may be intentionally vague or ambiguous. Government agencies may actually want to perpetuate vagueness. In order to maintain control over industries, institutions, and individual programs, federal agencies often prefer to decide questions on a case-by-case basis. The result, not surprisingly, can be regulations that are as vague as the statutes.

When a government agency wishes to extend its authority — perhaps beyond the explicit limits provided by the statute — it derives a certain degree of security if it does so by using language from the statute. For example, the Homeowners' Loan Act empowers the Federal Home Loan Bank Board to grant charters to new savings and loan associations. Under the terms of the statute

> no charter shall be granted . . . unless in the judgment of the board a necessity exists for such an institution in the community to be served, nor unless there is a reasonable probability of its usefulness and success, nor unless the same can be established without undue injury to properly conducted existing local thrift and home-financing institutions.
>
> Homeowners' Loan Act, §5(e).

The Act does not explicitly empower the Bank Board to grant permission for existing savings and loans to establish branch offices. Nonetheless, the Bank Board decided to issue regulations permitting savings and loans institutions to "branch out." Under the branching regulation, 12 C.F.R. §545.14(c), an applicant for a branch office must show:

> (1) a necessity for the proposed branch in the community to be served by it at the time it is opened;
> (2) the branch has a reasonable probability of success;
> (3) the branch can be established without undue injury to properly conducted existing local thrift and home-financing institutions; . . .

As you will note, the regulatory criteria for a branch office closely parallel — in both form and substance — some of the statutory criteria for a charter. Many of the vague and elastic terms of the statute ("reasonable probability," "necessity," "undue injury") are also used in the regulation without further definition. The Bank Board felt that it was safer to use existing statutory phraseology in enlarging its jurisdiction than to make up and define new terms. It may have felt that using new language to introduce additional powers for itself might cast doubt on the legal propriety of the regulation.

Detailed regulations usually possess the grammatical and semantic ear-marks of legal language (often further complicated by the presence of vocab-ulary from other technical jargons). These regulations, by the use of legal language and legal discourse style, and by the excessive use of detail, can serve political purposes: The detail lessens the scope of an industry's power to make decisions, and the legal language serves formal notice that it is the agency that possesses the authority to make the decisions. Here are two examples from a proposed regulation of the U.S. Environmental Protection Agency:

Example 1

(a) Any person who produces and disposes of no more than 100 kilograms (approximately 220 pounds) of hazardous waste in any one month period, or any retailer disposing of hazardous waste (other than waste oil), is not a generator provided that the hazardous waste:

(1) Is disposed of in an on-site or off-site solid waste disposal facility in a State with an approved State plan under Subtitle D of the Solid Waste Disposal Act, as amended, which facility has been permitted or otherwise certified by the State as meeting the criteria adopted pursuant to Section 4004 of the Act; or (2) Is shipped to and treated, stored, or disposed of in a facility permitted by the Administrator pursuant to the requirements of Subpart E of this part or permitted by an authorized State program pursuant to Subpart F of this Part.

Example 2

(1) Generators must send hazardous waste to a treatment, storage, or disposal facility permitted by the Administrator pursuant to the require-ments of Subpart E and shall comply with the requirements of this Subpart as follows:

(i) If the generator sends the hazardous waste to an off-site treatment, storage or disposal facility which the generator does not own or the generator owns but which is not located in the State where the genera-tion occurred, the generator shall comply with all requirements of this Subpart except §§250.23(d), (e), (f), (g), and (h) and 250.28.

Note the long sentences and complex sentence structure; the statement of exceptions within the rule; the overuse of the passive voice; the noun string "off-site solid waste disposal facility"; the use of "which" instead of "and this"; the legal preposition "pursuant to"; the legal terms "shall," "amended," "certified," "authorized"; and the peculiar way of describing a person who is *not* a member of a class and for referring the reader elsewhere (in the last paragraph of the second example). All of these language characteristics help to mark this as a regulation with the force of authority, and the use of legal language ostensibly reinforces the power and authority of the agency that created the regulation.

d. *Jurisprudential Factors*

Common law is built on precedent. In the law, terms, phrases, even whole chunks of discourse, mean what courts have decided they mean. While the common meaning of a word or phrase may still be the basis of a court's decision,[6] Chief Justice Hughes's statement that "a federal statute finally means what the Court says it means"[7] is probably more accurate, as the legal system actually operates.

Most nonlawyers would recognize the dictionary definition of the term *heir*:

> 1. *Law*. A person who inherits or is entitled by law or by the terms of a will to inherit the estate of another. 2. A person who succeeds or is in line to succeed a hereditary rank, title or office. 3. One who receives or is expected to receive a heritage, as of ideas, from a predecessor.[8]

However, the strict legal definition of *heir* differs in a number of ways from the common dictionary definition. An heir is a person entitled by statute to the land of someone who dies *intestate,* i.e., *without a will.* This means that a person who receives land under a will is not technically an heir according to the law. Furthermore, a person who receives personal property, even under the laws of intestate succession, is not technically an heir. Such a person is a *distributee* or *next-of-kin*.

There are numerous other instances where a definition decided either by the courts or by statute differs substantially from the common meaning of the term, e.g., *income, purchase,* and *domicile.* Another term with a strict legal definition built on precedent is *assault.* The dictionary definition accurately reflects common usage, describing assault as a violent attack that can be either physical or verbal. However, the legal definition, as set forth in the Restatement (Second) of Torts §21, is as follows:

> An actor is subject to liability to another for assault if
> (a) he acts intending to cause a harmful or offensive contact with the person of the other or a third person, or an imminent apprehension of such a contact, and
> (b) the other is thereby put in such imminent apprehension.

6. See Dickerson, Materials on Legal Drafting (1981).
7. C. Hughes, The Supreme Court of the United States 230 (1928).
8. American Heritage Dictionary of the English Language 611 (1973).

In other words, *legal* assault is an act coupled with an intention on the part of one person that produces a fear or expectation in another. It does not require physical contact, but cannot be solely verbal.

The interaction between jurisprudence and legal language is nicely illustrated in the often contradictory rules that courts use to interpret the meaning of statutory language. Among them is the *plain meaning rule,* which states that a statute means what it says on its face. However, this rule can often be countered with the *purpose of the statute rule,* which states that a statute should be interpreted to fulfill its underlying purpose. In addition to these two broad rules, the courts have created a host of maxims to take care of specific situations. One well-known maxim is *ejusdem generis,* which says that if a list of two or more items is followed by a more general term that includes the prior items, then the more general term is limited by the prior items (thus, "dogs, cats, and other animals" would probably not include amoebas because amoebas have so little in common with dogs and cats). Some other maxims are *expressio unius est exclusio alterius* — "a statement of one is an exclusion of another"; and *in pari materia,* which says, essentially, that two statutes on the same general subject ought to be construed in harmony with one another.

While the purpose of these rules is supposedly to provide "objective criteria" for resolving statutory ambiguity, courts often use these rules to support a particular interpretation *after* they have reached a decision. Consequently, different courts have, according to their various judicial philosophies, applied the various rules and maxims to the same term and have come up with a variety of contradictory meanings. For example, notwithstanding ordinary usage, courts have managed to totally confuse the meanings of *shall, may, must,* and *will,* so that *may* has been interpreted to have mandatory meaning *(must). Must* has been interpreted as *may,* and *shall* has been interpreted as *may, must,* or *will.* In *Kansas City v. J. I. Case Threshing Machine Co.,* the court decided that *may, must,* and *shall* are interchangeable in statutes without regard to their literal meaning.[9]

4. Attitudes Toward Traditional Legal Writing

Obviously you cannot escape existing legal documents, even if they are filled with grammatical and stylistic features that obscure meaning with confusing

---

9. 337 Mo. 913, 87 S.W.2d 195, 205 (1935). See also State ex rel. Hanlon v. City of Maplewood, 231 Mo. App. 739, 99 S.W. 2d 138 (1936); In re Vrooman's Estate, 206 Okl. 8, 240 P.2d 754, 756 (1952); and Ballou v. Kemp, 68 App. D.C. 7, 92 F.2d 556, 559 (1937).

constructions. You must use the information in existing documents as the foundation for your own legal analyses. The important thing is not to write that way yourself, if you can help it.

In this book, we introduce what some attorneys consider a revolutionary idea — that legal writing can be written clearly as well as effectively. You may feel, either now or later in your law school career, that the principles presented in this book are not important in law school or in the real world and that your ability to use traditional legal language is a marketable skill. In some ways this is true. There will be situations in which you will be discouraged from using clear, straightforward language. You may find yourself in that type of situation if you are writing for a conservative audience or creating documents from forms or models.

a. Conservative Audiences

You may find that some of your law school professors are reluctant to accept any attempts to alter traditional legal language. If you work for a law firm, you may find that a senior attorney will not allow you to change "remise, release, and forever discharge" to just "release," and he or she may send you to a form book or to the firm's files so that you can see how the firm expects a release to be written. In fact, some clients will not be satisfied with a document unless it contains the traditional *whereases* and *heretofors*.

You may run into similar problems in the courtroom. If you fail to use the appropriate boilerplate or terms of art, some courts may not be receptive to your document. If you have doubts about your writing, check with someone who has more experience before you submit a document.

The problems posed by conservative audiences do not invalidate the principles presented in this book. More and more law firms are becoming interested in improving the writing produced by their attorneys, and many courts prefer clear writing to boilerplate.

b. Forms and Model Documents

The amount of control you will have over your writing will also depend upon the kind of document you are creating. For example, some documents are used time and again with little variation. The audience comes to expect a certain format and certain language, and the writer will use well-established, previously litigated language so that he or she can be fairly sure of how the courts will interpret the language. This includes such documents as very simple contracts, deeds, leases, and wills. Even though you might be able to draft your own, clearer version of these documents, your firm may want you to fill in the blanks in a form or piece together portions of other documents to create a new one.

Thus, you may have little opportunity in your early years of practice to change the forms or models that your firm uses, even though they may contain poor writing, boilerplate, and unnecessarily difficult legal terms. There may come a time, however, when you will be able to change some of these forms. Professor David Mellinkoff describes how a new attorney might influence established legal language:

> One day you will be working on a contract, not writing a contract, but trying to find out what went wrong with a contract written by other lawyers, in other firms. Your client signed it, and now the contract is in court, the *Jones* case. In your memo, you point out that the contract is so wound up in long, long sentences, and three words for one, that it is impossible to find a single meaning. You say that they botched the job of writing the contract. It's ambiguous, and the road is wide open to testimony about what the parties meant. Your memo convinces the powers. Your client wins. You move up a notch in the pecking order. The next time around, the old man tells an associate, "Show it to what's-his-name, the young lawyer who wrote the memo in the *Jones* case."
>
> One day, you will be calling the shots. You will be in a position to insist that the writing the firm turns out be simpler, clearer, shorter, better.[10]

c. *Memos and Briefs*

If you are writing documents whose primary purpose is to inform, explain, or persuade, you will have a good deal more leeway. Memos and briefs are examples of these kinds of documents. You may be required to follow a certain format and use a formal tone and certain terms of art, but the writing itself is up to you. Because the audience for a brief or memo is expecting to have things explained, they are unlikely to be jarred or bothered if you deviate from the traditional way of saying things. Hence, you will generally be able to determine the style, vocabulary, and sentence structure of your document.

This book is designed to make you aware of *whom* you are writing for and *why* you might choose one or another way of expressing an idea or constructing an argument. It also provides guidelines to help you assess the

---

10. D. Mellinkoff, in Syllabus, A.B.A. Section of Legal Education & Admission to the Bar, vol. XIV, #2, June 1983, pp. 1, 8.

quality of the writing in documents written by others. Your ability to judge the quality of communication will, in turn, make you a more discerning and effective legal advocate.

B Categories of Legal Writing

The legal documents that law students and lawyers encounter most often can be divided into categories. We have listed some typical kinds of legal documents here. As you read through the list, note that most of the documents fall into one of two broad areas: Either they are intended to inform or to persuade. There are exceptions, of course. Briefs, for instance, attempt to do both. Interrogatories really do neither. And documents such as wills and contracts serve a recordkeeping function as well as an informative one. It can be helpful, however, to think in terms of these two broad areas when you consider different types of legal writing.

Client letters are sent to clients for a number of purposes. One major purpose is to *inform* clients about the status of their legal affairs. An attorney might write a letter to a client to keep the client apprised of what the attorney is doing or plans to do with the client's case. A specific kind of letter to a client is the *opinion letter*. This letter is sent to the client to explain the lawyer's understanding of the law as it applies to the facts of the client's case.

Private documents such as contracts and wills are documents that establish a *record*. They describe a client's wishes, rights, or obligations. They can be used as a reference by the client, third parties, or a court.

Pleadings are documents that the parties to an action file with the court to explain their controversy to the court and to each other. They serve different purposes. For example, a pleading may *inform* the court about the sort of case that is involved; *inform* the opponent and other interested parties that suit has been filed; *petition* the court to dismiss a case before litigation; *narrow and define* the legal issues in a given case. Three common types of pleadings are:

1. A *complaint* is used to initiate suit and to disclose to the court and to the defendant the facts upon which the plaintiff is basing the claim.
2. An *answer* is the defendant's response to the complaint, denying some or all of the allegations in the complaint.

3. A *demurrer* (a type of motion to dismiss) is used to challenge the legal
sufficiency of an opponent's pleading.

Interrogatories are written questions used by an attorney, usually in a civil
case. They are designed to *elicit* certain kinds of information from an adversary. The attorney serves these questions on the adversary, and the adversary
is required to respond within a specific period of time.

A *memorandum* or *memo* is an informative document written after researching the points of law or the facts for a particular case. Its major purpose
is to *inform* the reader, rather than to persuade, and to give the reader a
decision-making tool. The reader may use this information to construct a
brief or a pleading, to inform a client about the status of the case, or to decide
whether to take a client's case. A memo is usually requested by, and addressed to, another lawyer — often, a colleague or supervisor — but you
may use it yourself. In writing a memo, compile all the relevant information
you can find on each point and then sort out key cases in order to convey the
present status of the law. Next, discuss the different ways to apply the law to
the facts of the case and ways to interpret the law. You might also speculate
on how your opponent or the court would interpret the facts and law and
make some recommendations for future action.

An *appellate brief* is presented to an appellate court as a formal document
that states the facts of the case, identifies the relevant issues, and presents an
argument that is supported by statutes and previously decided cases. Its
function is to *persuade* the court that legal principles and precedents support
your client's position. Therefore, a good brief integrates the facts with the
relevant law. A brief also provides judges with reference materials — a list of
relevant cases and statutes and a documented, well-reasoned analysis of the
facts and the law.

A *memorandum of points and authorities* is a short adversarial document
much like a brief. It usually accompanies a motion and is designed to persuade the court (usually a trial court) that the motion should be granted. For
example, a defendant in a civil case who files a motion to dismiss under Fed.
R. Civ. P. 12(b)(6) will usually attach a memorandum of points and authorities to that motion. Similarly, a party against whom a motion has been filed
may wish to submit to the court a memorandum of points and authorities in
opposition.

II

3

Planning
the Document

A Determining Purpose

Defining the purposes of your document is one of the basic pre-writing steps. Writing before you have identified your purposes is like trying to plot a route on a road map without knowing your destination. Only if you know where you are going can you hope to construct the shortest, most expedient route. Good writers identify and articulate their purposes — what they want to accomplish — when they are first planning a document. This gives them the opportunity to make calculated decisions about content, tone, vocabulary, and sentence structure. Thus, the experienced writer knows at a very early stage just what he or she wants to accomplish, makes appropriate writing decisions based on this knowledge, and constructs a document that is likely to achieve precisely what the writer wants it to.

Legal documents serve a variety of purposes. Various legal documents are written:

to inform	to satisfy court rules, federal, state, or local law
to elicit information	to threaten
to persuade	to make someone act or not act
to record	to give notice
to describe	

A legal document can serve more than one purpose. For example, the purpose of a deed to real property is to convey title to that property from one person to another. However, when the deed is recorded, it also serves to place others on notice that a particular piece of land is owned by a particular person.

A letter written by an attorney to a client may inform the client about the merits of the client's case. It may also serve other purposes. For example, if the attorney feels that it is not in the client's best interests to pursue the matter further, he or she may try to persuade the client to drop the case. Thus, the letter would serve both to inform and to persuade the client.

A written contract serves a number of purposes. One purpose is to memorialize the contract so that the parties can refer to it to find out about their rights and obligations. Another purpose is to serve as a record of the agreement should a dispute arise. A final purpose for putting a contract into writing is to ensure that it will be enforceable. In many states certain types of contracts can be enforced only if they are in writing.

1. Specifying Your Purposes

One of the first steps in planning any document is to list every purpose you have for writing that document. Next, sort these purposes into categories so that you can decide how much value to assign to each one and how to relate one purpose to another. There are no rigid formulas for sorting out your purposes, but we suggest using the following guidelines, which are discussed in more detail in the next few pages.

1. Look at your ultimate or long-range purposes for writing the document. What do you want to gain in the end?
2. Examine your immediate or short-term purposes for writing. What are you trying to accomplish right away?
3. Sort through all of your purposes, both long- and short-term, and rank them according to their importance to you.

Start by thinking about your ultimate purposes for the document. For example, you write trial documents (briefs, memos, interrogatories, pleadings, etc.) with the ultimate goal of winning a client's case. The goal of contracts, wills, trust agreements, warranties, leases, and similar documents, on the other hand, is to create a permanent record of an agreement or a client's request and to establish and define certain legal relationships or legal statuses. Your ultimate goal is to ensure that your client's wishes are carried out and that your client is protected if there is a dispute.

Each document you write will probably also have an immediate purpose or purposes. You write client letters and memos to inform, briefs to persuade, interrogatories to elicit information, and so on.

How do your ultimate and immediate purposes relate to each other? Knowing your ultimate goals will help you decide how to accomplish your immediate purposes. If you lose sight of your ultimate goal when you design a document, you risk sacrificing your long-range effectiveness for the sake of an immediate result. For example, your ultimate goal in writing interrogatories is to help win your client's case, but the more immediate goal is to elicit useful information. Thus, you may design a set of interrogatories in the early stages of your client's case with the immediate purpose of obtaining as much information as you can. In your enthusiasm to do so, you design questions that elicit a wealth of information, but are framed in such a way that they give the opposition insight into how much you already know and what kind of trial strategy you are planning. In other words, you may have damaged your chances of accomplishing the ultimate goal of winning your client's case by creating particularly "successful" interrogatories.

Weighing your immediate purposes against your ultimate goals may sound simplistic, but it can be difficult to do in a field such as law, where strategy is crucial, the time span between events in a case can be very great, and an enormous number of documents interrelate to accomplish a final goal or goals. Thus, you may write your interrogatories *years* before your client's case finally comes to trial and culminates in a judgment. You should have that judgment in mind from the beginning and it should influence everything you write.

2. Ranking Your Purposes

Once you are aware of all of your purposes — both ultimate and immediate — establish a hierarchy, so that you will know which purposes deserve the most emphasis.

Establishing a hierarchy is a subjective activity: There are no rules to tell you how to do it. Your decisions will be based on the specific circumstances of each case. Following is an example of how an attorney might determine and articulate a hierarchy for a particular document.

Imagine an attorney who is representing the husband in a divorce case. The attorney is charging this client a flat fee. He has met with the client several times. Every time the attorney tries to discuss the details of a separation agreement and property settlement with him, the client becomes angry. He protests over and over again that his wife has refused to have relations with him for the last two years, verbally abuses him, and regularly commits adultery. However, he has admitted that he has committed adultery himself on several occasions. The client frequently telephones his attorney to tell him each new offense that the wife has committed.

The client has said that he does not want his wife to get any support payments or any personal or real property. He also wants custody of their two children. He says that if he does not get custody, he does not want to pay child support. In fact, he does not care if his wife and children lose the family home and car, since he feels that his wife will somehow find alternatives. He acknowledges that his wife makes a good deal less money than he does, but he feels that she deserves to struggle to make ends meet. So far, the client has been unyielding about accepting a more balanced proposal to present to his wife's attorney.

The husband's attorney must now draft a preliminary separation and property settlement agreement. The attorney's first step is to identify the ultimate goal of the agreement. In this case the attorney feels that this goal is to produce the best possible settlement for the client — one that is workable and unlikely to lead to repeated litigation and renegotiation.

Next, the attorney will probably think about other, more immediate purposes for the agreement, purposes that will contribute to achieving the ultimate goal. Here are some that the attorney has identified.

1. Informing the court of why the husband and wife have separated, and what they have agreed to.
2. Informing the client of his rights.
3. Persuading the client that he has to give up some of what he wants in order to negotiate with his wife and that concessions are reasonable and necessary.
4. Persuading the wife and her attorney that the client is being reasonable.
5. Persuading the court that the agreement is reasonable.
6. Settling property rights, alimony, attorney's fees, child custody, child support payments, and other issues arising from the dissolution of the marriage.
7. Describing the couple's possessions and other property with precision.
8. Recording the agreement for future reference.
9. Formalizing the separation and property agreement to effect a legal act.

Having identified major purposes for writing the separation and settlement agreement, the attorney creates the following hierarchy.

1. It is of the utmost importance for the attorney to persuade the client that he must make concessions, because the case cannot go any further until the two parties come to some agreement.
2. It is also important to settle rights and describe the property accurately so that the husband and wife will have something concrete to refer to and will better understand exactly what they are agreeing to.

3. The attorney wants to formalize the separation quickly, because he thinks that once the husband and wife are legally separated some of the tension between them will abate.

4. The attorney is somewhat less concerned about persuading the court that the agreement is reasonable. He knows from past experience that the court will accept the agreement if it is within certain reasonable bounds —and he knows how to draft within those bounds.

Once an attorney creates a hierarchy, he or she can use it, along with information about the audience for the document (see Section B) to determine how best to use the following elements:

> content
> organization
> sentence structure and style
> vocabulary
> tone

Skillful use of these elements can ensure that a document accomplishes what the attorney wants it to.

3. Accomplishing Your Purposes

Different purposes lead to different strategies for writing. Thus, if your purpose is to *inform*, you will have to

- find out what your audience does and does not know
- gather the relevant information, anticipating questions
- know the relative importance of each piece of information
- put the information in a logical sequence, either chronologically or so that the sequence emphasizes (or obscures) certain information
- highlight the information you want the reader to be most aware of
- guide the reader through the document

If your purpose is to *elicit information,* you will have to

- decide what information you need
- find out what information your audience is likely to have
- ask relevant questions
- order your questions to fit your needs

If your purpose is to *persuade,* you will have to

- review all available information and decide what will be most favorable to your case
- organize to stress the major points of your argument
- anticipate counterarguments
- develop a strategy to deal with counterarguments
- create a logical progression to lead readers to the conclusions you want them to reach
- present the available information in a way that is most favorable to your case
- choose words carefully for maximum connotative effect

If your purpose is to *draft a document as a record*, you will have to

- find out your client's desires
- translate the client's desires into legally accurate language
- define legal relationships
- anticipate possible contingencies
- eliminate undesired or irrelevant provisions
- comply with correct procedures and legal requirements

These are general guidelines for creating documents with different purposes. In later chapters we will present specific strategies for writing different types of documents.

4. Dealing with Conflicting Purposes

Sometimes the multiple purposes of a document will conflict, and it will be necessary to judge which ones should take precedence. If you do not make clear distinctions and choices, you risk including conflicting messages in your writing or hopelessly obscuring your meaning and intentions.

In the example of the attorney representing the husband in a divorce case, the attorney must accommodate multiple, conflicting purposes in order to accomplish the primary goal of persuading the husband to reach an agreement with his wife. The attorney must try to satisfy a client who is angry and unreasonable and at the same time try to convince the wife's attorney that the husband is willing to make a reasonable settlement. If the husband's attorney does not acknowledge this conflict and attempt to resolve it or to carefully balance these purposes, then the document may be weakened.

Conflicting purposes can influence all kinds of documents, under all kinds of circumstances. A doctor, for example, must inform a patient about the details of a medical procedure before performing that procedure. To avoid a future claim of malpractice, the doctor must make sure that the patient has not only consented to undergo the procedure, but also understands the procedure well enough to know what he or she has consented to.

Doctors frequently provide their patients with pamphlets or booklets that explain the details of a particular medical procedure. One purpose of these documents is to inform. The doctor wants the patient to understand what will occur and to be aware of the possible risks and side effects. Another purpose is to reassure the patient and, indirectly, to persuade a patient who really needs a procedure to submit to it, in spite of the risks.

The two purposes of these documents may conflict. The informative aspects may frighten the patient, so that he or she decides not to submit to the procedure or becomes so distressed that his or her physical and emotional health are affected. Unless it is written with care, the document may have an undesirable effect: The patient may know exactly what a necessary procedure will involve, but may refuse to consent to it out of fear. Only a writer who recognizes these conflicting purposes will be able to achieve the necessary balance.

A related issue in writing legal documents is the need that they be both legally sufficient and comprehensible. A legal document may sometimes require technical legal terms established by precedent or statute, but it should still be comprehensible to everyone who has to deal with it. Some lawyers believe that these purposes cannot be reconciled and that they must sacrifice comprehensibility for legal sufficiency. A major purpose of this book is to demonstrate that it is possible to achieve both.

5. Writing for Multiple Purposes: An Example

Jury instructions provide a good example of multiple purposes. Jury instructions are directions given orally by the judge to the jurors before they deliberate. The judge uses the instructions to inform the jury of the law that applies to the facts of the case. This major purpose includes two subpurposes: to provide the jury with instructions that are legally sufficient and to provide the jurors with instructions that they can understand.

Typically, jury instructions achieve the goal of legal sufficiency but not the goal of comprehensibility. Legal sufficiency is crucial: An appellate court can reverse a judgment if the appellant shows that the jury instructions were incorrect or imprecise. As a consequence, trial courts tend to use, verbatim, language that has been previously approved by appellate courts, even though the jurors may not be able to understand that language. However, recent research shows that jury instructions can be both legally sufficient and comprehensible, provided some changes are made in the way the instructions are written.[1]

Here is a typical jury instruction. It may be legally sufficient, but it is certainly difficult to understand.

> One test that is helpful in determining whether or not a person was negligent is to ask and answer whether or not, if a person of ordinary prudence had been in the same situation and possessed of the same knowledge, he would have foreseen or anticipated that someone might have been injured by or as a result of his action or inaction. If such a result from certain conduct would be foreseeable by a person of ordinary prudence with like knowledge and in like situation, and if the conduct reasonably could be avoided, then not to avoid it would be negligence.[2]

The first sentence contains 62 words and 9 subordinate clauses. Not only is the entire instruction difficult to read, it is even more difficult to follow if you are sitting in the jury box *listening* to it. Only in recent years have the courts come to recognize that many legally sound jury instructions are difficult for people to understand. The hypertechnical language may satisfy an appellate court, but it can lead to confused jury deliberations or an unjust verdict. The same results would probably be achieved without any instructions, since jurors tend to fall back on their own notions of the law when they cannot understand the court's instructions.

The same jury instruction can be written to insure it will be both legally sufficient and understandable. Keep in mind that these jury instructions are read orally to the jury, so that they are written in a different style than they would be if they were meant to appear only on paper.

> In order to decide whether or not the defendant was negligent, there is a test you can use. Consider how a reasonably careful person would have acted in the same situation. Specifically, in order to find the defendant negligent, you would have to answer "yes" to the following two questions:

1. Charrow & Charrow, Making Legal Language Understandable: A Psycholinguistic Study of Jury Instructions, 79 Col. L. Rev. 1306 (1979).
2. California Jury Instructions — Civil — Book of Approved Jury Instructions, §3.11 (5th ed. 1969).

1. Would a reasonably careful person have realized in advance that someone might be injured as a result of the defendant's conduct?

And

2. Could a reasonably careful person have avoided behaving as the defendant did?

If your answer to both of these questions is "yes," then the defendant was negligent. You can use the same test in deciding whether the plaintiff was negligent.

In a recent study, jurors who heard this modified instruction understood the law significantly better than those who heard the original version.[3] To see how it is possible to be both understandable and legally accurate, let's look in detail at what the writers did in producing the modified jury instruction.

Context. The original instruction lacks context. It begins by talking about "one test," which is totally new information for the jurors. They have never heard of any test before and have no idea what it is for until well into the instruction. People understand better if familiar information is used to introduce new information. If *all* information is unfamiliar, comprehension suffers severely. Since the jurors are familiar with the terms "defendant" and "negligence" by the time they hear this instruction, the rewritten instruction uses those terms to introduce the new idea of a test to determine negligence. Thus, the drafters have provided a context for the unfamiliar information.

Style. The style of the original instruction is impersonal; the message is not directed *to* anyone. It states, for example, that "one test that is helpful [to whom?] . . . is [for whom?] to ask and answer . . ." People understand information that is directed to them personally better than information that is directed to no one in particular. Furthermore, the impersonal phraseology is vague and could lead to an imprecise interpretation: The listener can't always tell to whom the information is addressed or who is being discussed. The modified version has a precise and personal style; it addresses the jurors directly as "you": "There is a test *you* can use." "*You* would have to answer 'yes.'"

Organization. The original instruction is not organized logically. Not only does it begin with unfamiliar information, it tells the listener to apply a test

3. Charrow & Charrow, Making Legal Language Understandable: A Psycholinguistic Study of Jury Instructions, 79 Col. L. Rev. 1306 (1979).

without first explaining it. The instruction first tells the listener to "ask and answer whether or not . . . a person of ordinary prudence" would have foreseen the possibility of injury. Only at the very end does the instruction explain that the defendant was negligent if the answer is "yes." There are no signals to alert the listeners to what is expected of them; people need to know that in order to carry out instructions properly.

The modified version provides a logical progression of ideas. It describes the purpose of the listeners' task before describing the task itself: "*In order to find the defendant negligent*, you would have to answer 'yes' to the following two questions." The modified instruction contains signals to guide listeners through the instruction. They know from the outset that they have to answer "yes" to two questions in order to find the defendant negligent; the two questions are separated and numbered; and, finally, the listeners are told again that if the answer to the two questions is "yes," the defendant was negligent.

Sentence structure. The original instruction consists of two long sentences, each containing many subordinate clauses in unusual order. The human mind can process only a few pieces of information at a time, and long, complex sentences like these put an undue burden upon the listener. The information in the modified instruction is divided into several shorter sentences, with fewer subordinate clauses. The words in the new sentences are arranged in a more normal order than the original. (See Chapter 5 for a discussion of word order.)

Vocabulary. The original instruction contains terms of art as well as unfamiliar and archaic phrases. It also contains legalistic doublets. None of the legalistic terms or phrases are necessary for the legal accuracy of the instruction. Therefore, the drafters of the modified instruction replaced the term of art *person of ordinary prudence* with the semantically equivalent phrase *reasonably careful person*. They eliminated the archaism *possessed of* and changed *like situation* to *the same situation*. They replaced the first doublet *foreseen or anticipated* with the phrase *realized in advance;* eliminated one term in the second doublet so that *by or as a result of* became *as a result of;* and changed *action or inaction* to the single word *conduct*.

The modified jury instruction was created systematically, following the principles that we present in this book. The drafters identified their purposes before they began to write and let those purposes shape their decisions about the organization, sentence structure, and vocabulary of the modified instruction. They did not ignore legal accuracy, but they did not sacrifice comprehensibility in order to preserve archaic boilerplate. Rather, the drafters chose to emphasize the informative purpose of the instruction, while carefully choosing words that would still accurately reflect the intent of the law.

EXERCISES

1. Read the MECO warranty on page 36 and the RDL warranty on page 37. Then do the following:
    a. List the purposes of these documents.
    b. Compare the documents. Is one more effective? If so, can you tell why?
2. Read the "Holder in Due Course Notice" below. It appears in consumer credit contracts. What do you think the purposes of this notice are? Does it achieve those purposes? Try to rewrite the notice so that it better achieves its purposes.

    > Any Holder of this Consumer Credit Contract is subject to all claims and defenses which the Debtor could assert against the Seller of goods or services obtained pursuant hereto or with the proceeds hereof. Recovery hereunder by the Debtor shall be limited to amounts paid by the Debtor hereunder.

3. Skim the airline ticket below. What are the purposes of this document? What can be done to help the document better achieve its purposes?

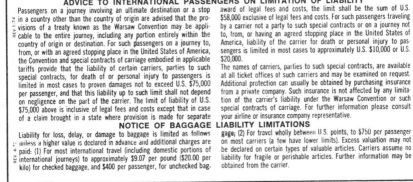

ADVICE TO INTERNATIONAL PASSENGERS ON LIMITATION OF LIABILITY

Passengers on a journey involving an ultimate destination or a stop in a country other than the country of origin are advised that the provisions of a treaty known as the Warsaw Convention may be applicable to the entire journey, including any portion entirely within the country of origin or destination. For such passengers on a journey to, from, or with an agreed stopping place in the United States of America, the Convention and special contracts of carriage embodied in applicable tariffs provide that the liability of certain carriers, parties to such special contracts, for death of or personal injury to passengers is limited in most cases to proven damages not to exceed U.S. $75,000 per passenger, and that this limit of liability shall not depend on negligence on the part of the carrier. The limit of liability of U.S. $75,000 above is inclusive of legal fees and costs except that in case of a claim brought in a state where provision is made for separate award of legal fees and costs, the limit shall be the sum of U.S. $58,000 exclusive of legal fees and costs. For such passengers traveling by a carrier not a party to such special contracts or on a journey not to, from, or having an agreed stopping place in the United States of America, liability of the carrier for death or personal injury to passengers is limited in most cases to approximately U.S. $10,000 or U.S. $20,000.

The names of carriers, parties to such special contracts, are available at all ticket offices of such carriers and may be examined on request. Additional protection can usually be obtained by purchasing insurance from a private company. Such insurance is not affected by any limitation of the carrier's liability under the Warsaw Convention or such special contracts of carriage. For further information please consult your airline or insurance company representative.

NOTICE OF BAGGAGE LIABILITY LIMITATIONS

Liability for loss, delay, or damage to baggage is limited as follows unless a higher value is declared in advance and additional charges are paid: (1) For most international travel (including domestic portions of international journeys) to approximately $9.07 per pound ($20.00 per kilo) for checked baggage, and $400 per passenger, for unchecked baggage; (2) For travel wholly between U.S. points, to $750 per passenger on most carriers (a few have lower limits). Excess valuation may not be declared on certain types of valuable articles. Carriers assume no liability for fragile or perishable articles. Further information may be obtained from the carrier.

MECO Black and White Television

LIMITED WARRANTY

Who Is Covered?

This warranty covers the original buyer of this MECO TV set.

What Is Covered?

This warranty covers your new MECO TV set for any defects in materials or workmanship.

What Is NOT Covered?

This warranty does not cover:

- the antenna
- the power cord
- any accessories used with the TV
- a broken cabinet
- parts damaged by misuse.

This warranty will not apply if the TV set was dropped, abused, or damaged when altered or repaired by anyone except an authorized MECO service center.

What MECO Will Do and For How Long

For the first 90 days, MECO will supply parts and labor free to repair or replace any defects in materials or workmanship.

After 90 days and up to 1 year, MECO will supply the part free but you will pay a $9.00 service charge. The $9.00 service charge must be paid when you bring or send in the TV.

After the warranty period (one year), you will pay for labor and parts.

At all times, you are responsible for bringing or sending your MECO TV in for repairs.

What You Must Do

The set must have been installed and used normally during the warranty period.

If you bring or send the TV in to an authorized MECO service center, it must be in its original packing case.

You must present an original sales receipt, showing the original date of purchase.

How To Get Warranty Service

Look in the Yellow Pages of your telephone book for the authorized MECO service center nearest you.

This warranty gives you specific legal rights, and you may also have other rights which vary from state to state.

The warranty that this product will work normally is limited to one year. No one has the right to change or add to this warranty.

Five Year Limited Warranty

These units have been properly designed, tested and inspected before they are shipped. Each speaker system is warranted free from defects (workmanship and material) for five years from date of delivery to the original purchaser. The warranty includes parts and labor for the first year. After the first year, and continuing through the fifth year of the warranty, the warranty extends to parts only and a nominal charge will be made for labor. The speaker system is to be delivered or shipped to us, or an authorized warranty station, for warranty repair, freight charges prepaid. The duration of all warranties other than this written warranty, whether express, implied or created by operations of law, trade usage or course of dealing is five years from date of delivery to the original purchasers. The Company shall not be liable for any loss or damage, direct, incidental or consequential arising out of the use of, or the inability to use the product, and The Company's obligation in any event is expressly limited to the repair of the product as provided herein above. The warranty is not extended to the cabinet or grill. This warranty does not apply to units which have been subject to misuse, abuse, neglect, accident or improper installation; nor does it apply to repairs or alteration by unauthorized personnel. We retain the right to make such determination on the basis of factory inspection. Any claims under this limited warranty must be asserted prior to the expiration date of this written warranty.

4. One of the purposes of a complaint is to disclose to the court and to the defendant the facts upon which the plaintiff is basing the complaint. The complaint should contain a concise, clear statement of the facts. Read through the statement of facts below. Identify any features that obscure its meaning and explain why each feature has this effect. Finally, rewrite the passage so that it is legally sufficient, but more comprehensible.

On or about September 3, 1980, at or about 6:20 PM, plaintiff Jack Marshall was operating his 1979 Chevrolet Citation automobile, license number 676 ABC, at, near, or about Springfield Boulevard northbound and near Royal Oaks Drive, in the County of Los Angeles, State of California, and at the said time and place, the defendant, Lawrence Cutler, so negligently, carelessly, and recklessly owned, manufactured, controlled, maintained, repaired, leased, used, rented, operated, permitted, entrusted, supervised, managed, and drove his said property on, about, or near said streets and highways, so as to cause the same to violently collide with the right rear side of the vehicle of the plaintiff, and to violently collide a second time with the right door of the vehicle of the plaintiff, and to violently collide a third time with the right front portion of the vehicle of the plaintiff, causing plaintiff to lose control of his vehicle and thereby damaging the vehicle and property of plaintiff and injuring plaintiff as hereinafter set forth.

That immediately thereafter and as soon as plaintiff was able to regain control of his vehicle, plaintiff pulled over to the right-hand side of Springfield Boulevard, in an effort to comply with the statutory requirements of the laws of the state of California to exchange information with the driver of the other vehicle, and plaintiff attempted to motion the defendant, Lawrence Cutler, to pull over his vehicle for said exchange of information, and the defendant, Lawrence Cutler, proceeded northbound on Springfield Boulevard, without stopping, and defendant Lawrence Cutler, as he passed the plaintiff herein, made a gesture to the plaintiff herein with the middle finger of his right hand, and proceeded to flee the scene at a high rate of speed.

B Identifying the Audience

Most courtroom lawyers develop some remarkable language abilities. They learn to change their verbal style so that they argue differently before an appellate court than before a trial court; they address a jury very differently from the way they address a judge. In addition, research by sociologist Brenda Danet of the Hebrew University in Jerusalem and by anthropologist

William O'Barr of Duke University has shown that trial lawyers change their questioning style considerably from direct examination to cross-examination.[4] They use different grammatical structures and different vocabulary — as well as a different tone of voice. Consciously or unconsciously, courtroom lawyers change their style and language to suit the purpose and the audience.

Many lawyers — even those with excellent courtroom skills — are not able to transfer verbal skills into writing. Because they cannot adjust their writing styles to fit the audience and the purpose, their writing often fails to communicate. Those lawyers who can adapt their presentations to appeal to specific audiences have an edge over other attorneys: They are better able to inform, instruct, or elicit information and, most important, they are better able to persuade. You can fine-tune your writing in the same way that skilled courtroom lawyers fine-tune their oral presentations. To do this, however, you must learn to identify your audience and its needs even before setting pen to paper.

1. Lawyers' Audiences

Lawyers write many documents for other members of the legal community. However, they do not communicate just with each other or with the courts. They produce numerous documents that are directed at nonlawyers. For example, lawyers regularly write to or for the following audiences.

1. *Individual clients:* Lawyers write letters to clients and create documents for clients to use — wills, leases, deeds, contracts, etc.
2. *Business clients* (such as insurance companies, private investigators, corporations, banking institutions): Lawyers write letters, articles of incorporation, by-laws, contracts, release agreements, etc.
3. *Government agencies:* Lawyers outside government agencies write, among other things, letters of inquiry and comments on regulations. Lawyers within agencies write regulations, guidelines, preambles, position papers, etc.
4. *Lay people who are not clients:* Lawyers write letters to nonlawyers on behalf of their clients. Lawyers also write documents such as journal articles, books, and speeches for the general public.

---

4. Danet, Language in the Legal Process, 14 Law and Society Review 445 (1980); O'Barr & Conley, When a Juror Watches a Lawyer, 3 Barrister 8 (1976).

Lawyers rarely write a document that is meant for only one audience. Even when they write for other members of the legal profession, they are often writing for various people with different backgrounds and different roles. Thus, a brief will be read by both the judge and opposing counsel, and each will use the document for different purposes.

Attorneys sometimes misperceive the expectations of the courts or other lawyers when they write, assuming that all lawyers speak the same language and are familiar with the same subject matter. Modern law is complex, and a lawyer who specializes in one area of the law may not be familiar with the nuances of other areas. And no matter how well versed attorneys are in the law, it will not help them decipher writing that is ambiguous, unclear, or badly written. The attorney who assumes that his or her peers will understand a document risks having it misunderstood by the court, misinterpreted to the client's disadvantage, or made the subject of a malpractice suit.

Even documents that one might suppose are written primarily for other members of the legal profession often have important nonlegal audiences. Thus, although some attorneys would argue that a will is written primarily for the probate court, it is important that the client, beneficiaries, executor, trustees, guardians, and other fiduciaries be able to understand it without continually turning to a lawyer for translation.

Picture the following situations.

1. An attorney drafts a will in typical legal language for an elderly client. She explains to the client that she has incorporated all the client's wishes in the will. Three months later, the client, pondering his decisions about his estate, decides to check his will and finds that he cannot understand it. He calls the attorney several times a day for the next week, asking questions about his will. The attorney realizes that although she had discussed all these matters with the client before drafting the will and before the client signed the will, the will is useless as a reference document for the client. Calling the attorney is time consuming and costly for both the client and the attorney.

2. A woman in her thirties has a will drafted in traditional legal language. Both she and her husband read it, but they do not really understand it and do not realize that it doesn't reflect what they want. Years later, the woman dies, and, much to the husband's dismay, the probate court follows the provisions of the will, refusing to accept the husband's arguments that these were not his wife's original intentions. The attorney who drafted the will has been dead for twenty years, and so the husband has no recourse.

These situations could have been avoided if the attorneys had written the wills so that they were comprehensible to their clients.[5]

a. *Writing for Multiple Audiences*

Because attorneys sometimes assume that the primary purpose of most legal documents is to communicate with the courts, they concentrate on using the language that is necessary to make a document legally sufficient. They may regard clear writing as a desirable, but secondary, goal. Some attorneys even believe that writing clearly and comprehensibly for nonlawyers is unnecessary. They consider it an attorney's function to serve as translator for the lay person and to act as a go-between for the lay person and the legal system.

As the will examples demonstrate, an attorney cannot always take the place of a legal document as a source of information. These situations are not farfetched. They demonstrate the kinds of unforeseen or poorly handled circumstances that often lead to lawsuits. There are other instances of poorly drafted language resulting in problems because an attorney is not always available to serve as a translator. An attorney cannot serve as an "interpreter" during jury deliberations, and judges will rarely do more than merely repeat an instruction. Many tenants have little or no idea of the terms of their leases, even though by signing them they have consented to those terms. Similarly, consumers often do not know exactly what a product warranty covers. Consumers and tenants would not normally think of consulting an attorney before there was a problem, even if they could afford to do so. Readable documents would help avoid many of the disputes and complications that clog the court system unnecessarily.

b. *Writing for Conflicting Audiences*

The problem of conflicting audiences is similar to the problem of conflicting purposes. Even though you may realize that a document should be addressed to more than one audience, you may feel that the needs of each are mutually exclusive. The solution is similar to the solution for dealing with conflicting purposes: You can frequently accommodate the needs of many audiences at once by knowing *how* to present the information.

If complex legal language does not really serve most of your audiences,

---

5. Although it is not an easy task, it is possible to write a complex will that is understandable to the testator and beneficiaries and is still legally sufficient. A number of experienced probate lawyers have created complex wills that satisfy these conflicting audiences, and, in fact, in March 1983, the American College of Probate Council tackled just this problem in a course it presented on "Drafting with Clarity." See also Squires & Mucklestone, Drafting a Truly Simple Will that Can Effectively Communicate to both Client and Court, Estate Planning, March 1983, at 80.

then what changes should you make? It is a good idea to start with the premise that you should design your document for the *audience that is least likely to understand it;* that way you will encompass *all* of your audiences. This is a sound strategy as long as it won't damage your credibility or render the document useless for some audiences. Usually, there will be no such threat: The modifications we suggest will not result in a simplistic or condescending tone, nor will they damage legal sufficiency. If properly used, they will merely clarify your message.

What if you feel that you absolutely cannot afford to gear your document to the audience that is least likely to understand it, because it will damage your credibility with a more sophisticated audience or because it will mean that you cannot include all of the material necessary for other audiences? If that is the case, you should ask yourself the following questions.

1. Can you rearrange the document? You might divide the document into sections addressed to different audiences. Alternatively, you might include a glossary of major terms and concepts for some audiences.
2. Do you really want just one document? Perhaps you should create several versions.
3. If you cannot write more than one document and it cannot be broken into sections, then you will have to do some weighing and balancing. Carefully review all of your audiences. Who is your most important audience? Whom do you have to be sure to address? Be careful not to make hasty assumptions about who does or does not matter.

2. Classifying the Audience

a. *Identifying Your Audience*

How do you decide who your audience is? First, list all possible audiences. Don't stop at the obvious ones or with those that appear to be primary; you may be neglecting other, equally important, audiences. For example, if you were an attorney working for a federal or state regulatory agency and you were corresponding with regulated industries, you would be aware that industries are the major audience. It might not immediately occur to you, however, that it could as easily be an engineer as an attorney who will read your letter.

There will be other audiences also — your superiors within the agency, for example. If you are writing a document for a case, the document may be discoverable, and your opponent may read it. You will surely want to choose your content and modify your style on the basis of this information.

Sometimes you may have trouble determining who your audience is, and you will need to do some research. For example, you may have to find out how the review system works in your agency to learn who will review your letters, or you may have to research the law to find out if a particular document is discoverable.

b. *Analyzing Your Audience*

Once you have identified all possible audiences, consider their different characteristics, needs, and expectations. If you are addressing a letter to your client, ask yourself about that client. Is the client a physician? Is the client another attorney who has hired you as counsel? An insurance agent? A criminal defendant? A retired farmer? A plumber? How would your writing differ for members of these groups?

There are other things you might want to consider when writing letters or other documents.

1. *Age.* Will the age of your audience affect how you write the document? If your reader is a child who is being asked to sign an assent form in an adoption case, is the form written in language a child can understand? If your client is elderly and has expectations about formality and respect, is the document written in a suitable style?

2. *Native language.* Does your audience have any problems with the English language? An attorney for the Immigration and Naturalization Service who writes forms and instructions for aliens or a practicing attorney who has a foreign client must keep in mind that his or her readers are not native speakers of English.

3. *Education and reading level.* Does your audience have any significant education or reading level characteristics for which you should tailor vocabulary and style? For example, is your client a person who can barely read or is your client a corporation with a highly sophisticated board of directors?

4. *Familiarity with subject matter.* Is your audience familiar with the subject of the document? If you are handling a medical malpractice case, is your client the defendant physician, or the plaintiff?

5. *Familiarity with legal language.* Is your client familiar with legal language? Is your client a judge or another attorney, or an airline pilot or school teacher who may never have had any dealings with the court system?

6. *Attitude.* What kind of attitude does your client have about documents such as the one you are creating? Is your audience composed of members of a regulated industry, who resent the paperwork and complicated regu-

lations that your agency produces? Are the members of your audience lay people who are annoyed or intimidated by legal documents that they can't understand?

7. *Physical or other problems.* Do the members of your audience have any physical, mental, or emotional problems that will affect the way you write? For example, does your client have vision problems that might make small print difficult to read? Does your client have a short attention span? Is your client sensitive about certain kinds of subject matter?

8. *Individual concerns.* Are there any other individual concerns or unique characteristics of your audience? Does your audience have obvious biases? Does your audience have a particular desire to be involved in what you are doing? Are there considerations associated with the audience's profession, gender, or marital status?

Sexist writing can be particularly offensive to many members of your audience. There are a number of ways to avoid sexist writing.

1. Rewrite the sentence so that you do not have to use the gender pronouns *he* or *she*. You can do this by repeating the noun instead.

   An attorney will often write a letter to the client in order to keep *him* informed.

   An attorney will often write a letter to the client in order to keep *the client* informed.

2. If possible, rewrite the statement in the plural.

   The student should bring *her* torts book to class.

   Students should bring *their* torts books to class.

3. If you are talking about or directly to your readers, address them in the second person.

   A *lawyer* must pass the state bar exam if *he* wants to practice law.

   You must pass the state bar exam if *you* want to practice law.

4. You can often replace third person singular possessives (*his* or *her*) with articles.

   A judge must wear *her* black robe while in court.

   A judge must wear *a* (or *the*) black robe while in court.

5. Avoid gender-specific titles such as *chairman, policeman,* or *stewardess.* You can often replace these terms with neutral terms such as *chair, police officer,* or *flight attendant.* Similarly, you can replace generic terms such as *mankind* with *the human race.* Avoid awkward constructions such as *chairperson* or *policeperson.* Use them only if you cannot find a better alternative.

6. You can sometimes use the passive voice to avoid a sexist construction. However, the passive voice can cause more problems than it solves (see Chapter 4).

7. You may sometimes use *he or she* and *his or hers.* However, *s/he* and *he/she* are awkward and you should avoid them.

8. Don't try to cure a sexist statement by using a third person plural pronoun to refer to a third person singular antecedent. For example:

> *A student* can work in a law firm or for a judge, depending on what *they* want to do when *they* graduate.

This construction is not grammatical and can make you appear illiterate.

c. *The Unfamiliar Audience*

If you know who your audience is, but don't know enough about it to list its relevant characteristics, then do some research. You might protest that you are not a researcher, and that you don't have time to perform such an analysis. However, audience analysis is really an extension of what most good attorneys do when they practice law — they evaluate people. Attorneys make judgments and draw conclusions about others in order to make sound business decisions and construct successful strategies. When an attorney talks to a client, the attorney probes for nonlegal information about that client: How intelligent is the client — will he make a good witness? Is she telling the truth? Is he emotionally stable? Will she pay me my fee? Should I take this case, or will it be more aggravation than it is worth? Lawyers systematically (sometimes unconsciously) use this data to make decisions about how to handle a case. The same information is also valuable for making decisions about how to write.

A conscious audience analysis is not reserved just for clients. If you become a litigator, you will learn a great deal by observing judges and juries, and over time you will learn to gauge their reactions. What does a certain judge expect from an attorney? How will this jury respond to a certain strategy or approach? Will emotion or logic be more effective?

If you cannot observe your audience directly, you may be able to find out about it by asking others, or by reading. You might ask another attorney for an assessment of a particular judge. However, if you are unable to assess your audience at firsthand or through another's experience, be wary of books or articles, especially on trial advocacy, that make generalizations that are not based on empirical research.

3. Writing for a Specific Audience: An Example

Here are examples of two documents that deal with essentially the same subject matter but are directed at different audiences. The first document is a portion of a medical consent form, used by the National Institutes of Health, for adults who volunteer to participate in medical research projects. When the patient signs the form, he or she gives legal consent to being treated as an experimental subject by NIH.

The second document is part of a child's assent form from NIH, which is used when the subjects chosen for the study are below the age of consent (i.e., their parents must consent for them). When the child signs the form, he or she is indicating willingness to participate as an experimental subject.

CONSENT FOR ADULTS

We invite you to participate in a research study conducted by the National Institutes of Health. It is important that you read and understand the following general principles, which apply to all participants in our studies: 1) participation is entirely voluntary; 2) it is possible that you may not personally benefit from participating in the study, although we may gain knowledge that will benefit others; and 3) you may withdraw from the study at any time without any consequences.

We will explain what the study is about, its risks, inconveniences, discomforts, and other relevant information. If you have any questions, please feel free to ask us.

What this study is about: This study attempts to discover the causes of neurological (nervous system) damage, which may be related to infections in pregnant women, children, and adults. It involves a physical examination and routine laboratory tests, including drawing 1-4 tablespoons of blood at the time of your first visit and at later times if necessary. We may also do cultures of sputum and of any lesions (sores) in the throat, eye, skin, or the urinary or genital tract.

We may find that it is necessary to do a lumbar (spinal) puncture in order to define the extent or possible cause of the illness. If we find it necessary to do a lumbar puncture, you will have to lie on your side, and we will insert a needle into the space between the bones in your lower back to collect spinal fluid. We will use a local anesthetic so that you won't feel very much pain.

Even though this is an outpatient study, we will ask you to stay in the hospital for one to three days if we do a lumbar puncture.

ASSENT FROM CHILD

How You Can Help Us

We are asking you to help us because we want to find out why some children have your illness. One way we can find out is to do some tests on children like you. These tests may not help you, but the things we learn may help other children.

This paper explains what we want to do to you. Read this paper and ask us questions about anything that you do not understand. Then you decide if you want to be in the test. You can stop being in the test any time you want. When you come to the Clinical Center, we will talk to you and your parents. We will examine you and we will explain more about the different tests we will do.

What We Will Do

The first thing we will do is stick a small needle in a vein in your arm to take 4 spoonfuls of your blood. The needle will hurt for a minute, but the pain will go away quickly. We may also take swabs from your throat, eyes, or skin. This means that we will use a tool like a big Q-tip to scrape off a few cells from your throat, eyes, or skin. You may feel a little uncomfortable when we do this, but it will not really hurt. You will go home as soon as we finish these tests.

You may have to stay in the hospital for a while if we decide to take some liquid from in between the bones of your spine (the bones that go down the middle of your back). The liquid is called spinal fluid. Before we get the spinal fluid, we will give you some medicine so you won't feel any pain. Then we will put a small needle between the bones of your spine in the lower part of your back. After we take out the fluid, we will ask you to lie down flat on your back for a few hours. If you feel any pain in your back or head, you should tell us.

You will notice that the two documents differ in the following major ways.

1. The adult form assumes that the adult will have some idea of why research studies are conducted, and what it means to be in a research study. But the child's assent form begins by telling the child *why* he or she is being asked to participate in the study, and what this means to the child. The child's form immediately connects the study to the child's own illness because it is easier to understand new information if it is tied to the reader's own experience.

2. The internal organization of the adult form reflects an adult way of thinking: The form first presents general principles regarding all NIH studies, then the rationale for this study, and then the procedures involved. In the description of procedures, there is little discussion of immediate consequences, such as pain. These are explained in a separate section which we have not reproduced.

The child's form has a different internal organization. It starts by relating the rationale for the study directly to the child's experience. It then talks about specific procedures, beginning with participation in the study and going on to the steps involved in the tests.

Because children are generally less adept than adults at making causal connections, the child's form fills in the gaps between procedures and results. The child is told right after each step whether he or she will experience discomfort. Because a child's experience is more limited, the form explicitly states information that would be self-evident to an adult.

3. The adult form contains a number of technical terms and concepts, such as "neurological damage," "lesions," and "lumbar puncture." These are terms that adults might understand or that they can figure out from the context provided by the rest of the document. Even so, the terms are clarified in the text. The child's form, on the other hand, contains none of these technical terms. Furthermore, because children tend to think about things in very concrete ways, the assent form gives a step-by-step description of each activity or process.

4. Neither of these forms contains long, complex sentences. The use of short, relatively simple sentences is particularly important in the child's form, because children are still learning to read and to decipher basic sentence structures, and complicated sentences are more difficult to follow. These forms were written with the help of writing experts and use many of the techniques we describe in this book in order to accomplish their purpose: communication with a specific audience.

4. Writing for Multiple Audiences: An Example

Following is a copy of a Massachusetts automobile insurance policy. Skim this document, then compare it with the modified version on pages 52-53. The modified version accommodates various audiences without sacrificing legal sufficiency or appropriateness for any individual audience.

Before comparing the policies, consider who the audiences for this type of insurance policy are. It has at least six readily identifiable audiences.

1. Consumers (insureds and potential insureds).
2. Insurance agents or employees who administer the policies.
3. Members of the Massachusetts Insurance Commission (the Commission regulates insurance companies and approves plans and policies).
4. Banks and finance companies that require anyone who takes out an automobile loan to have insurance on that automobile.
5. Other insurance companies (if the insured is covered by more than one company, companies often pay *pro rata* shares of the insured's liabilities).
6. Insurance company attorneys, private attorneys, and the courts, when questions or disputes arise.

Notice that only one of these audiences consists of people who are likely to have legal backgrounds. Members of the lay audiences have different backgrounds and varying degrees of familiarity with a legalistic writing style and with insurance terms and concepts. They are probably the least well equipped to deal with this document, yet, because they use the document frequently, these are the people who most need the information in the policy. Attorneys and insurance company employees can also have trouble interpreting insurance policies. Insurance company employees do not always understand the language of the policies generated by their own companies; they frequently rely on verbal explanations or written translations provided by the people who write the policies. A private attorney who does not regularly handle insurance cases might also have trouble deciphering the provisions. Even an attorney who is well versed in insurance law would probably be relieved to see some of the needless complexity removed.

The person who revised the Massachusetts insurance policy chose to modify the original so that the lay audiences could understand it, but the modifications do not damage the document's usefulness for any audience. Let's examine the modifications and the differences they make.

BLANK INSURANCE COMPANY

A . . . . insurance company herein called the company

In consideration of the payment of the premium, in reliance upon the statements in the declarations made a part hereof and subject to all of the terms of this policy, agrees with the insured named in the declarations as follows:

(For policy issued by two companies)

In consideration of the payment of the premium, in reliance upon the statements in the declarations made a part hereof and subject to all of the terms of this policy, severally agree with the insured named in the declarations as follows, provided the Blank Casualty Company shall be the insurer with respect to coverages . . . . and no other and the Blank Fire Insurance Company shall be the insurer with respect to coverages . . . .

PART I—LIABILITY, PERSONAL INJURY PROTECTION,

PROPERTY PROTECTION, MEDICAL PAYMENTS AND PHYSICAL DAMAGE

INSURING AGREEMENTS

1 Coverage A
Division 1—Bodily Injury Liability—Statutory—The Commonwealth of Massachusetts—(This Coverage is Compulsory)

The company will pay on behalf of the insured, in accordance with the "Massachusetts Compulsory Automobile Liability Security Act," Chapter 346 of the Acts of 1925 of the Commonwealth of Massachusetts and all Acts amendatory thereof or supplementary thereto, all sums which the insured shall become obligated to pay by reason of the liability imposed upon him by law for damages to others for bodily injury, including death at any time resulting therefrom, or for consequential damages consisting of expenses incurred by a husband, wife, parent or guardian for medical, nursing, hospital or surgical services in connection with or on account of such bodily injury or death, sustained by any person or persons during the policy period as defined in Item [3]² of the declarations and caused by the ownership, operation, maintenance, control or use of the insured motor vehicle upon the ways of the Commonwealth of Massachusetts or in any place therein to which the public has a right of access.

This division of coverage A is subject to the following provisions:

(1) No statement made by the insured or on his behalf, either in securing this policy or in securing registration of the insured motor vehicle, no violation of the terms of this policy and no act or default of the insured, either prior to or subsequent to the issuance of this policy, shall operate to defeat or avoid this coverage so as to bar recovery by a judgment creditor proceeding in accordance with the Laws of the Commonwealth of Massachusetts. The terms of this policy shall remain in full force and effect, however, as binding between the insured and the company, and the insured agrees to reimburse the company for any payment made by the company under this policy on account of any accident, claim or suit involving a breach of the terms of this policy.

(2) Notwithstanding the provisions of the Cancelation Condition of this policy, if this policy is canceled by the company and subsequently the effective date of cancelation is changed by an order of the Board of Appeal or by a decree of the Superior Court or Municipal Court of the City of Boston or a Justice of either, under the provisions of the Massachusetts Compulsory Automobile Liability Security Act, the insurance provided in this coverage shall be canceled as of the date of cancelation effective by such order or decree and premium adjustment shall be made accordingly; if after the issuance of notice of cancelation by the company, a finding that such cancelation is not proper and reasonable or is invalid is made under the provisions of said Act either by

the Board of Appeal from which finding the company takes no appeal, or by a decree of the Superior Court or Municipal Court of the City of Boston or a Justice of either, the company will continue the insurance provided in this coverage in full force and effect if such order or decree is based upon a complaint made prior to the effective date of cancelation stated in the company's notice, and will reinstate the insurance provided in this coverage in full force and effect as of the date specified in such order or decree if such order or decree is based upon a complaint made within the ten days after the effective date of cancelation stated in the company's notice. If the company shall cease to be authorized to transact business in the Commonwealth of Massachusetts, this policy shall be canceled and premium adjustment shall be made on or a pro rata basis as of the effective date of the new certificate of insurance filed by the named insured with the Registrar of Motor Vehicles in Massachusetts, or if no certificate is filed, then as of the effective date of the revocation of registration of the insured motor vehicle.

(3) This policy, the written application therefor, if any, and any endorsement, which shall not conflict with the provisions of said Massachusetts Compulsory Automobile Liability Security Act and all Acts amendatory thereof or supplementary thereto, shall constitute the entire contract between the parties.

(4) The Other Insurance Condition of this policy shall be applicable to this coverage only in the event that other insurance referred to therein is carried in a company authorized to transact insurance in the Commonwealth of Massachusetts.

(5) This agreement is made in accordance with Sections 112 and 113 of Chapter 175 of the General Laws of Massachusetts.

Division 2—Personal Injury Protection—Statutory—(This Coverage is Compulsory)

The company will pay, in accordance with Chapter 670 of the Acts of 1970 of the Commonwealth of Massachusetts and all Acts amendatory thereof or supplementary thereto, subject to any applicable deductible, all reasonable expenses incurred within two years from the date of accident for necessary medical, surgical, X-ray and dental services, including prosthetic devices, and necessary ambulance, hospital, professional nursing and funeral services, and, in the case of persons employed or self-employed at the time of an accident, any amounts actually lost by reason of inability to work and earn wages or salary or their equivalent, but not other income, that would otherwise have been earned in the normal course of an injured person's employment, and for payments in fact made to others, not members of the injured person's household, and reasonably incurred in obtaining from those others ordinary and necessary services in lieu of those that, had he not been injured, the injured person would have performed not for income but for the benefit of himself or members of his household, and, in the case of persons neither employed nor

Context. The original policy does not provide a context for the information in the policy. There is nothing to explain to the reader what the document is about. It begins with a statement about an agreement of some sort that the insurance company has with the insured. The statement is never discussed, nor is it labeled with an informative heading. There is no introduction to explain what the policy is for, what divisions or sections it contains, or what kinds of coverage it provides. Instead, the policy jumps from the agreement boilerplate into "Coverage A." The reader isn't told how many different kinds of coverage there are, why there are different kinds of coverage, or how each kind fits into the overall scheme.

In contrast, the modified policy clearly labels the agreement provision with a large title in boldface type and explains exactly what the insurer and insured are agreeing to. This section also provides the reader with a definition of what an insurance policy is (i.e., a contract) and tells the reader exactly what this contract consists of.

The main body of the modified policy also has a boldface title and contains an introduction. This section defines compulsory insurance and provides a roadmap for what is ahead: It tells the reader how many parts the policy contains and where to find information on coverage and costs.

Tone. The tone in the original policy is impersonal — the information is not directed to anyone in particular. In addition, the sentences do not always tell *who* is being discussed. For example, Coverage A, Division 2 states that "The company will pay [to whom?] . . . subject to any applicable deductible [whose deductible?] all reasonable expenses incurred within two years [by whom?] from the date of the accident [whose accident?] for necessary medical, surgical, x-ray, and dental services."

The modified policy has a personal tone; it addresses the insured as "you" and refers to the insurer as "we." The sentences all contain subjects and objects, so that the reader can always tell who is being addressed and who is being discussed. For example, Part 1 opens with the following statement: "Under this Part, *we* will pay damages *to people injured* or killed by *your* auto in Massachusetts accidents. The damages *we* will pay are the amounts *the injured person* is entitled to collect."

Organization. The original policy presents information in an illogical order, without natural topic or section divisions. It is divided into broad sections that cover a hodgepodge of different subjects. Part 1, for example, has the following heading: LIABILITY, PERSONAL INJURY PROTECTION, MEDICAL PAYMENTS AND PHYSICAL DAMAGE INSURING

2 Our Agreement

This policy is a legal contract under Massachusetts law. Because this is an auto policy, it only covers accidents and losses which result from the ownership, maintenance or use of autos. The exact protection is determined by the coverages you purchased.

We agree to provide the insurance protection you purchased for accidents which happen while this policy is in force.

You agree to pay premiums and any Merit Rating surcharges when due and to cooperate with us in case of accidents or claims.

Our contract consists of this policy, the Coverage Selections page, any endorsements agreed upon, and your application for insurance. Oral promises or statements made by you or our agent are not part of this policy.

There are many laws of Massachusetts relating to automobile insurance. We and you must and do agree that, when those laws apply, they are part of this policy.

Compulsory Insurance

There are four Parts to Compulsory Insurance. They are called Compulsory Insurance because Massachusetts law requires you to buy all of them before you can register your auto. No law requires you to buy more than this Compulsory Insurance. However, if you have financed your auto, the bank or finance company may legally insist that you have some Optional Insurance as a condition of your loan.

The amount of your coverage and the cost of each Part is shown on the Coverage Selections page.

Your Compulsory Insurance does not pay for any damage to your auto no matter what happens to it.

**Part 1.
Bodily Injury
To Others**

Under this Part, we will pay damages to people injured or killed by your auto in Massachusetts accidents. Damages are the amounts an injured person is legally entitled to collect for bodily injury through a court judgment or settlement. We will pay only if you or someone else using your auto with your consent is legally responsible for the accident. The most we will pay for injuries to any one person as a result of any one accident is $5,000. The most we will pay for injuries to two or more people as a result of any one accident is a total of $10,000. This is the most we will pay as the result of a single accident no matter how many autos or premiums are shown on the Coverage Selections page.

We will *not* pay:

1. For injuries to guest occupants of your auto.

2. For accidents outside of Massachusetts or in places in Massachusetts where the public has no right of access.

3. For injuries to any employees of the legally responsible person if they are entitled to Massachusetts workers' compensation benefits.

The law provides a special protection for anyone entitled to damages under this Part. We must pay their claims even if false statements were made when applying for this policy or your auto registration. We must also pay even if you or the legally responsible person fails to cooperate with us after the accident. We will, however, be entitled to reimbursement from the person who did not cooperate or who made any false statements.

If a claim is covered by us and also by another company authorized to sell auto insurance in Massachusetts, we will pay only our proportional share. If someone covered under this Part is using an auto he or she does not own at the time of the accident, the owner's auto insurance pays up to its limits before we pay. Then, we will pay up to the limits shown

AGREEMENTS. This vast area is then divided into different coverages that are in turn subdivided. There is no roadmap to clarify the logic or meaning of these divisions for the reader.

Moreover, the information in each section of the original policy is rarely presented in an effective manner. Each division consists of tightly packed paragraphs that are not divided into useful parts. For instance, one key fact — that the accident must occur on property open to the public in Massachusetts — is almost lost at the bottom of the first paragraph in Coverage A, Division 1. It occurs at the end of a 162-word sentence.

The modified version, on the other hand, is divided into logical, manageable sections. The reader is told from the outset that the policy has four parts. Each part covers only one subject or a few closely related subjects. Part 1, for example, covers only "Bodily Injury to Others." The modified policy further sorts information into short sections that highlight important points and that are useful to the reader. Part 1 is divided into sections explaining what the policy covers and what it does not cover. The reader does not have to dig out information; the policy clearly states, for example, that "We will not pay: For accidents outside of Massachusetts or in places in Massachusetts where the public has no right of access."

Sentence structure. The original policy contains many long sentences. For instance, the second paragraph in Coverage A, Division 1 consists of one 251-word sentence. It contains many phrases and subordinate clauses and is extremely difficult to follow.

However, it is not length alone that makes the sentences hard to read. Inserted phrases add complexity. The sentence that constitutes paragraph three is somewhat shorter but has so much verbiage between the subject and verb, and such an unusual ordering of ideas, that it is painful to read.

(3) *This policy,* the written application therefor, if any, and any endorsement which shall not conflict with the provisions of said Massachusetts Compulsory Automobile Liability Security Act and all Acts amendatory thereof or supplementary thereto, *shall constitute the entire contract* between the parties.

Readers have to get to the end of the sentence before they realize why all of this information is given: These documents make up the whole contract between insurer and insured.

The modified policy breaks all of its information into relatively short sentences and uses a standard word order. The sentences also have an internal logic; for example, the reader is told at the beginning of the following sentence that the topic is the content of the insurance contract.

> *Our contract consists* of this policy, the Coverage Selections page, any endorsements agreed upon, and your application for insurance. Oral promises or statements made by you or our agent are not part of this contract.

Vocabulary. The original policy is full of technical legal terms and concepts. For example, the policy mentions "consequential damages," "compulsory coverage," and "default of the insured." None of these is explained or defined. In addition, this policy lists full citations for the Massachusetts laws that govern particular provisions. These citations disrupt the flow and are of little or no use to many of the audiences that use the policy.

The modified version has eliminated much of the technical language and has provided explanations for terms that could not be eliminated. The modified version also has eliminated the full citations of Massachusetts law. Instead, the policy retains its legal integrity by incorporating the applicable laws by general reference at the end of "Our Agreement." The audiences that need the citations can get them from another source.

Layout, type style, etc. The layout of the original policy consists of large blocks of print, with little white space to break up the text and few visual cues to guide the reader through the document. The few headings do not contrast much with the rest of the text, so they don't really stand out.

The typesize is tolerable, but the type style is quite hard to read — the letters are tall and thin, giving words and sentences a "crowded" look.

The overall effect is of a mass of dense type that is hard on the eyes and that is certainly uninviting — and possibly intimidating — to the reader.

In contrast, the layout of the modified policy consists of smaller, discrete chunks separated by visible markers — lines and white space. Major headings, at the tops of the pages, are large and bold. Subheadings, in boldface type, are "hung" in the wide left margin, where they are easily visible and can provide signposts through the document.

The typesize is larger than in the original policy, and the type style is far more readable; even elderly policyholders should have no difficulty reading the modified policy. The overall visual effect is pleasant, even inviting, to the reader.

EXERCISES

1. Describe the purposes of the following document, and then list the audiences for the document.

```
                                                             1 0 4
         MARY A. DOE                        _____ 19____
         1000 STONEY STREET
         ANYTOWN, USA 00000                          65-309
                                                     ──────
                                                      580
 PAY TO THE
 ORDER OF_____| $_____

 _____ DOLLARS

 1st BIG Bank
 ANYTOWN, USA 00000

 FOR _____

 ⑆058000502⑆  ⑈04⑈ 1958574⑈  42101⑈
```

2. The document reproduced below is an agreement for legal services between a lawyer and a client. The rules of legal ethics encourage lawyers to put such agreements in writing in order to avoid disputes that otherwise might arise over the fee or the services that the attorney will render. Obviously, it is extremely important to *both* parties that a client fully understand what he or she is signing. Read through the agreement, then comment on how well you think this document addresses its major audience. What changes might make the agreement more effective?

RETAINER AGREEMENT

THIS AGREEMENT is made for the purpose of retaining the law firm of _____, to represent us in our claim for damages which were sustained as a result of injuries and property damage due to an accident which occurred at _____, at approximately _____ o'clock _____.m., on the _____ day of _____, 198___ ___.

Said Law Firm is hereby retained on a contingent basis and is to receive an amount equal to Thirty-three and one-third Percent (33⅓%) of any amount which is recovered for us, by settlement; an amount equal to Forty Percent (40%) of any amount which is recovered for us if this matter goes to trial and a favorable verdict is rendered; and an amount equal to Fifty Percent (50%) of any amount which is recovered for us if this matter goes to trial and then an appeal is taken. It is further understood and agreed that we will pay all reasonable and necessary costs arising out of the handling of this claim by our attorneys, including any expenses incurred during litigation of this matter. We agree that said Law Firm has made no promises or guarantees regarding the outcome of our claim. We understand that _____, will investigate our claim and if, after so investigating the claim does not appear to said Law Firm to have merit, then said Law Firm shall have the right to cancel this Agreement.

IN THE EVENT NO RECOVERY IS MADE, IT IS UNDERSTOOD THAT WE ARE NOT OBLIGATED TO PAY ANY FEE TO SAID LAW FIRM.

IN WITNESS WHEREOF, we hereunto set our hands and seals this _____ day of _____, 198_____.

WITNESS:

_____   _____

_____   _____

Accepted: _____
                          (name of firm)

By: _____

C Identifying Constraints

Obviously, we cannot discuss — or even imagine — *all* of the possible constraints that you might encounter when writing a legal document. However, there are some constraints that writers of legal documents encounter more often than others, and these are the ones to keep in mind and attempt to accommodate. We concentrate on the most common constraints, but the strategies described for dealing with them can also help you identify and prepare for unique constraints.

1. Constraints of Time and Space

In your first year of law school, you will learn firsthand about two of the most significant constraints affecting those who write in the legal profession: *time* and *space*. When your professor assigns the first memo or brief, he or she will probably give you a rigid deadline and possibly a rigid page limit. These limitations are established for practical reasons — most professors have neither the time nor the desire to grade voluminous memos — but primarily so that you will learn to think and write efficiently.

Most practicing attorneys as well, will tell you that they conduct a running battle to keep up with deadlines and the obligations that come with each client, as well as balancing the needs of all their clients. Because of time and resource constraints, attorneys must write efficiently — to produce high quality work in a limited time. Furthermore, the readers of legal documents — judges, law clerks, senior partners, clients, and others — also have time constraints. A busy judge, for example, will not have the time or the inclination to wade through pages and pages of writing to find the relevant information. You will have more success with a document that is well organized, concise, and to the point.

Learn as much as you can about your time and space limits before you start writing. Budget your time early so that you can allot enough to each major issue. Be sure to leave adequate time for revising, since legal documents tend to grow and change as you refine your research and even while you are writing. And of course leave time for typing and editing.

You should also budget your writing space with care. If your memo can be only 15 pages long, keep this fact in mind from the moment you start planning the memo until you complete the final draft. Throughout the time you are researching and gathering materials, organizing the content, and drafting, you should continually question the relative value of each piece of information and the time and space you can devote to it. Be ready to shift and reallocate as you rethink your writing strategy or reevaluate your research materials. Expect to write more than one draft. And expect to be making changes until you complete your last draft.

2. Format Requirements

The constraints imposed by format requirements are also important. There are formal and informal rules for the format of legal documents; you should be aware of them before you write.

Formal rules. Most courts and agencies have requirements for the format of specific documents and rules for how to write them. For example, courts and agencies specify a page limit for certain documents and prescribe the divisions and titles you must create, the size and kind of paper you must use, the size and style of type, and where certain provisions must appear in the document.

To get some idea of how precise and demanding format requirements can be, look at the following excerpt from the Rules of the Supreme Court of the United States. This passage is just a small part of Rule 33, which prescribes format requirements for the major documents that are submitted to the Court.

RULE 33

Form of Jurisdictional Statements, Petitions, Briefs, Appendices, Motions, and Other Documents Filed with the Court

1. (a) Except for typewritten filings permitted by Rules 42.2(c), 43, and 46, all jurisdictional statements, petitions, briefs, appendices, and other documents filed with the Court shall be produced by standard typographic printing, which is preferred, or by any photostatic or similar process which produces a clear, black image on white paper; but ordinary carbon copies may not be used.

(b) The text of documents produced by standard typographic printing shall appear in print as 11-point or larger type with 2-point or more leading between lines. Footnotes shall appear in print as 9-point or larger type with 2-point or more leading between lines. Such documents shall be printed on both sides of the page.

(c) The text of documents produced by a photostatic or similar process shall be done in pica type at no more than 10 characters per inch with the lines double-spaced, except that indented quotations and footnotes may be single-spaced. In footnotes, elite type at no more than 12 characters per inch may be used. Such documents may be duplicated on both sides of the page, if practicable. They shall not be reduced in duplication.

(d) Whether duplicated under subparagraph (b) or (c) of this paragraph, documents shall be produced on opaque, unglazed paper $6\frac{1}{8}$ by $9\frac{1}{4}$ inches in size, with typed matter approximately $4\frac{1}{8}$ by $7\frac{1}{8}$ inches, and margins of at least $\frac{3}{4}$ inch on all sides. The paper shall be firmly bound in at least two places along the left margin so as to make an easily opened volume, and no part of the text shall be obscured by the binding. However, appendices in patent cases may be duplicated in such size as is necessary to utilize copies of patent documents.

2. (a) All documents filed with the Court must bear on the cover, in the following order, from the top of the page: (1) the number of the case or, if there is none, a space for one; (2) the name of this Court; (3) the Term; (4) the caption of the case as appropriate in this Court; (5) the nature of the proceeding and the name of the court from which the action is brought (e.g., On Appeal from the Supreme Court of California; On Writ of Certiorari to the United States Court of Appeals for the Fifth Circuit); (6) the title of the paper (e.g., Jurisdictional Statement, Brief for Respondent, Joint Appendix); (7) the name, post office address, and telephone number of the member of the Bar of this Court who is counsel of record for the party concerned, and upon whom service is to be made. The individual names of other members of the Bar of this Court or of the Bar of the highest court in their respective states and, if desired, their post office addresses, may be added, but counsel of record shall be clearly identified. The foregoing shall be displayed in an appropriate typographic manner and, except for the identification of counsel, may not be set in type smaller than 11-point or in upper case pica.

If you violate formal rules of format for legal documents, you risk having your document rejected. This can mean that the document has been permanently rejected or that you have to redo and resubmit it. Resubmitting a document to a court or an agency can result in additional complications: You can end up missing a filing deadline before you are able to resubmit. Obviously, you must make it your business to find out what the formal rules for the format of a document are. Often you can find these by consulting volumes that contain court rules and other rules of procedure. If you are unable to find the information in the books, you can try telephoning the agency or talking to the court clerk.

Informal rules: Rules of usage and tradition. There are other format rules that are not strictly prescribed but have evolved over the years into accepted or expected standards. For example, many courts do not prescribe a rigid formula for a brief, but most attorneys follow a basic format, with minor variations. Informal guidelines can be as important as formal rules, because the reader often expects a particular type of document to follow certain patterns. At best, an unfamiliar arrangement may slow the reader down; at worst, the reader may feel that the document is insufficient or inappropriate.

Before writing, find out the informal format rules for your document. For briefs and memos, law professors can often provide you with outlines or sample documents, or you may be able to obtain a memo or brief from a practicing attorney. This book has two sample briefs and two sample memos, and you may find other books that also have samples. However, you must choose carefully when you use a document as a model. Not all "model" briefs are well organized, well written, or well formatted. The same is true of documents you find in form books: Many are full of antiquated provisions and archaic language. The goal of this book is to teach you how to create your own documents and to help you recognize and choose good models to follow.

3. Citation Constraints

Because our legal system is based on case law and statutes, legal arguments and explanations are derived from or based on these sources. A writer must include complete, precise references or citations to supporting materials whenever they are used.

Citation form. Citations can be placed either in the text or in footnotes, depending upon the type of document. For example, law review articles and legal treatises are footnoted, while most citations in briefs and memos are in the text itself. You will find most of the rules for citing legal sources in *A Uniform System of Citation* by the Harvard Law Review Association.

There are rules that you can follow to keep your references from disrupting the flow of the text. One general rule for using footnotes is to write the textual part of the document so that it stands on its own — that is, the footnotes should elaborate on the text, but the reader should be able to follow the text without them. Otherwise, you force the reader to continually switch from text to footnotes in order to understand the document. Many law review articles contain good examples of text that can stand on its own. This system allows the reader to cover the text fairly quickly for a superficial review of the article or to read footnotes together with the text for more thorough coverage.

Avoid using long string citations within the text itself. String citations are lists of sources that are meant to substantiate a particular point or statement in the text. String cites are bad style; they can disrupt the flow of your text.

Furthermore, they may cast doubt upon the credibility of your claims because they can give the impression that your case is so weak that you have to substantiate it with every source you can find. You can substantiate your claims far more effectively by using only one or two of your strongest sources.[6]

Referencing and cross-referencing. Legislation, regulations, codes, and other similar documents and texts often contain complex cross-referencing. If improperly used or overused, references to other parts of the text can disrupt the flow of the document.

Here is an example of what can happen when the text contains so many references that the reader must turn to them just to understand what is going on. Section 179 of the 1977 Internal Revenue Code reads as follows:

§179 **Additional first-year depreciation allowance for small business**
  (a) General rule — In the case of section 179 property, the term "reasonable allowance" as used in section 167(a) may, at the election of the taxpayer, include an allowance, for the first taxable year for which a deduction is allowable under section 167 to the taxpayer with respect to such property, of 20 percent of the cost of such property.

The term "section 179 property" is not defined until part (d) of section 179 and, if you want to know what is in section 167, you must flip through many pages. In other words, you must read forward to section (d) and backward to section 167 before you can finish the first paragraph of section 179.

These kinds of reference problems can be avoided. If you have to refer to other sections of the document or to different documents in your discussion, try giving a short description of what is in the reference or refer to it by its title. That way, the reader can follow the flow and logic of your discussion without having to search for the actual reference. For example:

General rule for section 179 property (tangible personal property, as specifically defined in (d)):

  If the taxpayer chooses, the term "reasonable allowance," as used in section 167(a) (for figuring a reasonable depreciation deduction for exhaustion, or wear and tear of business property) may include an allowance of 20 percent of the cost of that property, for the first taxable

6. For additional details on choosing your strongest sources, see H. Weihofen, Legal Writing Style 292-295 (2d ed. 1980).

year for which section 167 allows the taxpayer a deduction for that property.

4. Constraints on Content

There are constraints imposed by the kinds of information that go into legal documents. You will often find that you do not have access to all of the information that you may think you need: The law may be vague, in flux, or ambiguous, so that you cannot find the legal "answers" that you want. The facts of a case may be incomplete or distorted, so that you do not have a clear picture of what has happened.

Clients can seldom provide a complete picture of the circumstances surrounding an event. And even if a client knows all the details and is able to articulate them, he or she is naturally going to see the events from only one point of view. You can use discovery to get additional information from your adversary, but even that is unlikely to provide you with a full picture of the facts. There is also the chance that a client or witness will intentionally withhold information, unintentionally invent information to fill in gaps or to please the attorney, or simply lie.

Legal writers who ignore the constraints on content can fall into the trap of "filling in the gaps" in the facts or the law themselves. They may assume that certain things are true or that certain events occurred, or they may draw unfounded inferences from information that they do have.

Before you write a legal document, you need to know what information exists and what is missing and to plan how to present what you do know in the best possible way. One way to do this is to acknowledge a lack of information and then argue the *likelihood* that something has occurred. Then build your case around "logical" inferences or "reasonable" assumptions. Here is an example of what we mean.

Attorney X represented the estate of Brian Smith in a wrongful death case with the following facts. Smith's car was moving in an intersection on the road perpendicular to the road the defendant was on. Smith's car was struck broadside by the defendant's car after the defendant allegedly ran a red light. The only witness to the accident was a police officer who saw the incident while sitting at the intersection. He was on the same road as Smith, coming from the opposite direction. The police officer was waiting for the light to change. Here is a map of the intersection. The **A** represents Smith's car, **B** is the defendant's car, and **C** is the police car. Just before the accident, the police officer noticed that his own light had turned green. He saw Smith

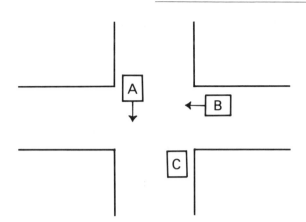

move forward into the intersection. Before he could move, the defendant sped across the intersection. The police officer is ready to testify that the defendant ran a red light.

In his brief Attorney X wrote that the defendant had violated a traffic law by running a red light. He used this information as a foundation for his theory that the defendant was driving with reckless disregard for the safety of others and was thus liable in tort for the plaintiff's death.

The defendant's brief, however, destroyed the very foundation of the plaintiff's argument: The only witness, the police officer, did not *see* the defendant's traffic light turn red. He only deduced that it had. The attorney for the defendant pointed out that the defendant's traffic light could have been malfunctioning and may never have turned red at all.

Attorney Y, representing the plaintiff in an identical case, wrote her brief with a different strategy. First, she realized that there were facts missing: No one had seen the traffic light change. Second, Attorney Y was careful not to draw conclusions about what had happened. Instead, she acknowledged the gap in information. She then proceeded to argue *around* the missing information by showing that all of the facts pointed to a high probability that the defendant had run a red light. She noted that it is extremely rare for lights on the perpendicular roads of an intersection to be green at the same time. She also made use of the occupation and experience of her witness, the police officer, stating that the police officer was familiar with the area and with road conditions and had learned a great deal about accidents in his work. She also emphasized his credibility and honesty. She built the rest of her case upon the "highly reasonable assumption" that the defendant ran a red light. She was thus able to overcome the constraints on content and to win her case.

EXERCISES

1. Look at the pleading on page 66. As you may remember, a pleading is a legal document used to state the facts that make up a plaintiff's cause of action or a defendant's defense. In other words, pleadings give each party an opportunity to tell his or her story to the court — to articulate grievances or deny accusations.

    A pleading can be fairly complicated or quite simple, depending upon the particulars of the case or the kind of case. The pleading reproduced here is a simple, relatively informal complaint that can be filed in a trial court if the case involves uncomplicated facts, small damages, or is the kind of case that is routinely handled in that particular court. Because these cases are fairly small or routine, an attorney can create a pleading by merely filling in the blanks.

    To complete the sample, the plaintiff's attorney has to supply the "particulars" or relevant facts of the case in concise form. The space on this form under the title "Statement of Claim" has room for approximately 200 words. As a practice exercise, write up a 200-word summary of the relevant facts contained in the following attorney-client interview. Keep in mind that the case is one involving *bailment*, a situation in which one person (the *bailee*) holds the property of another person (the *bailor*) for a particular purpose.

    The elements of a bailment are

    1. a delivery of the property by the bailor to the bailee
    2. a contract, express or implied, that the bailee will keep the property for a given purpose and, after the purpose has been fulfilled, will return the property to the bailor, account for the property, or keep the property until the bailor claims it, depending upon the circumstances

    The bailee has certain obligations or duties to the bailor: If the bailment is for the mutual benefit of the bailor and the bailee, the bailee must exercise ordinary due care in keeping the property. In State X, this has been interpreted to mean that the bailee must treat the property with as much care as a person of ordinary prudence would use in taking care of his or her own property. If the bailee fails in this duty to the bailor, then the bailee is guilty of negligence.

    Do not try to analyze the law and facts, but do try to use the elements

File original and one copy for each defendant

DISTRICT COURT OF MARYLAND FOR.................................

City/County

FORM NO. 3

Located at.. Case No. ....

Court Address

(1) ....
Exact name of individual or corporation

Trade name of party suing

Full mailing address

City/Town, State, Zip Code   County

(2) ....
Full name of individual or corporation

Trade name of party suing

Full mailing address

City/Town, State, Zip Code   County

Plaintiff

Sues

(1) ....
Exact name of individual or corporation

Address for service

City/Town, State, Zip code   County

Name, title & address of agent to be served

(2) ....
Full name of individual or corporation

Address for service

City/Town, State, Zip Code   County

Name, title & address of agent to be served

Defendant

STATEMENT OF CLAIM

Clerk: Please docket this case in an action of ☐ contract ☐ tort ☐ replevin ☐ detinue
The particulars of this case are...
....
....
....
....
....
....
....
....
....
....

The Plaintiff claims:

☐ $........... with interest of $........... and attorney's fees of $........... plus court costs of $...........
☐ Return of the property and damages of $........................ for its detention in an action of replevin.
☐ Return of the property, or its value, plus damages of $................ for its detention in an action of detinue.
☐ Other ....
....

....
Signature of Attorney   Address of Attorney

....
Signature of Plaintiff   Telephone No. of Plaintiff or Attorney

WRIT OF SUMMONS

TO THE DEFENDANT: You have been sued and you are hereby notified that the trial will be held in the District Court.

IMPORTANT NOTICE:

If you intend to be present at the trial, at which time you may present a defense to the claim, you must notify the court in writing within 21 days of receiving this notice. (You may use the form below.) If you fail to file such notice, judgment by default may be given against you for the amounts claimed above.

To addressee's postal agent: If you signed the postal receipt for this summons and cannot deliver it or make its contents known to the defendant in time for the defendant to appear as directed, please advise the Court at once in writing, giving reasons.

....
Date

....
Clerk

NOTICE OF INTENTION TO DEFEND

Case No. ....   Trial Date........................

I intend to be present at the trial of this case and demand proof of the Plaintiff's claim.

....
Defendant   Attorney for defendant

....
Address   Telephone No.   Address   Telephone No

CV-1 (Rev. 6/78)   (complete reverse side)

Exact full names of parties must be given

If more space is needed please affix an additional sheet as a part of the particulars

of bailment as guidelines for selecting the facts to include in your summary. For example, the fact that the garage had signs of previous break-ins is relevant to whether the owner used ordinary care in the way he kept the plaintiff's car. On the other hand, the fact that the plaintiff never saw the place where the car was wrecked is not relevant.

Attorney (A):   Tell me about your problem.

Client (C):   My car was stolen and totalled.

A: When?

C: On March 3.

A: Have you reported this to the police?

C: Yes — actually, I didn't have to. They called me at 1:00 in the morning — Saturday morning — to tell me that they had found it wrecked on a back road — way out somewhere. Anyway, my mother and I later drove out to check to see where the road was, but we never could find it. It must be a small farm road or something.

A: Where did the police take the car after they found it?

B: To a towing place. That's where I went to get it after they called me. I never saw the place where it was smashed. It hit a tree.

A: And the police made a report?

C: Yes. But only after we towed the car again, back to Schmidt's.

A: Schmidt's?

C: Where the car was when it was stolen. It was being repaired there. It was stolen late Friday night. It was supposed to be picked up on Saturday. They had finally fixed it.

A: How long had it been at Schmidt's?

C: Well, I called them on that Monday and asked if they could fix the car and they said yes, bring it by.

A: Who told you this?

C: Jimmy, the mechanic. He said he was really busy, but to bring it over and he'd try to fit it in sometime during the week.

A: And he did, I take it. You say he worked on it Friday?

C: Yes, finally. He said to call every evening and he'd let me know if he got to it that day. I called all week, but he didn't work on it til Friday.

A: Where was the car all this time?

C: In their parking lot. It was on the very edge of the lot. You know, the thing that gets me is that nobody seemed to take this very seriously. When we got the car back to Schmidt's, all the mechanics were looking at it and going "wow," and they all took turns sitting in it.

A: What about the policeman?

C: He didn't care. Everybody was just joking around. I don't think anybody was taking it too seriously. I heard several guys saying that Schmidt's gets broken into all the time, that stuff happens a lot.

A: Guys?

C: The mechanics.

A: Have there been other car thefts?

C: Not that I know of. But one of the mechanics said that he came in one day in December and the door of the office part of the garage had been bashed in. And another guy said that another time someone got in and took an adding machine, and that tires are stolen all the time.

A: Do you know the names of these people or do you remember what they look like?

C: One's name is Bruce. He drove the tow truck. I don't know about the other one. Schmidt is Bruce's father-in-law.

A: Is there a fence or anything around the lot?

C: No. It's right off the street.

A: How did they start your car? Do you know how it was taken?

C: They got the key when they broke into the garage.

A: Wait a minute — you mean that someone broke into the garage first?

C: Yes.

A: How did they get in?

C: They just broke a pane of glass in the bay door of the garage and pulled a lever inside. Then you can just slide the door up. From the garage, you can walk right into the office. The keys are all on a keyboard up on the wall. I think that that kind of thing has happened before because one of the other panes of glass in the bay door was replaced by plexiglass.

A: Can you see the keys from outside?

C: Oh yes. The office is like in a gas station. It's mostly glass. The keys are right on the wall.

A: Did anyone else hear these comments that the mechanics were making?

C: My mother was with me.

A: Have you talked to the owner of the place?

C: Yes, and he said his insurance would pay for the car. But the insurance company called me and said that it wouldn't because Mr. Schmidt wasn't liable or responsible, that it wasn't his fault. Anyway, at least Schmidt paid for the towing.

A: Do they light their lot at night?

C: Well, the cop told me that Plunket Donuts, next door, used to be open all night and their lights used to light up the garage's lot too, but since Plunket started closing at ten, things get dark around the area. Schmidt doesn't have his own lights.

2. Using the interview in question number 1, come up with 10 interrogatories that you would like to ask Mr. Schmidt, the owner of the garage. Each interrogatory must ask for only one thing: You cannot disguise two questions as one (for example, you cannot ask: "Are you married and how many children do you have?"). Also, try to ask the most pertinent questions you can because you will want to use your limited number of interrogatories to find out all kinds of background and additional information, as well as to verify the information that your client gave you.

4

Getting

Organized

After going through the steps in Chapter 3 you will have answered the following questions.

1. What are you writing about? What is the *topic* (the main idea)? What is your *thesis* (the point you want to make)?
2. Who is your audience?
3. What is the purpose of the document? Are you presenting information, or trying to elicit it? Is the document a teaching device? Does it simply present pros and cons, or are you arguing for or against an idea?

The answers to these pre-writing questions will help to determine the way you organize a document.

A Why Organize?

You must always impose order on your writing. Legal documents, in particular, demand a tight, logical structure. In other documents poor organization may interfere with readers' comprehension, but in legal documents poor organization can cause even greater problems. In an adversarial document, for example, your opponents will be looking for any weak spots they can find. A gap in your logic caused by poor organization can give your opponents an opening for attack. In a nonadversarial document, poor organization can make the reader believe that either your knowledge and research are not thorough or that your thinking is not logical. While you are in law school, your professors will be judging the organization and logical progression of your writing assignments and examinations.

One of the best ways to organize a document is to create a written outline. This can be a simple list or something more elaborate, with many topics and subtopics. The complexity of the outline usually depends on the complexity of the document.

When you create an outline, you give yourself the opportunity to organize and reorganize your ideas to provide the most effective focus for the document. If you are constructing a document intended to persuade, writing and rewriting an outline will help you build a more effective argument and will also help you spot any gaps or weaknesses in your logic. Outlining can in itself suggest new ideas and fresh perspectives.

When should you organize? You should start organizing material into an outline as soon as you have identified the main issues and decided what points you want to make. No doubt you will revise this outline as you continue to research and even after you have started writing. That is both normal and useful: The document will evolve in a thorough, systematic manner. Minutes invested in outlining will save you hours later. A well-developed outline will make your writing task easier and will keep you from going off on tangents in research or in writing.

B How to Organize an Expository Document

Let's start with a basic type of document — one that has the purpose of simply informing, not of persuading or eliciting information. Here is an example of an outline for an expository document.

1. Introduction providing a context
   - introduces the topic
   - amplifies the topic
   - gives some background
   - states the thesis
   - sets out a "roadmap" explaining what the document will cover and the order in which the material will be covered
2. First event or idea
   - information to amplify event or idea
3. Other events or ideas
   - information to amplify events or ideas
4. Closing or conclusion

1. Providing a Context

It is essential to provide a context at the beginning of every legal document for the information that is to follow. You can never assume that your readers will know beforehand what you are writing about. If they have to read far into the document before they discover the topic and the purpose of the document, then you have not done a good job. If the reader has to deduce the context or guess at it, then your document may be ineffective.

Sometimes an informative title can provide enough context. Other times a document may require several pages of introductory material. How much context you need depends on the purpose, audience, and length of the document.

The purpose of providing a context is to link new information to information that you know the reader has or is very likely to have. Thus, in general, you should begin by telling the reader, as specifically as possible, what you will be talking about. Then, depending upon how complex the document is and how familiar the reader is with the topic, you can amplify the topic by providing more information about the ideas you will be covering in the body of the document.

If it is appropriate, you might then want to provide a small amount of background. This could consist of a sentence or two briefly outlining the history of the issue you are dealing with, describing the extent of the problem, or providing any other type of background information the reader might need. If this is a document in which you will be making a point, state your thesis, or what you are proposing, here. In a memo especially, it is helpful for the reader to know what your position is from the beginning. And, in fact, experienced readers will expect a *short answer* — a condensed version of your conclusion — at this point. (See Chapter 9.)

Finally, if you are writing a fairly long document, you should set up a "roadmap" of what will follow: Tell your readers what you will cover and the order in which you will cover it. It is also helpful to refer to "signposts" — section headings or chapter headings — in which specific information is to be found. (See Chapter 8.) Following is a proposed rewrite of the introduction to a trade regulation rule for proprietary vocational and home-study schools. Notice how this introduction describes what is in each section of the rule.

WHAT THIS RULE IS ABOUT

The purpose of the Rule is to provide students with information that will enable them to make an informed decision on whether to buy a course, to discourage abusive sales practices by representatives of vocational schools, and to give the student the right to cancel at will without a heavy financial loss.

The Rule is organized in the following way: The first section lists a number of the unfair and deceptive acts and practices that schools have engaged in. The next section tells when and how this Rule becomes effective. The third section defines the schools, courses, and students covered by the Rule. All of the subsequent sections deal with the specific steps a school must follow to avoid violations: the kinds of records a school should keep to comply with the Rule; the rules a school must follow when it advertises a course and makes job or earnings claims; what a school must do when a student applies; the special rules a school must follow if it furnishes a student with course materials during the cooling-off period; and what the school must do if a student cancels an enrollment contract during or after the cooling-off period. The Rule is followed by appendices that contain forms which the school must use to comply with the Rule.

2. Presenting the Substance of the Document

The next part of a document contains the information or ideas you want to present — the substance of the document. If there is a thesis or main point to the document, the information you present here will explain the basis for it.

How do you decide what is a logical order for the events, ideas, or information you are presenting? First, write down all the ideas, events, or pieces of information that you think are relevant to your topic or thesis.[1] Next, decide on an "organizing principle" — the principle that will unify your material and govern its order. In choosing an organizing principle, look for a conceptual relationship among the ideas, events, or pieces of information you are dealing with. Analyze the material to see if the pieces of it are strongly related or ordered by any of the following.

1. *Cause and effect*: Totally different events B, C, and D all appear to have happened as a result of incident A.
2. *Time*: A, B, and C follow each other in a time sequence.
3. *Similarity of events or ideas*: Several events appear to have similar characteristics.

---

1. See N. Brand and J. O. White, Legal Writing: The Strategy of Persuasion 6, 57 (1976), for information and exercises on how to "brainstorm" an idea or issue, that is, how to come up with all the arguments, points to consider, and supporting evidence.

4. *Priority:* A, B, and C are all exceedingly important and must be considered together, separately from D, E, F, and G.

There are other possible ways of grouping material. The point is to have a reasonable plan for organizing information. Look for any unifying factors. For example, if Party A and Party B are both involved in an action, you can use "parties" as your overall organizing principle, discussing all of the information concerning Party A first, then dealing with the information that is relevant to Party B. You might also order your information by legal issue or by action, if there is more than one. Sometimes your organizing principle will be dictated or influenced by outside sources. For example, usually the most logical and efficient way to order a reply brief is to follow the order of the arguments in your opponent's brief. That way, you can answer the arguments point by point.

One way to make the process of organizing and grouping information easier is to put each piece of information on an index card. You can then try out different groupings and subgroupings of information by rearranging the cards. You will find that some groupings are more logical or more satisfying than others.

Once you have chosen an organizing principle for a document, do not depart from it in the overall structure of the document. In other words, if your organizing principle for a memo is *priority,* make sure that each major issue is presented in order of its importance. Don't suddenly start presenting events in the order in which they happened (unless that order coincides with priority).

The same general principles apply to grouping and organizing material within each subpart of your document. However, once your overall organizing principle has been set out clearly, you can then use different organizing principles *within* a given subpart or paragraph. For example, your overall organizing principle for a memo may be order of importance of issues, but the organizing principle within a discussion of one issue might be cause-and-effect.

3. Writing the Conclusion

Finally, provide a conclusion or closing statement for the document. The nature of your conclusion will depend upon the length and the complexity of the document. If the document is short and fairly straightforward, you might close by telling the reader what will happen next or by inviting the reader to ask questions. If the document is long or complex, it is a good idea to briefly summarize the information you have presented in the document and restate your main point or thesis and the reasons for it.

4. Organizing an Expository Document: An Example

Read the following letter written by an attorney to a client. After the letter, we discuss the way it is organized in terms of the outline we have presented.

Dear Mr. Williams:

I am writing to summarize the status of your discrimination suit against Wambush, Inc. and to tell you about what we have to do next. As I mentioned to you in our telephone conversation of July 29, Wambush filed two motions seeking to dismiss your lawsuit and we intended to vigorously oppose both motions. I am pleased to report that the court denied both of Wambush's motions to dismiss.

In its first motion, Wambush sought to have your lawsuit dismissed for improper venue. Wambush tried to convince the court that we should have filed this lawsuit in San Francisco rather than in Washington, D.C. In its motion Wambush argued that since its principal place of business was San Francisco, California, this lawsuit should have been brought in San Francisco. However, the law on that point is fairly clear. Under Title VII of the Civil Rights Act of 1964, you are entitled to file a lawsuit in any federal court located in the state where the act of racial discrimination occurred. Since you unsuccessfully applied for a job with Wambush's Washington, D.C. office, then the act of racial discrimination, if one is proven, occurred in the District of Columbia. The court agreed with our interpretation of the law and denied Wambush's motion to dismiss for improper venue.

In its second motion, Wambush claimed that it was not an "employer" within the meaning of Title VII of the Civil Rights Act of 1964. As I mentioned to you during our earlier telephone conversations, Title VII only applies to companies that have 15 or more employees. Wambush argued that since its Washington, D.C. office had only nine employees, it is not covered by Title VII. In response, we argued that for Title VII purposes you must count all of a company's employees, no matter where they are employed. Since Wambush's San Francisco office employs 275 people, we argued that Wambush was clearly an employer and was obligated to abide by the provisions of Title VII. Once again, the court agreed with our position and denied Wambush's motion.

Yesterday, I received a letter from Wambush's attorneys indicating that they would like to take your deposition. In a deposition a party like yourself is questioned under oath by the attorney for the other side. The attorney's questions and the witness's answers are recorded by a court stenographer and a typewritten record is then made. It is important that I spend at least a full day with you preparing you for the deposition. Please call my office as soon as possible so that we can arrange a seven- or eight-hour block of time during which I will fully prepare you for the deposition.

If you have any questions concerning any of the matters that I have discussed in this letter, please do not hesitate to contact me.

Sincerely yours,
Elizabeth A. Brown

The *context* for the letter is provided by the introductory paragraph. Sentence 1 tells the *purpose* of the letter and the *topics* to be discussed — to summarize the status of the suit and discuss plans. Sentence 2 provides *background,* which in this case is the lawyer's and client's shared understanding of the contents of a previous conversation. Sentence 3 presents the outcome (the court denied both motions) of the events mentioned in that conversation. This is also the *main point* of the major part of the letter.

The next three paragraphs present the *substance* of the letter — the important points that the lawyer wishes to tell the client. Paragraph 2 presents and elaborates on Event 1. Sentence 1 describes the event — that Wambush tried to have the lawsuit dismissed for improper venue — and sentences 2-7 amplify it. Sentence 2 explains what "improper venue" means in terms of the client's own case. Sentence 3 elaborates, explaining the content of the motion and summarizing Wambush's argument. Sentences 4-6 recount the lawyer's counterargument. All of the sentences lead up to the next one, sentence 7, which tells the outcome: The court agreed with the lawyer's argument and denied the motion. Paragraph 3 follows the same pattern as Paragraph 2.

Paragraph 4 elaborates on the second topic referred to in the introductory paragraph — the deposition that will take place. Sentence 1 informs the client about the coming deposition and sentences 2-3 give a brief explanation of what is involved. Sentences 4-5 present an important point — what the client and attorney must do before the deposition. Paragraph 5 *concludes* by giving the client an opportunity to ask questions.

The overall organizing principle for the letter is a time sequence: These two events have occurred, this third event will occur. The organizing principles *within* the paragraphs are different: Paragraphs 1, 2, and 3 are based primarily on cause-and-effect sequences, while paragraph 4 is basically a time sequence.

C How to Organize a Complex Legal Document

For more complex legal documents, the basic outline for an expository document must be expanded. For persuasive documents, such as briefs and motions, and for documents that present pros and cons, such as memoranda and law examinations, the main section of the document requires a special type of structure. Instead of the events or ideas that make up the main section of an expository document, the main section of a complex legal document will consist of an analysis of issues or subissues. Thus, the outline for a complex legal document might look like this:

1. Introduction providing a context
2. First claim
    a. What is the *claim* you are making? How are you proposing to resolve the issue or subissue? This can be further subdivided into
        i. A statement of the particular *issue* or subissue you have identified. At this point you may also wish to state how you believe the issue should be resolved.[2]
        ii. The *rule* of law that is most pertinent to the situation.
        iii. Why the rule should be *applied* to the facts of your case.
        iv. A *conclusion* based upon your analysis and the application of the law to the facts.
        IRAC is the mnemonic for this method of organizing a claim.
    b. What are the *objections* and counterarguments to your claim?
    c. What is your *response* to the objections and counterarguments?
    d. What is your *conclusion?* This section summarizes your reasoning and restates your claim.
3. Second claim
4. Conclusion

---

2. This is especially important in persuasive writing, where you want to make a forceful opening statement.

This model works well for any level of analysis, from the general analysis of a whole problem down to the analysis of specific subissues. When you have used this model to analyze all of the issues or subissues, you will then be able to come to a conclusion.

1. Identifying and Presenting Issues

Your first step in setting up the structure of a complex legal document is to identify the important issues that you will be discussing in your document. Here is an example of a fact situation and the issues that should be analyzed in a brief.

Jones worked as a salesman for the Southern Corporation. His job required him to provide his own car and deliver perishable supplies to customers on his route. Jones had been told a number of times by his supervisor at Southern that it was extremely important that he stay on a strict time schedule with his deliveries.

On March 10, Jones made a delivery during normal working hours. He returned to the parking lot in which he had left his car and found that Warner's car was blocking his car. After waiting ten minutes for Warner to return, Jones finally decided that he had to leave. Jones tried to move his car, but put a large dent in Warner's bumper and broke one of Warner's headlights in the process. Warner returned just as Jones broke the headlight. Warner demanded payment for the damage to his car and refused to move his car so that Jones could leave. Jones angrily got out of his car and moved towards Warner, yelling that he was already late for his deliveries and that it was Warner's fault. Warner angrily shook his fist at Jones and again demanded payment for the damage to his car. Jones, in anger, hit Warner, knocking him to the ground. Warner had Jones arrested.

After Jones's arrest, Southern Corporation learned from the local police that Jones had been convicted of aggravated assault three years before Southern had hired him. When Southern hired Jones, the corporation did not inquire into his background. Warner is suing Southern for the personal injuries he suffered as a result of Jones's attack.

ISSUE 1:   Did the defendant commit an intentional tort when he knocked the plaintiff to the ground, or was the action privileged?

ISSUE 2: Is an employer liable for injuries that its employee intentionally inflicted upon the plaintiff while the employee was trying to make deliveries on behalf of the employer?

ISSUE 3: Can the defendant employer be held liable for negligence in hiring and retaining an employee who has a criminal record for assault if the employer did not investigate the employee's background and does not know of the record?

Once you have identified the main issues, you may find that you can deal with them more easily by breaking them down into smaller, more manageable subissues (or sub-subissues). For example, you might see the following subissues under Issue 1.

1. Did the act of the plaintiff in shaking his fist at the defendant place the defendant in imminent threat of physical injury?
   a. If the plaintiff's act placed the defendant in imminent threat of physical injury, did he have a duty to retreat?
   b. If the defendant did not have a duty to retreat, did he use excessive force in repelling the imminent threat?
2. Did the act of the plaintiff in refusing to move his vehicle constitute the tort of false imprisonment?
3. Did the act of the plaintiff in refusing to move his vehicle constitute the tort of trespass to chattel?

2. Presenting the Rule

The rule of law that you use in your analysis can come from case law or enacted laws. Once you have established the applicable rule in a particular case, you should present it in a way that will make it easy to apply the law to the facts. For example, if you are discussing a particular tort or crime, or the definition of a particular legal concept, describe it by breaking it up into its elements. Thus, if the issue is whether a defendant has committed a battery, a good way to present the rule would be to take the definition from section 13 of the Restatement (Second) of Torts.

> §13 **Battery: Harmful Contact**
> An actor is subject to liability for battery if
> (a) he *acts intending* to cause harmful or offensive contact with the person of the other or a third person, or an imminent apprehension of such a contact, and

(b) a harmful contact with the person of the other directly or indirectly *results* (emphasis added).

If you have to synthesize the rule from case law, this will probably take more time and space. This is because you will often need to go through the steps that you took and the sources that you used in your distillation of the rule.

3. Application: Analyzing Facts and Law

The next step is to examine the facts and decide whether a rule is satisfied or the elements of an offense or tort are present. You should organize this section so that it follows the order of the elements of the rule. For example, you could discuss the facts in the Jones case by applying them to the elements of battery.

> First, the defendant, Jones, *acted* when he attempted to strike the plaintiff in the parking lot. Second, the defendant *intended* to harm the plaintiff, since he spoke angrily to the plaintiff, shook his fist at the plaintiff, and then struck him. Third, the defendant struck the plaintiff and knocked the plaintiff to the ground. Thus, the defendant's act *resulted in* the harmful contact to the plaintiff.

The application section of your document is the most crucial, for it is here that you have to convince your audience that your analysis is sound and that your conclusions follow logically. We have presented only the most basic application of facts to law in the example above. In Chapter 6 we will cover sophisticated and specialized techniques for applying the facts to the law so that you can guide your reader smoothly from your claims to your conclusions.

4. Anticipating Counterarguments

One of the best ways to ensure that you have treated an issue thoroughly is to try to anticipate all possible counterarguments and defenses. Put yourself in your opponent's position: List all of the ways that you can attack or weaken your own argument. Be ruthless. After you compile the list, develop responses or rebuttals for each area of attack.

There are a number of counterarguments that the defendant might raise in the battery case. The defendant might attack the way in which you applied the law to the facts; or the defendant might raise the defense that he was using reasonable force to prevent the plaintiff from committing a tort against his property (the plaintiff refused to let the defendant remove his car from the lot) or against his person (the plaintiff prevented the defendant from leaving by holding something of great value to the defendant).

5. Providing a Conclusion

The contents of your conclusion will depend upon the length and complexity of the information that you have presented in the other portions of your analysis. For example, if your application section is long and intricate, then you might want to refresh your reader's memory by briefly recounting the steps in your reasoning. If the application section is short, however, you would probably not want to reiterate your reasoning. In either case, you would finish with a statement of your position or your interpretation of the facts and the law. Here is an example of a simple way to conclude the battery issue:

> Because all three elements of battery are present in the defendant's conduct, the defendant is liable for the tort of battery.

6. Organizing a Complex Legal Document: An Example

Now that we have presented and explained the different parts of the model on page 77, look at the following fully developed issue analysis. This analysis follows the standard IRAC — issue, rule, application, conclusion — outline.

[Issue]
The issue presented in this case is whether one spouse can sue the other for injuries caused by the negligence of the other spouse.
[Rule]
In *Sink v. Sink,* 239 P.2d 933 (1952), this court held that neither spouse may maintain an action in tort for damages against the other. Although a number of states have recently enacted legislation which allows these suits, Kansas has not joined them. This can be seen in the fact that the Kansas legislature has just enacted, in 1981, a law which authorizes any insurer to exclude coverage for any bodily injury to "any insured or any family member of an

insured" in its insurance policies. Even though this law does not go into effect until January 1, 1982, it is clear that Kansas's position on interspousal tort immunity has not changed.

[Application]

In the present case, the plaintiff, who is the defendant's wife, was injured when the car the defendant was driving crashed into a telephone pole. The plaintiff was sitting in the passenger seat at the time of the accident. She sustained a broken leg and cuts and bruises. Although the defendant may have been negligent, the accident obviously involved injuries inflicted by one spouse upon another.

[Conclusion]

Therefore, this case clearly falls within the mandate of *Sink,* and the plaintiff's case should be dismissed on the basis of Kansas's very viable interspousal immunity.

[Counterargument]

The plaintiff has claimed that a decision upholding interspousal immunity violates logic and basic principles of justice. She notes that the new law has not yet gone into effect, so that it does not apply to the present case. She also contends that the foremost justification for immunity laws is illogical, since it is based on the premise that personal tort actions between husband and wife would disrupt the peace and harmony of the home. She cites the Restatement of the Law of Torts, which criticizes this justification by stating that it is based upon the faulty assumption that an uncompensated tort makes for peace in the family.

[Response]

However, it is no more logical to contend that family harmony will be better served if a husband and wife can drag each other into court and meet each other as legal adversaries. In addition, the plaintiff has overlooked a far more persuasive argument for interspousal tort immunity: under Kansas law, any recovery that the plaintiff-wife would obtain if this action were allowed to proceed would inure to the benefit of the defendant-husband. All property acquired by either spouse during the marriage is "marital property" in which each spouse has a common ownership interest. If the injured spouse (plaintiff) should die, the surviving spouse could maintain an action for wrongful death, and could share in any recovery of losses. This result would allow a negligent party to profit by his own actions. This is a result which would be truly offensive to anyone's sense of justice.

[Conclusion]

The doctrine of interspousal immunity is as viable today as it was when initially enunciated by this court. It not only fosters family harmony, but also prevents a spouse from profiting from his or her own negligence.

For some types of documents, you will want to abbreviate the scheme presented above. For example, if you are answering an opponent's brief, you could begin by stating the opponent's objections and then follow with your own claims and conclusions. With this order, the response section is no longer necessary.

Some caveats. There are several caveats to consider when you use IRAC or any similar outline to analyze the issues in a law school problem. Students sometimes get the impression that they have done a complete, well-rounded analysis of a question once they have taken the obvious issues through the IRAC outline. IRAC can give you a false sense of security if you mistake the thorough analysis of an issue for the thorough analysis of a whole problem or question. Once you have completed analyzing the obvious issues, make sure that you reread the problem to search for subissues or elements of issues that you might have overlooked. These are important and can influence the outcome of your problem.

IRAC is merely a framework within which to build your analysis: It should not appear to your readers that you have merely plugged information into a rigid formula. Edit your writing to eliminate the mechanical effects of a series of statements that the issue is W, the rule is X, the analysis is Y, and that, therefore, the conclusion is Z.

D The Importance of Headings

We have talked about providing a "roadmap" in your introduction to tell the reader what is going to be covered in your document. You can also use informative headings and a table of contents to show your organization to your readers. In fact, rules of court may require that you use headings and a table of contents in documents that you submit to the court.

Headings guide the reader through the text by describing what is included in each section of the document. For some documents the headings can then be collected and used as a table of contents. The table of contents tells the reader where things are located and gives the reader an overview of the contents of the whole document. Headings and tables of contents are particularly useful in reference documents such as memos, statutes, regulations, treatises, and any other document in which a reader might want to find specific information quickly. Even documents that are not usually used as references benefit from informative headings and a table of contents, especially if the documents are long. The example below is a table of contents from a very long will.

Table of Contents

Item 1: Declarations
   1.1 My will
   1.2 My family
Item 2: Payment of Funeral and Administrative Expenses, Debts, and Taxes
   2.1 Funeral and Administrative Expenses
   2.2 Debts
   2.3 Taxes
Item 3: Specific Gifts
   3.1 Personal property to my wife
   3.2 Personal property to children if my wife does not survive
   3.3 Discretion of executor
   3.4 Resolution of disputes
Item 4: Disposition of My Residuary Estate
   4.1 Beneficiaries
   4.2 Use of the residuary trust income and principal
   4.3 Invasion of principal for the benefit of my wife
   4.4 Limitation on a trustee-beneficiary
   4.5 Time limit of the residuary trust

Headings should mark logical divisions in a text. If you have outlined your document well and have chosen a good organizing principle, it will be fairly easy to decide where the headings belong and what the levels of these headings should be (full heading, subheading, run-in heading, etc.). In fact, if you have trouble deciding where to put headings, it may be a sign that your document needs to be reorganized.

Once you have determined where headings belong, make them as informative as possible and try to make headings at the same level parallel in structure (see Guideline 8 on using parallel structure). Headings should tell the reader something. A single word or short string of nouns is usually not informative. On the other hand, sentences — statements or questions — make particularly informative headings. The headings in the following table of contents are from a student's term paper. These short headings tell the reader nothing.

Table of Contents

Briefs must have headings, and the headings should be informative and persuasive. They cannot be single words or labels; they must spell out the lawyer's conclusion on each question addressed in the brief. If a brief is particularly long or complex, it should contain informative subheadings as well. The headings and subheadings, taken together, then serve as a table of contents that summarizes the lawyer's position. Below are the headings from a Supreme Court brief. In this case the respondent was indicted on charges of armed robbery of a bank and was jailed before trial in the Norfolk City Jail. An FBI agent asked an inmate who had previously acted as a paid informant to be especially alert to any statements made by the respondent and several other federal prisoners, but not to initiate conversation or ask questions about the charges against them. The informant later told the FBI agent that the respondent had talked openly about the robbery. The informant testified at the respondent's trial. The respondent's conviction was appealed on the basis that the FBI had violated his Sixth Amendment right to counsel.

Table of Contents

Some attorneys like to use the parties' names in an issue statement in order to personalize the argument, to differentiate the actors if there are many of them or if the facts are complicated, and for other similar reasons. However, other attorneys do not favor this practice. They believe that headings should never be personalized because one function of an appellate brief is to give the court an opportunity to convert issue statements into rules of law that can be applied to anyone in the future.

EXERCISES

1. "If John mows Fred's lawn on Tuesday, Fred will pay him $10.00." Based on this sentence, construct an agreement for Fred and John. Provide a context — e.g., purpose, parties, location, etc. Provide for contingencies; add any missing information. Then group and organize all the material and supply informative headings.

2. Break up and reorganize the leash law below. Insert informative headings in appropriate places.

LEASH LAW

No animal of the dog kind shall be allowed to go at large without a collar or tag, as now prescribed by law, and no person owning, keeping, or having custody of a dog in the District shall permit such dog to be on public space in the District, unless such dog is firmly secured by a substantial leash not exceeding four feet in length, held by a person capable of managing such a dog, nor shall any dog be permitted to go on private property without the consent of the owner or occupant thereof.

3. Before trial, a party can ask an adversary to stipulate (agree to) certain things, such as that certain documents are genuine, or that certain pieces of evidence can be admitted into court, or that certain facts are not really in dispute. In other words, the parties can formally agree that certain things are not really at issue. This way, trial time is not wasted on facts, evidence, or documents that are already accepted by both parties.

The adversary must meet with the party asking for the stipulation at a time that is determined by the date of the trial notice. (Trial notice is notice given by one party in an action to an adversary, stating that he or she intends to bring a cause to trial at the next term of the court. The adversary generally learns of the specific trial date by finding out from the court when the case has been set on the docket.)

If the adversary does not meet to stipulate as the party has requested, then the party can file an order for the adversary to show cause why the documents, evidence, or facts should *not* be accepted by the court. If the adversary ignores the show cause order, then the court will automatically accept the documents or facts.

Following is a rule that deals specifically with stipulations. Read the rule, then rewrite and reorganize the rule so that it is easier to read and follows a logical order. In addition, indicate what organizing principle you have chosen and explain why you think it is appropriate.

(1) If a party, by the date of issuance of trial notice
(2) in any case pending in this court, or within ten days
(3) thereafter in the case of an expedited trial notice,
(4) fails, after having been duly served with a request by
(5) his adversary, to meet and confer for the purpose of
(6) stipulating to the genuineness of documents or to the
(7) admissibility of evidence or to undisputed facts, the
(8) party serving the request may within 50 days, but not

(9) less than 35 days, prior to the date set for the call
(10) of the case from the trial calendar, file with the
(11) court a motion for an order to show cause why the
(12) documents, evidence, or facts covered in the request
(13) should not be accepted as proved for the purposes of
(14) the case.

4. Below are the facts and law from an employment discrimination case filed in a federal court in the District of Columbia. This information is in no particular order. The plaintiff claims that he was denied employment by the defendant employer. Assume that you are the plaintiff's attorney and that you must use this information to write a brief. Begin by identifying the issue and rules. Then use the factual statements to create an application section and a conclusion. Create a strong argument that shows why the plaintiff's case should not be dismissed because of improper venue. Show the outline (IRAC) for your argument in the margin of your paper. If you do not have all of the information that you think you need, then make reasonable assumptions and argue on the basis of these assumptions.

The defendant employer is a member of a joint apprenticeship committee of printing unions and employers. This committee consists of six people, three of whom are officers of printing unions and three of whom are officers of print shops that are members of the print shop trade association. The committee meets in the District of Columbia and engages in at least the following activities in the District.

1. interviewing apprenticeship candidates
2. evaluating apprenticeship candidates
3. selecting and recommending apprenticeship candidates to be employed by member companies

A person cannot be hired as an apprentice by a member company unless he or she has been approved by the joint apprenticeship committee.

The defendant employer runs a print shop.

Under Rule 12(b)(3) of the Federal Rules of Civil Procedure, the defendant has moved this court for an order dismissing the employment discrimination action against it on the grounds of improper venue under §706(f)(3) of Title VII of the Civil Rights Act of 1964, as amended, 42 U.S.C. §2000e-5(f)(3).

The defendant employer has all of its offices and facilities in Virginia. It hires, fires, and promotes all employees in Virginia.

There are four criteria for venue under §706(f)(3) of Title VII. In summary, the action may be brought

1. In any judicial district in the state in which an unlawful employment practice is alleged to have been committed *or*
2. In the judicial district in which the employment records relevant to the alleged practice are kept *or*
3. In the judicial district in which the plaintiff would have worked but for the alleged unlawful employment practice *or*
4. In the judicial district in which the defendant has his principal office, if the defendant is not found within any of the above districts.

The plaintiff sought to be hired as an apprentice by the defendant but failed to gain the approval of the joint apprenticeship committee.

The joint apprenticeship committee was created by a collective bargaining agreement entered into by all of the employees and all of the unions. This agreement was entered into in the District of Columbia.

In *Trucking Management, Inc.,* 20 FEP Cases 342 (D.D.C. 1979), the defendant companies were members of a trade association. The companies were not located in the same state as the association. Nevertheless, the court found that membership in a trade association that negotiated a collective bargaining agreement on behalf of its members provides a sufficient nexus among the out-of-state defendants to satisfy the venue requirements of Title VII. Specifically, the court stated:

> From the beginning of this litigation, the negotiation of the NMFA [trade association] in the District of Columbia was the only alleged "unlawful employment practice" providing a sufficient nexus among the defendants to satisfy the venue requirements.

5. Arrange the following disjointed pieces of information into a coherent whole, then come to a conclusion about the facts and law in the case. Be sure to supply a logical organization and transitions for your argument.

The elements for a prima facie case for conversion are:

1. An act by a defendant that interferes with the plaintiff's right to possess a particular chattel. The act must be serious enough to warrant that the defendant pay for the full value of the chattel. Interfer-

ence is established if the defendant exercises control or dominion over the property for a substantial amount of time.

2. The defendant must intend to commit the *act* leading to conversion. The defendant does not have to intend to convert the plaintiff's property.

3. The defendant's act must cause the interference or set in motion those forces that interfere with the plaintiff's possession of the chattel.

Stealing, embezzling, selling, or destroying chattel all qualify as acts that interfere with the plaintiff's possession of chattel.

Harvey bought a tape deck from Larry.

Right after Harvey got the tape deck, he sold it.

Larry had stolen the tape deck from Mike.

Harvey did not know that the tape deck was stolen property.

Mike is suing Harvey for conversion.

Chattel is tangible personal property or is intangible property that has been reduced to some physical form (e.g., a stock certificate).

6. You are an associate working for the law firm of Smith, Smythe, and Smooth. Your senior partner has given you this client letter, which was written by one of your colleagues. The partner asks you to comment on how well it is written. He also wants to know whether you think Mrs. Bush will understand it. Make a list of all the problems you find in the letter, reorganize it, and rewrite it.

Smith, Smythe, and Smooth

Attorneys at Law

160 Pennsylvania Avenue, N.W.

Washington, D.C.   20001

Telephone: (202) 555-2318

August 5, 1984

Mrs. Marion Bush

1400 Ft. McNavy Drive

Bethesda, Maryland

Re: Alimony for medical bills

Dear Mrs. Bush:

You asked if there was a way to recover your medical expenses from Admiral Bush. The normal procedure would be to garnish his wages. That means that his employer would withhold money and pay it into the court.

The problem is that your ex-husband's employer is the United States Navy. Under a doctrine of law called "sovereign immunity," you cannot sue the Government unless they consent to it. Congress recently passed a law permitting garnishment for alimony or child support only.

Admiral Bush's obligation to pay your medical bills comes from your property settlement agreement. When your divorce became final, the settlement agreement became part of the decree. U.S. law defines alimony as "periodic payments of funds for the support and maintenance of the former spouse." The medical payments fall within the state scheme of spousal support.

We have presented this information to Judge Stern and now await his ruling. If he holds that the medical payments are in fact "alimony" within the meaning of U.S. law, you will be able to garnish Admiral Bush's pay until the bills are fully paid.

Of course, if you have any questons, please contact me.

Sincerely yours,
Robert C. Shaw

III

5

Writing
Clearly

This chapter contains 13 guidelines for clear legal writing. They have been selected because they are particularly useful for writing and reviewing all types of legal documents, including exams, memoranda, briefs, pleadings, client letters, legislation, contracts, and leases. These guidelines are tools that you use when you want to write for a specific audience or audiences, accomplish a well-defined purpose or purposes, and create well-organized, logical legal documents.

Thirteen Guidelines for Clear Legal Writing

1. Write short sentences.
2. Put the parts of each sentence in a logical order.
3. Avoid intrusive phrases and clauses.
4. Untangle complex conditionals.
5. Use the active voice whenever possible.
6. Use verb clauses and adjectives instead of nominalizations.
7. Use the positive unless you want to emphasize the negative.
8. Use parallel structure.
9. Avoid ambiguity in words and sentences.
10. Choose vocabulary with care.
11. Avoid noun strings.
12. Eliminate redundancy and extraneous words; avoid overspecificity.
13. Use an appropriate style.

A Guideline 1: Write Short Sentences

You will often see two- and three-hundred-word sentences in all forms of legal writing, from hornbooks to judicial opinions, briefs, and memos. Probably no other single characteristic does more to needlessly complicate legal writing than these long sentences.

Research in linguistics and psychology has shown that the average reader can hold only a few ideas at a time in short-term memory.[1] After two or three ideas, the reader needs to pause and put together what he or she has read. The period at the end of a sentence is one signal for such a pause. When there are no periods in long strings of thoughts, the reader will try to break up the sentence into smaller pieces in order to understand it. However, the reader may not know where to pause or which ideas to group together. Readers often get lost in very long sentences.

In addition to the burden imposed by sheer length, most long sentences violate other guidelines for writing clearly. Structural complexities such as complex conditionals, passives, unclear references, and nonparallel constructions add to the reader's difficulties.

Although you see long sentences in all kinds of traditional legal writing, there is nothing in the nature of the law itself that requires you to express all of your thoughts in one sentence. Your writing will be legally accurate whether you use one sentence or several sentences. Legal convention, however, will sometimes require you to put a lot of information in one sentence. For example, you may have to put each issue statement in a brief in its own sentence. This convention has resulted in some of the longest, most cumbersome sentences you will see in legal writing.

Here are two examples of overly long sentences that we have revised. The first example is a subsection from a will that we have broken into several sentences.

POOR: The trustee may pay all or part of the income to or for the benefit of the beneficiary or may accumulate all or part of the income, distribute trust principal (even all of it if necessary) to or for the benefit of the beneficiary for the beneficiary's maintenance, support, education, comfortable living, business or professional needs, or general welfare, and if there is more than one beneficiary, pay income or distribute principal to or for the benefit of the beneficiaries as it determines (even excluding one or more of the beneficiaries) without regard to any principle of law requiring impartiality among beneficiaries of the trust.

1. Miller, The Magical Number Seven, Plus or Minus Two: Some Limits on Our Capacity for Processing Information, 63 Psychological Review 81 (1956).

BETTER: The trustee may pay all or part of the income to or for the benefit of the beneficiary or may accumulate all or part of the income. The trustee may distribute trust principal (even all of it if necessary) to or for the benefit of the beneficiary for the beneficiary's maintenance, support, education, comfortable living, business or professional needs, or general welfare. If there is more than one beneficiary, the trustee may pay income or distribute principal to or for the benefit of the beneficiaries as it determines (even excluding one or more of the beneficiaries), without regard to any principle of law requiring impartiality among beneficiaries of the trust.

Notice that just dividing the passage into shorter sentences makes it easier to read. Breaking up the last sentence and making it into a new paragraph further clarifies the drafter's meaning.

If there is more than one beneficiary, the trustee, in addition to the powers noted above, may pay income or distribute principal to or for the benefit of one or more of the beneficiaries, as the trustee determines. The trustee may exclude one or more of the beneficiaries from these payments or distributions, even if the law requires that the trustee treat all beneficiaries equally.

Sometimes breaking up a long sentence into shorter sentences makes the entire passage longer. There is nothing wrong with this: The goal is *clarity* and not brevity for its own sake.

The second example is an issue statement that we have rewritten so that it is shorter and easier to understand. It can be very difficult to put an issue statement in one sentence. If you create a sentence that is very long and very complex, keep rewriting it until you have put the parts of the sentence in a logical order and have removed all extraneous words.

POOR: The district court was correct in holding that the statute of limitations for medical malpractice begins to run at the time of the tort or when treatment ceases which was prior to the plaintiff's conception thereby foreclosing the right for her to bring a cause of action.

BETTER: Since the district court was correct in holding that the statute of limitations for medical malpractice begins to run at the time of the tort or when treatment ends, and since the plaintiff was conceived after both of these events, the plaintiff has no right on which to base a cause of action.

EXERCISES

Break up the following long sentences into shorter sentences. Rearrange the parts of the sentences and add words if necessary.

1. Where, upon the trial of such a case as is indicated above, there was evidence from which the jury was authorized to find that the defendant's agent went to the plaintiff's home and knowing that she, a child of 11 years of age, was at home alone, attempted to gain entrance to the home for the announced purpose of repossessing a television set, and when the child refused to admit him by the front door that he went to the rear door and wrote a note which he exhibited to the child through a window of the door and in which he threatened to go for the police and have her put in jail if she did not admit him so that he could take possession of the television set, and that the child became so frightened by this threat that she became extremely nervous, fearful of leaving the house, and unable to sleep at night, the jury would be authorized to find that the conduct of the defendant's agent, who was acting within the scope of his authority, was willful misconduct under the circumstances, and that the child's resulting nervousness and distress was a natural and probable consequence of such willful misconduct. (203 words)

2. A court order forcing the student editor of the Lincoln Weekly Star to publish candidate Jones' preferred advertisements would clearly violate and destroy the discretionary editorial privilege guaranteed to newspapers by the First Amendment and consistently upheld by the Supreme Court of the United States.

3. It is the judgment of this court that a lawyer who addresses a women's organization on the subject of divorce and whose address includes a description of the services the lawyer is willing to provide to members of the organization and includes the fees that are charged therefor, and who subsequently contacts all of the members of the organization who attended the meeting, is within the broad protections guaranteed by the First and Fourteenth Amendments to the U.S. Constitution, and has not violated the Code of Professional Responsibility's prohibition against soliciting business.

B Guideline 2:
Put the Parts of Each Sentence
in a Logical Order

Some sentences are ineffective or difficult to read because they lack internal logic. It is very important to put the parts of a sentence in a logical order. Start each sentence with information that is familiar to your audience or that will tell the reader where you are going with the sentence. If the sentence is the first in your document, begin it with information that will provide a context. If the sentence is in the middle of a document, begin the sentence by tying it to the information in the previous sentences or paragraphs. The following sentence from a letter provides the reader with a context that ties the content of the letter to the reader's own past action.

In response to your request of April 10, 1985, I am sending you copies of the pleadings and some additional documents.

Don't make your reader read through an entire sentence in order to discover its purpose.

Here is an example from a student memo. It is the opening paragraph of the student's Discussion section.

Since the instant action arose in Connecticut (the employer and employee are located in Virginia, but the alleged discrimination occurred in Connecticut), the initial issue to be resolved in determining what limitations period applies in a section 1981 action in federal court in Virginia is which state's law applies.

The main idea in this sentence — the initial issue that will be considered in the memo — is buried in the middle of the sentence. The student should have begun the sentence with a statement of the issue and then recounted the specific facts of the case.

The issue in this case is what limitations statute applies in a section 1981 action brought in federal court in one state if the cause of action arose in another state. In this case, the suit was brought in federal court in Virginia. The employer and the employees are located in Virginia, but the alleged discrimination occurred in Connecticut.

This guideline applies to groups of several sentences, or even paragraphs, as well. Look for a logical sequence — a time sequence, a cause-and-effect relationship, an order of priority — and arrange the sentences or paragraphs in that order. As with a single, longer sentence, begin with information that the reader already knows and use that as a context for information that follows. Tie the sentences to each other with the proper transitions (and, but, because, however, moreover, nonetheless, furthermore, therefore, thus, etc.).

EXERCISES

Put the parts of each sentence into a more logical order.

1. The fact that the *Rutgers* publication was a newspaper and the present publication is a law review and requires special selection of the type and quality of its articles is what distinguishes the two cases and will probably be the crucial factor in the court's decision.
2. The ultimate verification of the inquiries at the hospital was the damaging factor.
3. Whether or not the method of gathering data would be objectionable to the reasonable person is the question that must be asked by the court.

C Guideline 3: Avoid Intrusive Phrases and Clauses

One reason that a sentence can be too long is that it may contain a phrase or clause that has been inserted in the middle of the main clause. These additions, exceptions, or pieces of incidental material disrupt the logical flow of the sentence and make it difficult for readers to understand what is meant.

Sometimes even relatively short sentences contain intrusive phrases or clauses. The italicized words in the example below make up the main sentence. The date comes in the middle of the verb. The address comes between the verb and its object. Notice how much clearer even a short sentence can become when the intrusive phrases have been moved so that they no longer separate the parts of the main clause (subject, verb, and object) from each other.

POOR: Interested *attorneys may,* on or before (date), *submit* to the Clerk, (address), *written comments* regarding the proposed change in court procedures.

GOOD: Interested attorneys who want to comment on the proposed
          change in court procedures may send comments in writing to
          the Clerk, (address), by (date).

Intrusive phrases occur in abundance in all kinds of legal documents. In
the following example from a law student's memo, the student tried to cram
too much information into one sentence.

POOR: One of the main questions presented in this memo is whether
          28 U.S.C. §636(b)(1)(B), *which allows a district court to decide a*
          suppression motion based on the record developed before a mag-
          istrate, the magistrate's proposed findings of fact and recom-
          mendations, and the defendant's written and oral objections
          before the district court, violates the Due Process Clause.

The italicized information is inserted in such a way that it interferes with
the continuity of the main part of the sentence. Because the subject of the
sentence is separated from the verb by 37 words, the reader does not know
where the sentence is going until the very end. The student should have
broken up the sentence and reordered the information logically.

BETTER: One of the main questions presented in this memo is whether
          28 U.S.C. §636(b)(1)(B) violates the Due Process Clause. This
          section allows the district court to decide a suppression motion
          based on the record developed before a magistrate, the magis-
          trate's proposed findings of fact and recommendations, and the
          defendant's written and oral objections before the district
          court.

The reader of the rewritten version knows immediately what the point of
the passage is. A related problem is illustrated by the following sentence.

POOR: Petitioner's argument *that exclusion of the press from the trial*
          and subsequent denial of access to the trial transcripts is, in
          effect, a prior restraint is contrary to the facts.

In this sentence, the subordinate clause, which is in italics, intrudes into the
middle of the main clause. The verb phrase of the subordinate clause
("is . . . a prior restraint") is perilously close to the verb phrase of the main
clause ("is contrary to the facts") and makes the sentence very confusing to
read. This type of subordinate clause construction is called *self-embedding,*

and psycholinguistic research[2] has shown that self-embedding is very difficult for the human mind to process. The writer could easily have avoided self-embedding in that sentence.

BETTER: Petitioner argued that excluding the press from the trial and subsequently denying access to the trial transcripts is, in effect, a prior restraint. This argument is contrary to the facts.

In general, the best way to deal with any type of sentence with intrusive phrases is to remove the inserted material and put it into a new sentence.

EXERCISES

Underline the intrusive phrase(s) and rewrite the sentence.

1. In light of the prevailing jurisprudence, including that of the District of Columbia, contrary to our position that the district court should look to District of Columbia law (jurisdiction where the action arose), I conclude that a summary judgment motion relying on the applicability of the limitations provisions of the forum state (Maryland) is more likely to succeed than one relying on the law of the state in which the action arose.

2. The court held that the agreement whereby she would support him financially and provide household services while he wrote a German textbook, in return for which he would support her when he reestablished his professional career, was enforceable.

3. Although the Court stated that it need not reach the question of whether strict scrutiny was required because even under the most exacting standard of review the Minority Business Enterprises (MBE) provision passes constitutional muster, nowhere in the court's opinion is there any indication that it applied the strict scrutiny necessary to determine whether the MBE provision was in fact constitutional.

---

2. Psycholinguistic research is the study of how language is perceived and understood, using the methods of experimental psychology. See Miller and Isard, Free Recall of Self-Embedded English Sentences, 7 Information and Control 292 (1964); Schwartz, Sparkman, and Deese, The Process of Understanding and Judgment of Comprehensibility, 9 Journal of Verbal Learning and Verbal Behavior 87 (1970).

D Guideline 4:
Untangle Complex Conditionals

A conditional is a statement that establishes an *if* . . . *then* relationship between pieces of information; a complex conditional is a conditional with many conditions (*if* statements) or many rules or consequences (*then* statements). A conditional or complex conditional may not always contain the word *if*. Some conditionals introduce a condition with *when, where, whether,* or other words or phrases. Many conditionals also lack the word *then* in the rule or consequence statement. For example,

> When both parties are residents of the same state, there is no diversity of citizenship.

This sentence could be rewritten:

> *If* both parties are residents of the same state, *then* there is no diversity of citizenship.

As long as the sentence states a condition and a rule or consequence, it is a conditional.

Readers often have problems understanding complex conditionals. The more conditions or rules and the more combinations of *ands* and *ors* that a sentence contains, the more difficult it is to understand.

Here is an example of a complex conditional from the Federal Rules of Civil Procedure, Rule 6(b).

POOR: *Enlargement.* When by these rules or by a notice given thereunder or by order of court an act is required or allowed to be done within a specified time, the court for cause shown may at any time in its discretion (1) with or without motion or notice order the period enlarged if request therefor is made before the expiration of the period originally prescribed or as extended by a previous order, or (2) upon motion made after the expiration of the specified period permit the act to be done where the failure to act was the result of excusable neglect.

To untangle a complex conditional like this one, it is often useful to list each provision. It can also help to physically separate each condition and rule on the page itself. This rule would be much easier to understand if it were rewritten with these suggestions in mind.

GOOD: *Extending a time period.* This rule applies to acts that may or must be done within a certain time when that time is specified by:

- the Federal Rules *or*
- a notice issued under the Federal Rules *or*
- a court order.

If a party wishes to extend the time period, the party must show cause to the court to do so. The court may then, at its discretion, extend the time under two different sets of circumstances:

1. *If the request is made before the time period expires,* then the court may extend the original time period (or a previously extended time period) with or without motion or notice.

2. *If the request is made after the time period expires,* then the court may extend the original time period, but only if failure to act was the result of excusable neglect and if a motion is made.

EXERCISES

Rewrite the following complex conditionals so that they are easier to understand.

1. Where a contract is made for the satisfaction of a preexisting contractual duty, or duty to make compensation, the interpretation is assumed in case of doubt, if the pre-existing duty is an undisputed duty either to make compensation or to pay a liquidated sum of money, then only performance of the subsequent contract shall discharge the pre-existing duty; but if the pre-existing duty is of another kind, the subsequent contract shall immediately discharge the pre-existing duty, and be substituted for it.

2. If a person, whether a child or adult, against whom any warrant has issued out of a juvenile court cannot be found within the jurisdiction of the juvenile court out of which the warrant was so issued, but is or is suspected to be in any other part of the nation, any judge or deputy judge of a juvenile court within whose jurisdiction such person is or is

suspected to be or if there is no juvenile court having jurisdiction in such place, then any justice within whose jurisdiction such person is or is suspected to be, upon proof being made on oath or affirmation of the handwriting of the juvenile court judge or other officer who issued the warrant, shall make an endorsement on the warrant, signed with his name, authorizing the execution thereof within his jurisdiction.

Rewrite this complex conditional from a will to make each condition and consequence clear and easy to find.

TWENTIETH: PROVISION FOR DISABILITY. If at the time set for any distribution of income or principal of my estate, or the trust hereunder, the beneficiary entitled thereto (other than my wife as beneficiary under Clause TWELFTH) shall be less than 21 years of age or shall have been adjudicated an incompetent or shall be, in the judgment of my Executors or Trustees, as the case may be, otherwise unable to apply such income or principal to his or her own best interest and advantage, the title to the property to be distributed shall vest in such beneficiary, but during the existence of such condition or disability the income or principal to which the beneficiary is entitled may be retained by my Trustees who in that event shall hold, invest, or reinvest it and use as much of such income or principal as they, in their sole discretion, may deem appropriate for the beneficiary's maintenance in health and comfort, or for his or her education, or for any emergency needs of the beneficiary. My Trustees may do so either by the direct payment of bills or by making payments to such person or persons as my Trustees may select, without the intervention of a guardian, committee, or other fiduciary.

E Guideline 5:
Use the Active Voice Whenever Possible

The *passive voice* is an interesting grammatical construction. It is a way of changing the *focus* of a sentence without changing its meaning, by rearranging and adding words. Here are examples of active sentences and their passive counterparts.

Active: John hit Morris.
Passive: Morris was hit by John.

Active: Alice will eat the entire cake.
Passive: The entire cake will be eaten by Alice.

The passive voice allows the writer to focus on the object of the sentence rather than on the "doer" or the agent of the action. A passive construction can be in any tense; it can refer to a single action or to continuous action. For example:

The building will have been destroyed by the city by that time (future perfect tense).

The supplies are being eaten by rats (present continuous tense).

Because the passive does something unusual to the focus of a sentence, a passive sentence can be difficult for the reader to understand. Use the passive voice only when you want to focus on the object of the sentence.

When you use the passive voice, you can *truncate* the sentence by leaving out the doer of the action. For example, the full passive sentence

Morris was hit by John

can be made into the truncated passive

Morris was hit [   ].

The full passive

The building will have been destroyed by the city by that time

becomes the truncated passive

The building will have been destroyed [   ] by that time.

Using a truncated passive allows a writer to speak in general terms, in cases where it does not matter who the doer of the action is. For example:

In most law schools, law *is taught* by means of the Socratic method.

The writer can also avoid stating who is responsible for the action in cases where the identity of the actor does matter. The writer may intentionally "pass the buck" linguistically or may simply forget to identify the actor.

The effects of using the passive voice inappropriately can be particularly significant in legal writing. Many legal documents are concerned with the rights and responsibilities that govern the past, present, or future actions of specific individuals or entities. A contract, for example, spells out the rights and responsibilities of individuals under certain carefully defined circumstances. However, this vital information can be obscured by the use of passives, especially if they are truncated.

The following passage is an example of a very familiar kind of contract: It is part of an insurance policy. One of its major purposes is to describe the rights and responsibilities of the insurer and insured. However, the passage fails to focus on this important information. It is unclear who "incurred," who "lost," who "earned," and who "made payments."

> The company will pay, in accordance with Chapter 670 of the Acts of 1970 of the Commonwealth of Massachusetts and all Acts amendatory thereof or supplementary thereto, subject to any applicable deductible, all reasonable expenses *incurred* within two years from the date of accident for necessary medical, surgical, X-ray, and dental services, including prosthetic devices, and necessary ambulance, hospital, professional nursing, and funeral services, and, in the case of persons employed or self-employed at the time of an accident, any amounts actually *lost* by reason of inability to work and earn wages or salary or their equivalent, but not other income, that would otherwise have been *earned* in the normal course of an injured person's employment, and for payments in fact *made* to others, not members of the injured person's household and reasonably *incurred* in obtaining from those others ordinary and necessary services in lieu of those that, had he not been injured, the injured person would have performed not for income but for the benefit of himself or members of his household (emphasis added).

Similarly, when an attorney describes the past actions of an individual in the fact statement or analysis section of a memo or brief, it is important that the reader know exactly who did what. The passive voice may do more than just confuse the reader about each individual's actions; the passive voice can dilute the impact the attorney is trying to achieve. A plaintiff's attorney should describe the actions of the defendant so that they seem real and direct. The attorney wants the court to know that a particular individual committed a particular act. If the attorney writes in the passive voice, the focus will be on the act instead of on the person who committed the act.

Here is an example: The plaintiff, Jean, is suing her mother's doctor because the doctor prescribed the drug DES for her mother, Mrs. *M*, six months before Mrs. *M* became pregnant with Jean. The fact statement in the plaintiff's brief contained the following passage:

> On January 15, 1958, the plaintiff's mother, Mrs. *M*, consulted the defendant about the medical complications that she had experienced as the result of a miscarriage in March of 1957. Since Mrs. *M* was again pregnant, the drug DES *was prescribed* for her to take orally to prevent another miscarriage. Assurances *were made* to Mrs. *M* that the drug was completely safe. The prescribed drug *was taken* from January 16, 1958, until approximately February 28, 1958, when another miscarriage occurred. In August of 1958, Mrs. *M* became pregnant with the plaintiff.

This passage becomes far more effective when the passive voice is replaced by the active voice. It becomes clear who did the prescribing and assuring and who took the prescription and acted on the assurance. As a result, the defendant is directly indicted.

> Since Mrs. *M* was again pregnant, *the defendant prescribed the drug DES* for her to take orally to prevent another miscarriage. The *defendant assured* Mrs. *M* that the drug was completely safe. Mrs. *M* took the prescribed drug from January 16, 1958, until approximately February 28, 1958, when Mrs. *M* had another miscarriage.

You can use the active voice as part of your strategy to persuade your audience when you write documents like briefs and memoranda. As you begin to consciously identify the passive voice in legal documents, you will see the subtle effects you can achieve with this grammatical construction. Be attuned to writers who use the passive indiscriminately, because these writers may be diluting the forcefulness of their arguments and analyses. Being aware of the passive is especially important when you analyze an opponent's brief.

Learn to make your own arguments more convincing by following these rules:

1. Use the active voice whenever possible.
2. Avoid truncated passives. Reveal who is responsible for a particular action and put this "doer" into the sentence.
3. Use the passive voice only when you are speaking in general terms, when you want to stress the receiver of the action and not the actor, or when you want to downplay the actor.

EXERCISES

Identify the passive verbs in the following sentences. Rewrite the sentences in the active voice. If the original sentence is ambiguous or just unclear, make a reasonable assumption and rewrite the sentence accordingly.

1. A renewal clause was incorporated into the contract by the parties as well as the changes that were made in the delivery dates.
2. It can be argued that since the building wasn't owned but was leased by our client, permanent occupancy was not intended.
3. An official file shall be established for each client. To the extent that retained copies of documents do not represent all significant actions taken, suitable memoranda or summary statements of such undocumented actions must be prepared promptly and retained in the file.

F   Guideline 6:
Use Verb Clauses and Adjectives Instead of Nominalizations

Another interesting construction that is overused in legal documents is known as nominalization — the creation of nouns from verbs and adjectives.

the verb	can be made into the noun
determine	determination
resolve	resolution
apply	application
enforce	enforcement
inquire	inquiry
reverse	reversal

the adjective	can be made into the noun
enforceable	enforceability
distinguishable	distinguishability
applicable	applicability
specific	specificity
important	importance

As with the passive voice, these constructions are grammatical and so are the sentences that contain them. But, as with the passive voice, writers who overuse nominalizations weaken their writing.

Nominalizations make sentences difficult to understand, because they do not communicate a "scenario" — a scene that the reader can picture. Like truncated passives, nominalizations eliminate information about who did what.

Nominalizations make sentences less persuasive. Because nominalizations are nouns, they are *static,* giving the reader little or no feeling that an *action* is involved. Here are a few examples of sentences containing nominalizations. For the reader to fully grasp that someone *did* something, it is necessary to use verbs. Notice how direct the sentences become once the nominalizations are replaced with verb clauses.

POOR: *Recovery* by our client is predicated upon *circumvention* of the current interpretation of the adultery statute.

GOOD: Our client can *recover* if he *circumvents* the current interpretation of the adultery statute. (Note that some nominalizations are appropriate, such as *interpretation* in this sentence, because it cannot easily be replaced with a verb clause.)

POOR: Appellant did not authorize the *compilation* or *dissemination* of her credit report expressly or by *implication* when she submitted her *application* for insurance.

GOOD: The appellant did not expressly or implicitly authorize [whom?] to *compile* or *disseminate* her credit report when she *applied* for insurance.

POOR: The case's *significance* is in the fact that it demonstrates the court's *recognition* of the great *importance* of the right to privacy.

GOOD: The case is *significant* because it demonstrates that the court *recognizes* the importance of the right to privacy. (Here, too, one nominalization, *importance,* is appropriate.)

As you can see in the second of these examples, nominalizations often lead to other awkward or wordy constructions. Here, the simple verb *applied* has become *submitted her application.* Similarly, *decide* may become *make the decision; interpret* may become *construct an interpretation; sign* may become *affix one's signature,* etc. After making a noun out of the meaningful verb, the writer has to hunt around for another verb to make the sentence or clause grammatical. Often, the writer ends up using an "empty" verb — one that has no specific meaning, e.g., do, make, give, necessitate. This type of writing makes the action seem remote from the actors in the sentence; this, in turn, makes it harder for the reader to picture the scene. If you find nominalizations in your own writing, try converting them into their original form as verbs or adjectives. In most cases this will make your sentence more direct and easier to understand.

EXERCISES

Identify the nominalizations in the following sentences. Rewrite the sentences to eliminate them.

1. The appellee and W. C. Frederick entered into a contract for the delivery of ice by the appellee to Frederick and, before the expiration of the contract, Frederick executed an assignment of the contract to the appellant; and on the refusal of the appellee to deliver ice to the assignee it brought an action on the contract against the appellee.
2. We must construct an interpretation of the expiration date of a lease for years, with an emphasis on the applicability and legality of an ambiguous, inexact option for renewal clause.
3. This case involved a direct prior restraint imposed by a trial judge on reporters prohibiting publication of information already in their possession about a criminal trial.

G Guideline 7:
Use the Positive Unless You Want to Emphasize the Negative

Most people can easily understand a strong negative imperative ("Do not do that"). Negative statements, however, are generally more difficult for readers to process than positive statements. Furthermore, two negatives within a single clause are more than twice as difficult to understand as the corresponding positive statement.

Occasionally it is legitimate to use double negatives to capture subtleties of meaning. When you say that you are "not unhappy," for example, you do not necessarily mean that you are happy. The double negative expresses a state that is between happy and unhappy.

In general, however, you should avoid using two negatives when you can make a positive statement. The words *unless, except,* and *until* are negatives, as are words such as *failure, absent,* and *deny.* Here is a very simple example.

POOR: Plaintiff contends that it could *not* properly demand an equitable adjustment *until* after the completion of the project.

GOOD: Plaintiff contends that it could demand an equitable adjustment only after the project is completed.

More than two negatives make a clause exceedingly difficult or even impossible to understand. Yet legal writing is full of double and multiple negatives. Take a look at this example from a jury instruction:

POOR: *Failure* of recollection is a common experience, and innocent *mis*recollection is *not* uncommon.[3]

BETTER: Failure of recollection is a common experience, and innocent misrecollection is also common.

Following is an example of a triple negative from a law student's memo:

POOR: It is *un*likely that a Maryland district court would *ignore* the clear language of these opinions in the *absence* of convincing authority to the effect that a different rule applies where the action arose outside of the forum state.

GOOD: The Maryland district court will probably follow the clear language in these opinions unless there is convincing authority that a different rule applies where the action arose outside of the forum.

You may occasionally want to use multiple negatives to make a command or proscription more forceful. For example, in some circumstances you might want to use the double negative:

3. California Jury Instructions — Civil — Book of Approved Jury Instructions §2.21 (5th ed. 1969).

No client letter is to be sent out *unless* a senior partner has approved it.

Rather than the more positive:

A client letter is to be sent out *only* after a senior partner has approved it.

EXERCISES

Rewrite the following sentences in the positive.

1. We cannot but think that the Court in *Robson v. Drummond* went to the utmost length to which the principle can be carried.
2. A will shall not be valid unless it is signed by two witnesses.
3. There are few lawyers who would not agree that there are situations where "it is more important that the applicable rule of law be settled than that it be settled right."

H Guideline 8:
Use Parallel Structure

Sentences or clauses that bear the same conceptual relationship to some major idea should have parallel grammatical structure, e.g., all infinitives, all active voice, all gerunds (the *-ing* form of the verb used as a noun), etc. Sentences with parallel structure are much easier to read and remember. Here is a simple example:

POOR: To write a legal memo
- Identify the legal issues (imperative)
- Doing the correct research is your first priority (gerund and copula)
- You should make sure to read all cases and statutes with care (active sentence)
- Shepardize any cases that you use in your memo (imperative)
- It is important to use the correct citation form (stative sentence)

GOOD: To write a legal memo
(all   • Identify the legal issues
imperatives) • Do the correct research
             • Read all cases and statutes with care
             • Shepardize any cases that you use in your memo
             • Use the correct citation form

Parallel structure is important in lists. It is also important within a sentence and among sentences in a paragraph. Following is an example from a student memo. The student is discussing whether or not certain items in a rental property would be considered as fixtures:

POOR: Mr. Smith *used* the carpeting in his store, the air conditioner *was used* to cool the store, and the toilet in the back room *was intended for use* in the store.

The student used both the active and passive voice. The sentence is more effective and easier to understand if all the verbs are simple active verbs.

BETTER: Mr. Smith *used* the carpeting in his store, *used* the air conditioning to cool the store, and *intended* to have the toilet in the back room available for use in the store.

Parallelism is one of the best devices for effective, persuasive writing. First, a writer can use parallelism to test the cogency of his or her reasoning. Putting ideas into a parallel structure can help reveal to the writer whether those ideas are actually parallel. Once several ideas are lined up in a series, with the same grammatical structure, the writer can often tell whether he or she has forced dissimilar ideas into the same framework.

Second, a repeated grammatical structure emphasizes important information. When the arrangement of words in one sentence is repeated in another sentence, the repeated structure tends to stand out. In fact, a writer can achieve an emotional impact by arranging words, phrases, or sentences in structurally similar groupings. By repeating these groupings, the writer can build a powerful statement.[4]

Here is an example of an artful use of parallelism. It is from a speech by Winston Churchill to the House of Commons at the start of World War II. Notice how Churchill used parallelism in the overall structure of the passage

---

4. For more details on how to use parallelism effectively, see H. Weihofen, Legal Writing Style 319-322 (2d ed. 1980).

by asking a question and then answering it. This provides a powerful framework for his ideas. He also used parallelism within sentences to emphasize concepts and to build them to a climax. The parallel structures are italicized.

> *You ask, what is our policy?* I *will say:* It is *to wage* war, by sea, land, and air, *with all* our might and *with all* the strength that God can give us; *to wage* against a monstrous tyranny, never surpassed in the dark, lamentable catalogue of human crime. That is our policy. *You ask, what is our aim?* I *can answer* in one word: Victory — *victory* at all costs, *victory* in spite of all terror; *victory,* however long and hard the road may be; for without victory, there is no survival. Let that be realised; *no survival* for the British Empire; *no survival* for all that the British Empire has stood for, *no survival* for the urge and impulse of the ages, that mankind will move forward towards its goal. But I take up my task with buoyancy and hope. I feel sure that our cause will not be suffered to fail among men. At this time I feel entitled to claim the aid of all, and I say, "Come, then, let us go forward together with our united strength."[5]

EXERCISES

Correct the lack of parallelism in the following passages.

1. Upon vacating, the Tenant agrees to pay for all utilities services due and have same discontinued; to see that the property is swept out and all trash or other refuse is removed from the premises; that the doors and windows are properly locked or fastened; and that the key is returned to the Landlord or Agent.

2. The test used in determining whether the bookcases could be removed from the rental property was whether or not they became a fixture under the tests used in determining fixtures:

   1. alterations made to the property to facilitate installations of equipment;
   2. who bore the cost of expense;
   3. removal without damage to the premises;
   4. whether the item is particularly adapted to the particular present use — in that it would not be equally useful elsewhere.

5. Churchill, Speech to the House of Commons, May 13, 1940, reprinted in Their Finest Hour 22 (1977).

3. The trend is towards recognizing the rights of citizens to privacy and for punishing unwarranted intrusions thereon.

I Guideline 9:
Avoid Ambiguity in Words and Sentences

An ambiguous word or sentence can be interpreted in more than one way. If you want to be certain the reader understands your meaning, you should know the causes of ambiguity and how to deal with them.

1. Ambiguity at the Word Level

There are many kinds of ambiguity. Ambiguity at the word level is prevalent in legal language because the law gives common, everyday words special legal meanings. For example, a motion in legal language is a particular type of pleading, not a movement or gesture, nor a proposal for action in a parliamentary setting.

When words have different meanings in different contexts, readers will understand exactly what is meant only when they are familiar with the context. This applies not only to legal language itself, but to technical words and phrases that you may use in drafting a legal document for a particular trade.[6] Shipping or construction contracts, for example, may use terms that mean something different in that trade than in everyday usage. It is important that the trade meaning be clear — not only for the benefit of the parties to the contract, but in case it is ever necessary to interpret rights and obligations under the contract.

Avoid using shall. One source of ambiguity is the use of the word *shall*. In writing legal documents, it is traditional to use *shall* to establish a legal obligation. However, many lawyers use *shall* incorrectly. They use it inconsistently — to mean both *must* (obligatory or mandatory action) and *will* (future action). This ambiguous use can cause legal problems.

To complicate matters further, lawyers sometimes use *shall* along with *must* and *will* in the same document. Because most people do not use *shall* in

6. See Frigaliment Importing Co. v. B.N.S. International Sales Corp., 190 F. Supp. 116 (S.D.N.Y. 1960), where one party to a contract thought that the word "chicken" in the contract referred only to broiling and frying chickens, while the other party insisted that in the trade the term also included stewing chickens.

ordinary speech or writing and therefore do not use it properly in legal documents, we suggest that you do not use it at all. Use *must* when you mean the action is obligatory; use *will* when you intend future (nonobligatory) action; use *may* for permissible action. In the negative, use *must not; will not;* and *need not* or *does not have to. May not* is often ambiguous. It can mean either "must not" or "does not have to." For example, the following sentence can be interpreted in two ways.

If you give incorrect information on your application to take the bar exam, we may not accept your application.

The sentence can mean "we are barred from accepting it" or "we have the option of refusing it."

Don't use elegant variation. In legal documents it is important to use only one term for any concept. Call the car that struck your client "the car" every time you mention it; don't refer to it as "the car" in one place and as "the vehicle" in another place. As Mark Twain said, "Eschew elegant variation." Referring to the same thing by different names may confuse the reader; it may also create legal problems. For example:

I conclude that we should argue that the limitations period of the forum state applies, rather than that of the *state where the action arose.* However, if we argue for the limitations period of the *accrual state,* we will have to rethink our strategy.

The writer assumed that the reader would understand that the state where the action arose and the accrual state are the same thing, but the reader may assume that they are two distinct states or become confused enough to give up trying to understand the passage.

2. Ambiguity at the Sentence Level

Misplaced words or unclear structure. Ambiguity can also occur at the sentence level. If you misplace words or fail to indicate what a word or phrase refers to, you will confuse the reader.

Misplacing words such as *only* and *exclusively* can make a sentence ambiguous. For example:

Describe the client's property only in section II of the will.

Does this mean to describe the property and no other asset in section II, or to describe the property in section II and nowhere else? *Only* is a useful word, but it can create ambiguity.

You can also create ambiguity by using *more than* or *less than* carelessly. Be sure that the reader knows what is being compared. For example:

> I love Devil Dogs more than Marcia

can mean "more than I love Marcia" or "more than Marcia loves Devil Dogs." If the meaning of a sentence with *more than* or *less than* is not clear, fill in the missing words that will make it clear.

Pronouns. You must also be careful when you use pronouns. Make sure the reader will know which noun the pronoun refers to. If you have not made it clear which noun is the pronoun's antecedent, you can confuse the reader. For example:

> If the argument is made that the law of the forum state should be applied, I believe that *it* will be attacked by our opponent.

The reader may be unsure whether *it* refers to the law of the forum state or to the argument. Although most readers will work this one out correctly, they will waste time in doing so.

Make sure each pronoun is in the same person (he, she, it) and number (he, they) as the noun it refers to. For example, in the following sentence the pronouns *they* and *their* do not agree with the antecedent *one.*

> If one of the expert witnesses were to be used in this trial, they would be asked to show their qualifications.

It is also important to make sure that there is a clear concept for the pronoun to refer to.

> While there is no support in the Eighth Circuit for our position that the Minnesota statute of limitations period applies, I think we should assert *this* as our primary argument.

Here, the concept that the pronoun *this* refers to has not been clearly articulated. Sentences like this are not only examples of poor writing; they may indicate fuzzy thinking.

Misplaced clauses.   Yet another type of ambiguity arises from misplacing subordinate clauses. Position a subordinate clause so that it is clear which words you want the clause to modify. For example:

> The second type of fringe benefit is the receipt of goods, services, or money, not as a salary, *which is indirectly related to the performance by the employee of his duties on his job.*

> Our client is questioning the $2,000 requested for heat treatments for the plaintiff's arm *based upon Dr. Smith's itemized medical report.*

In each of these sentences, it is unclear exactly what the subordinate clause refers to. Does "which is indirectly related" in the first sentence refer to "salary" or "receipt" or "benefit"? Does "based upon Dr. Smith's itemized medical report" in the second sentence modify "the $2,000" or "requested" or "heat treatments"? Each sentence should be rewritten so that only one interpretation is possible.

Conditionals.   Conditionals can be especially ambiguous if they contain both *ands* and *ors*. For example:

> If a client is receiving alimony or is receiving child support and has been divorced for more than one year, then this section of the rule does not apply.

This sentence can be interpreted two ways. It can mean:

This section of the rule does not apply if the client
1. Is receiving either alimony or child support *and*
2. Has been divorced for more than one year

Or the sentence can mean:

This section of the rule does not apply if the client
1. Is receiving alimony *or*
2. Is receiving child support and has been divorced for more than one year

Nothing in the original sentence tells the reader which conditions belong together.

To avoid ambiguity in conditionals, make it clear where conditions begin and end. You can use punctuation, but that is not the best solution. A better solution is to use *syntax* to clarify the message. For example, you can repeat the subject of the sentence before each full condition.

> *If the client* is receiving either alimony or child support and *if the client* has been divorced for more than one year, then this section of the rule does not apply.

Or you can use *layout* to make the conditions clear. We used layout above to demonstrate the two possible interpretations of the alimony example. The best solution is to use a combination of syntax and layout to get your message across unambiguously.

Writing exceptions requires even more care. Exceptions are negative conditions (if not . . . then; if . . . then don't). Exceptions cause confusion because the reader must shift gears from "apply this rule" to "don't apply this rule." A shift like this can be particularly confusing if the exception appears in the same sentence as the rule.

POOR: The same cost accounting period shall be used for accumulating costs in an indirect cost pool as for establishing its allocation base, *except* that the contracting parties may agree to use a different period for establishing an allocation base, provided:
1. The practice is necessary . . .
2. The practice . . . etc.

Rather than joining exceptions into the same sentence as the rule, you should state the rule and then start a new sentence with "However, if . . ." or "Nonetheless, if . . ." The above example would be much clearer if it were rewritten as follows:

BETTER: Use the same cost accounting period for accumulating costs in an indirect cost pool as for establishing its (whose?) allocation base. However, the contracting parties may agree to use a different period for establishing an allocation base, if all of (or any one of) the following conditions hold:
1. The practice is necessary
2. The practice . . . etc.

3. Intentional Ambiguity

Ambiguity can have a valid place in legal writing. Legislation is often designed to be ambiguous so that it will be flexible enough to cover unforeseen circumstances. Ambiguity can also be useful to the writer who *wants* to obscure his or her meaning, as in the case of an attorney who is answering interrogatories. However, using intentional ambiguity takes a great deal of skill and care: Inappropriate or unsophisticated use can backfire. A piece of ambiguous legislation, for example, could exclude or include the wrong conditions, situations, or people. Unskillfully drafted answers to interrogatories may obscure neutral pieces of information while revealing too much about sensitive issues.

EXERCISES

Find and eliminate the ambiguities in the following sentences. Also use the other guidelines to make the sentences clearer.

1. Except as may be otherwise provided by statute or this subchapter, costs may not be incurred prior to the execution of the agreement by both parties thereto.
2. No person shall be a representative who shall not have attained to the age of 25 years, and been 7 years a citizen of the United States, and who shall not, when elected, be an inhabitant of that state in which he shall be chosen.
3. This tax credit may be claimed by any corporation or any limited partnership engaged in interstate commerce which has reinvested not less than the greater of $100,000 or 5 percent of its total gross income during the taxable year.

J Guideline 10: Choose Vocabulary with Care

From law school onward, members of the legal profession often unthinkingly emulate the writing that they come across in legal treatises, opinions, and casebooks. And often the language used in these documents is ungrammatical, unnecessarily complex, or archaic. Choose your vocabulary carefully. Try not to indiscriminately follow the models you see just because they look and sound "legal."

1. Eliminate or Change Archaic or Unnecessary Words

There are a number of words that commonly occur in legal documents that are archaic. These words can often be left out entirely. If you can't just leave them out, replace them with commonplace words or phrases. The following is by no means an exhaustive list of words of this kind. You will no doubt come across others. Try to keep them out of your own writing.

aforesaid	hereinbefore
henceforth	hereinafter
herein	heretofore
hereafter	thereto
thereby	thereunto

verbs ending in -*eth*
said, same, such (when you mean *the*)
one (before a person's name)

2. Replace Difficult Words or Legal Jargon with Words Your Readers Will Know

This principle is often stated as "use short words," but it is not really length that causes problems. It is unfamiliarity that causes problems. As it happens, less familiar words tend to be longer than common words.

This principle should be tempered by your knowledge of the audience. The purpose of a document is to communicate to the people who must read it. When people write only for other people in their field, it is appropriate to use technical words and specialized ways of communicating. Brevity and precision both are served by the use of specialized language if the reader and the writer give the same interpretation to that language. However, even lawyers can have trouble understanding specialized legal terms. For example, a criminal lawyer might have trouble understanding a document meant for tax lawyers.

Furthermore, many of the documents that lawyers produce are meant to be read by nonlawyers, who are unlikely to understand legal vocabulary and terms of art. The lay audience may also be confused by words or phrases that look familiar but that have a special meaning to lawyers. The list below will give you an idea of how you can substitute simpler terms for complex or specialized terms. The words in this list will not always be perfectly interchangeable. Nevertheless, it is a good rule of thumb to try the simpler term first to see if it works as well as the more difficult one. You will find that your audience will not be insulted if you use *after* instead of *subsequent to,* no matter how sophisticated that audience is.

3. Define or Explain Technical Terms

There are times when you cannot eliminate or change technical terms or legal terms of art, even though you know that some part of your audience will not be familiar with those terms. A definition, explanation, or example can help. If the definition for a technical term is fairly short, you can insert it right after the technical term the first time that term appears. You can do this with or without parentheses.

The following excerpt from a bank's loan note includes two examples of technical terms that are defined or explained in the sentence ("refinanced" and "rule of 78").

> *Prepayment of Whole Note:* Even though I needn't pay more than the fixed installments, I have the right to prepay the whole outstanding amount of this note at any time. If I do, or if this loan is *refinanced — that is, if I take out a new loan to pay off my old loan —* you will refund the unearned finance charge, figured by *the rule of 78 — a commonly used formula for figuring rebates on installment loans.* However, you can charge a minimum finance charge of $10.

You can provide a fuller explanation or example by making it a main part of the text itself, as in the following rewritten jury instruction.

> There is a type of negligence that involves the conduct of the plaintiff, rather than the defendent. It is called *contributory negligence.*
>
> If a plaintiff is negligent, and his negligence helps cause his own injury, we say that the plaintiff is contributorily negligent.
>
> A plaintiff who is contributorily negligent cannot recover money for his injury.

The following explanation of *default* from the rewritten bank note also illustrates how a term can be defined or explained within the main part of the text.

> *Default:* I'll be in default
>   1. If I don't pay an installment on time; or
>   2. If any other creditor tries by legal process to take any money of mine in your possession.

TABLE 5-1

Some Words and Phrases You Can Change

Don't use this word	if this word will work as well	Don't use this word	if this word will work as well
accord	give	institute	begin
adequate amount	enough	in the event that	if
afford	give	maintain	keep, continue,
aggregate	total		support
allocate	give, divide	necessitate	require
applicable	that applies	on or before	by
as to	about, relating to	on the part of	by
attain	reach	originate	start
attributable to	from, by	per annum	a year
by reason of	because of	prior to	before
cease	stop	procure	get
commence	begin	promulgate	issue
constitute	make up	provided that	however if
deem	consider	pursuant to	under
effectuate	carry out	retain	keep
exclusively	only	render	make, give
expiration	end	shall	must, may, will
for the duration		solely	only, alone
of	during	sufficient	enough
for the purpose		submit	send, give,
of	to, for		contend
for the reason		subsequent to	after
that	because	said, same, such	the, this, that
furnish	give, provide	terminate	end, finish
has the option of	may	unto	to
indicate	show	utilize	use
in excess of	more than	without the	outside the
initiate	begin	United States	United States
in lieu of	instead of		

EXERCISES

1. Underline the inappropriate or unnecessarily difficult vocabulary in this passage. Rewrite the passage.

CONSENT OF MINOR CHILD TO ADOPTION

I, Jane Smith, age 11, born on March 1, 1971, do hereby consent to my adoption by John Jones. I understand that if this adoption is granted, the relationship of parent and child will be established between myself and John Jones the same as if I had been born to him and further that all rights of my mother, Mary Jones, will be reserved unto her.

I further consent to the change of my name to Jane Jones.

2. Underline and mark with the appropriate letter any words or phrases that you think are: a) totally unnecessary; b) necessary but need to be defined or translated.

KNOW ALL MEN BY THESE PRESENTS:

That the undersigned, individually and as parents or guardians of John Smith, a minor of the age of 12 years, residing at 1800 Oak Street, for and in consideration of the sum of Eight Thousand Dollars lawful money of the United States of America, to them in hand paid for and on behalf of said minor, the receipt whereof is hereby acknowledged, do hereby remise, release, and forever discharge Asa Luntz from any and all claims which are a result of a certain accident or event which occurred on or about June 5th, 1980, at 4700 Chestnut Street.

K Guideline 11: Avoid Noun Strings

Not only can nouns be used in place of verbs (nominalizations), it is also possible to use nouns as adjectives. For example, *client interview form* — here the first two nouns modify the final noun, *form*. Two or more nouns in a row are called a noun string.

When a writer strings together more than two nouns, especially with an occasional adjective added to the string, it becomes difficult for the reader to understand the relationships among the nouns. Noun strings are grammatical, but the longer the string, the harder it is for the reader to understand what is going on. Some of the worst noun strings appear as the names of institutions or programs: *Family Planning Services Delivery Improvement Research Grants Program.* Here are other examples of noun strings from student memos and briefs:

• Qualified scholarship funding bonds
• The District of Columbia Human Rights Law limitations period
• Intrusive pretrial discovery methods

This is what one of these noun strings looks like in the context of a sentence:

> There is no precedent to support our position that the District of Columbia Human Rights Law limitations period applies to section 1981 actions.

Noun strings lack the "little words" — usually prepositions, sometimes the possessive *'s* — that clarify *how* the nouns are related to each other. Noun strings may shorten a sentence, which may appear to simplify it, but removing the little words actually makes the sentence more complex. The reader has to laboriously untangle the noun string and reconstruct the original relationships. The reader puts back the prepositions or possessives mentally, and that takes time and energy. Noun strings can also make a sentence ambiguous, so that readers sometimes untangle them incorrectly. A good example is the name *International Ladies Garment Workers Union.* Is this a union of ladies who work on garments or a union of workers who work on ladies' garments? Are the ladies, the union, the workers, or the garments international?[7]

The solution is to unstring noun strings whenever possible. For example,

POOR: There is no precedent to support our position that the *District of Columbia Human Rights Law limitations period* applies to section 1981 actions.

GOOD: There is no precedent to support our position that the limitations period of the District of Columbia Human Rights Law applies to section 1981 actions.

7. Another example is *Federal Employers Liability Act.* Is this an act that regulates federal employers or a federal act that regulates certain employers?

POOR: Not all information is available to the consumer for *consumption or purchasing choice decisions.*

GOOD: Consumers do not have all the information they need to decide what to use or what to buy.

Notice that noun strings often include nominalizations. When you unstring the noun string, you should also look for the verb underlying the noun and make sure that it is necessary. In the last example, for instance, "consumption" comes from the verb *consume,* which really means to use up or to eat, "purchasing" comes from the verb *purchase,* which really means to buy, and "choice" comes from the verb *choose,* which is redundant because it means the same here as *decide,* which appears as the noun "decisions."

EXERCISES

Identify the noun strings in the following sentences and unstring them.

1. The State bar client grievance committee is an attempt at a voluntary professional self-regulation program.
2. The Supreme Court held in *Ohralik v. Ohio State Bar Association,* 436 U.S. 447 (1978), that the state could prohibit attorney in-person client solicitations.
3. This is a request for public comment on a proposal for an industry self-regulated voluntary informational labeling program.

L # Guideline 12:
Eliminate Redundancy and Extraneous Words; Avoid Overspecificity

Legal drafters often use two words that have almost identical meanings where one is really enough (aid and abet, false and untrue). There is a historical reason for these pairs. One term is usually Anglo-Saxon, while the other is Latin-based through Norman French. In the Middle Ages when British common law had to deal with English-speaking yeomen and French-speaking aristocrats, doublets like these may have been necessary. In twentieth century America, they usually only add redundancy. Here are some of the more common pairs to be aware of:

each and every	false and untrue
any and all	excess and unnecessary
aid and abet	final and conclusive
authorized and empowered	type and kind
full and complete	absolutely and completely
order and direct	null and void

Bureaucrats and academicians are also guilty of using two words where one will do. The temptation to say things twice is often very hard to fight, but extra words that do not add any information should be left out. For example:

personal opinion	honest opinion
next subsequent	positive benefits

Some of these examples are truly redundant. You could not use the opposite of the adjective and have a meaningful phrase. For instance, what are negative benefits? In other cases, the adjective is informative only if you are stressing that attribute, e.g., "This is my personal opinion, not that of the group."

The use of extraneous words can also overload a sentence and obscure its meaning. Extraneous words often appear as meaningless sentence introductions.

> *It is possible that* you may not be able to file your brief on time.
> *This is to inform you that* your case has been put on the docket.
> *There are* four people *who* would like to testify.
> *It was* in the fall of 1978 that she revised her will.

You can tell that an introduction is extraneous if you can remove it and still communicate the same information.

Extraneous words can appear anywhere in a sentence. For example, one law student wrote:

> The *matter presented* for this Court's *determination in the case at bar* is the *question* of *allowing* a cause of action for a preconception tort in Minnesota.

The student could have eliminated many of the italicized words and rewritten the sentence as follows:

> The court must decide whether the plaintiff can recover under Minnesota law for negligence that occurred before the plaintiff was conceived.

A good way to edit out extraneous words is to think of how you would express the concept orally. Often this will enable you to eliminate words that only serve to pad your sentences.

Another, related problem is overspecificity — that is, listing every possible instance of a general concept. Some attorneys fear that they won't be "covered" unless they list every possibility.

KNOW ALL MEN BY THESE PRESENTS:

That John Smith, hereinafter designated as the Releasor, for and in consideration of the sum of $8,000, the receipt whereof is hereby acknowledged, has *remised, released, and forever discharged,* and by these presents *does remise, release, and forever discharge* the said Releasee *of* and *from* all *debts, obligations, reckonings, promises, covenants, agreements, contracts, endorsements, bonds, specialties, controversies, suits, actions, causes of actions, trespasses, variances, judgments, extents, executions, damages, claims, or demands,* in law or in equity, which against the said Releasee, the Releasor *ever had, now has,* or hereafter *can, shall, or may have, for, upon, or by reason of* any *matter, cause, or thing* whatsoever, from the beginning of the world to the day of the date of these Presents.

Not only is this overspecificity unnecessary, it can be dangerous: The drafter can easily leave out an important item or action, and because he or she has been so specific, the omission would probably be interpreted as intentional. If a litigated document contains such omissions, the omissions can be used by your opponents to their advantage.

Rather than specifying every instance, we suggest that you use a general term and perhaps one or two examples, or several general terms, e.g., " . . . released from all obligations, suits and other claims . . . " Remember that under the rule of ejusdem generis, courts will often construe general terms that follow terms of a particular or specific meaning as being defined or limited by these specific terms. That is, the general terms will be interpreted as applying only to things that fall into the same class as those specifically mentioned first. For example, if a list includes "dogs, cats, and other animals," "other animals" would probably exclude amoebas. The more general item is limited by the prior terms.

EXERCISES

Eliminate redundancy, superfluous words, or overspecificity in the following exercises. Also replace or eliminate any unnecessary legal jargon.

1. Any and all persons operating motor vehicles of any type and kind whatsoever in the District of Columbia shall obtain liability insurance.
2. The findings and determinations hereinafter set forth are supplementary and in addition to the findings and determinations previously made in connection with the issuance of the aforesaid order and of the previously issued amendments thereto; and all of the said previous findings and determinations are hereby ratified and affirmed, except insofar as such findings and determinations may be in conflict with the findings and determinations set forth herein.
3. §550.10   Trees, shrubs, plants, grass, and other vegetation. (a) General injury. No person shall prune, cut, carry away, pull up, dig, fell, bore, chop, saw, chip, pick, move, sever, climb, molest, take, break, deface, destroy, set fire to, burn, scorch, carve, paint, mark, or in any manner interfere with, tamper, mutilate, misuse, disturb, or damage any tree, shrub, plant, grass, flower, or part thereof, nor shall any person permit any chemical, whether solid, fluid, or gaseous, to seep, drip, drain or be emptied, sprayed, dusted or injected upon, about, or into any tree, shrub, plant, grass, flower, or part thereof, except when specifically authorized by competent authority; nor shall any person build fires, or station, or use any tar kettle, heater, road roller or other engine within an area covered by this part in such a manner that the vapor, fumes, or heat therefrom may injure any tree or other vegetation.

M Guideline 13:
Use an Appropriate Style

It is important to choose the right style when you write legal documents. The style you use will depend upon your audience and purpose. Once you choose an appropriate style, stick with it throughout the document. Following are several guidelines to the style you should use when you write memos, briefs, letters, and other documents.

1. Use the Correct Point of View, Labels, and Pronouns

The point of view, labels, and pronouns that you use in legal writing will depend upon the type of document you are writing. For example, the rules are slightly different for briefs and memos. You should generally write briefs in the third person (he, she, or it) from the point of view of an observer of the facts and the law. This will give the document a professional tone that will help convince your reader that you have drawn your conclusions from research and reasoning rather than by relying on your own biases and emotions.

This means that you should avoid referring to yourself with the personal pronoun *I* or *me* or to yourself and your client as *we* or *us*. Instead, formally refer to the client as petitioner, respondent, appellant or appellee, or, better still, use the client's last name. Also avoid using phrases that suggest that your statements are your personal observations: *I feel, It is my opinion, It is our belief.* Present your contentions more objectively by referring to yourself and your client in the third person: *Petitioner contends, Appellee suggests.* Be careful about being overly cautious in the way you present your contentions. Do not use phrases such as *It appears that, It seems likely that, It is suggested* to keep from committing yourself. Although cautious statements are occasionally necessary, they are usually used as a safety device, i.e., the user of such a statement cannot later be proved wrong. The consequence of hedging your bet this way is that the reader perceives the statement as just what it is — an equivocation. Your assertion is robbed of force. This is especially undesirable in a brief, where you are trying to persuade your audience.

POOR: Now that I have reviewed the facts, it appears that the petitioners have failed to establish undue influence, overreaching, and misrepresentation.

GOOD: The evidence shows that the petitioners have failed to establish undue influence, overreaching, and misrepresentation.

You should use the same style when you write memos. Even though you are not writing for an adversary or for the court, you still want to convince your audience that your analysis is impersonal and well reasoned. However, because memos are often internal documents, you may have more leeway for informality. For example, a law firm may allow you, or even expect you, to express your conclusions or recommendations as your own opinions. For instance, you might offer the following conclusion:

> It is my opinion that the petitioners have failed to establish undue influence, overreaching, and misrepresentation.

When you are writing letters to a client or a loan agreement for consumers, you can relax the rules presented above. In fact, it may be quite appropriate to present your document in the first person (I) or in the second person (you).

You can also use personal pronouns to give a document a tone of directness and personal interest. People may be more motivated to read a document that they feel is addressed to them. Using personal pronouns will also force you to write active rather than passive sentences (see Guideline 5). In a regulation or set of instructions, you can define *you* to mean all of the various participants. This can save space because then it is not necessary to repeat a cumbersome list many times.

In the revised regulations for Citizens Band (CB) radio operators, (47 C.F.R. §95.423 (1979)), the heading of each section is a question that the CB owner might ask. The body of each section is the answer. Both the first person pronouns (I, my) and the second person pronouns (you, your) refer to the CB owner.

> §95.423 **What address do I put on my application?** You must include your complete mailing address and station address in the United States on your CB license application.

In some revised bank forms and insurance policies, the company is writing to the consumer. *We* refers to the company and *you* means the consumer. Compare these two versions from a homeowners' insurance policy:

BEFORE: *Company's options.* It shall be optional with this Company to take all, or any part, of the property at the agreed or appraised value and also to repair, rebuild, or replace the property destroyed or damaged with other of like kind and quality within a reasonable time, on giving notice of its intention to do so within 30 days after the receipt of the proof of loss herein required.

AFTER: *Our option.* If we give you written notice within 30 days after your signed, sworn statement of loss, we may repair or replace any part of the property damaged with equivalent property.

Unfortunately, there is no standard way to use pronouns. Sometimes the consumer is *I* and the company is *you*. This lack of consistency in the use of pronouns from one document to the next may be confusing to readers. There is also some evidence that readers find it difficult to remember who is who as they get further and further into a document that has both *we* and *you* in it. For most documents a good solution is to call the reader *you* and refer to your firm, company, or agency by name or initials.

2. Use the Correct Tense

Legal writing has specific rules for when you should use the present and past tenses in memos and briefs.

1. If you are writing your own argument or analysis or if you are writing about your opponent's argument, use the present tense.

> Petitioners *argue* that common sense *dictates* that respondent's activities be classified as commercial.

2. If you are writing about a rule or statute that is still in force, use the present tense.

> According to §2-513 of the Uniform Commercial Code, a person who *buys* goods *has* a right to inspect the goods before *accepting* or *paying* for them.

3. If you are writing about a case that the court has already decided, use the past tense.

> In *Weisberg v. Williams, Connolly & Califano*, 399 A.2d 992, 995 (D.C. 1978), the court *held* that the statute of limitations for legal malpractice will not run if the defendant fraudulently concealed improprieties.

4. If you are writing about the actions of the people involved in a case, use the past tense, unless the actions are still going on. Discuss ongoing actions in the present tense.

> While it *is true* that the respondent *might have profited* from her activities, this *was not* the respondent's primary motive.

3. Use a Formal but Not Pompous Style

Aim for a style that is neither too chatty and colloquial nor too formal or inflated. It is difficult to describe the happy medium between these two extremes. To get an idea of the proper style, look at the sample memo and briefs presented later in this book. Here, however, we point out a few characteristics to avoid.

1. Avoid inappropriately "chatty" language.

> The most recent appellate court decision wasn't very good for our side. It will be a lot of trouble for us to argue around it.

2. Try to avoid inflated language. Using an inflated term like "telephonic communications" for telephone calls can give your writing a pompous tone.

> The attorney's subsequent *telephonic communications* were nothing more than the further dissemination of information to a special group.

3. Avoid cliches and mixed metaphors. You can damage your credibility if you use them. Cliches tell the reader that your thinking is not original. Metaphors are difficult to create, and if your metaphor doesn't work, or if you mix metaphors, you risk looking foolish. Here are examples from student memos that contain cliches and mixed metaphors. Note that in the second one the student also misquotes the metaphor, using *unchartered* instead of *uncharted*.

> A recurring theme in petitioner's appeal is that the courts have been flexible in their response to changing times. That flexibility is evidenced by *the slow and grudging wheels of Justice* is but a romantic notion of Justice responding to *every hue and cry*.

> Whether this small number of jurisdictions represents a trend or a *minority rushing blindly into unchartered waters* remains to be seen.

4. Use an Appropriate Approach

Begin your analysis or argument by dealing directly with the facts and law. Do not begin an analysis or argument with philosophical discussions as in the following example.

Since a lawyer's primary function is protecting and advising a client in the client's best interest, it is always of the utmost importance to first determine what it is, exactly, that the client needs or wants. Before assuming lawsuits and potential liability it is necessary to examine alternative procedures that may, in fact, serve the client as well or better than winning a particular day in court.

Legal briefs and memos are not term papers; don't write them like term papers. In term papers, students are usually expected to do library research on a topic and then write up all that they have discovered about that topic. The student may be encouraged to philosophize, cite people's opinions, or give a history of the topic. Here is an example in which a student used a term paper approach. The student was arguing that recognizing the specific tort of invasion of privacy is not necessary, because a plaintiff can currently use other tort actions and existing statutes to enforce the right of privacy.

> The right of privacy is an important value which has been gleaned from the Bill of Rights and developed throughout our nation's history. Arguing against it is like arguing against American notions of freedom, liberty, and justice.
>
> Historically, a tort action of privacy never existed in common law. Kalven, Privacy in Tort Law — Were Warren and Brandeis Wrong?, 31 L. & Contemp. Prob. 326, 327 (1978). The first major work done on the subject was motivated by the author's displeasure with stories of his daughter's marriage. Warren & Brandeis, The Right to Privacy, 4 Harv. L. Rev. 192 (1890). Out of this article arose the tort called invasion of privacy, which some courts began recognizing some thirty years later.

In the law, the reader's expectations are different, and hence the writer's approach must be different. The writer should include only information that is necessary for analyzing the facts and the law. The writer should leave out irrelevant material, no matter how interesting it may seem.

REVIEW EXERCISES

Identify all of the problems in each passage and then rewrite the passage.

1. Recent developments in Wisconsin law have made some progress in

clearing up the problems encountered in the construction of the drunk driving statute and will aid the resolution of our client's problem.

2. In *Marsh v. Alabama,* 326 U.S. 501 (1946), it was found that the town was not unlike others in its accessibility and functions to the public.

3. In this determination, state membership or representation on policy-making bodies and state powers over institutional decision making would be important factors for examination.

4. To examine more closely the objectionable methods of data gathering, reflect upon the attainment of private mental records from a state entity.

6

Writing
Effectively

A Step One: Developing a Logical Argument

As an attorney, you will be required to convince your audience to accept your point of view in documents ranging from letters to clients to briefs for the court. In this chapter we present a variety of techniques for constructing and writing persuasive legal documents.

In law you will rarely work with unambiguous situations or rules because most real-life situations are ambiguous. Your job as an advocate is to persuade your readers that your description of the facts is closest to what occurred, that the law or rule you have chosen to apply to a particular situation is the most appropriate one, that your understanding of the law is the most accurate, and that your overall interpretation of the situation is superior to any other interpretation, especially that of an adversary. To be persuasive, you must

1. Develop a logical argument.
2. Choose the most appropriate and effective information to emphasize in your argument.
3. Use writing techniques that will help you make the most of your position.

When you write a persuasive document, you must give that document a logical structure. For example, the IRAC framework (Issue, Rule, Application, Conclusion) that we discussed in Chapter 4 can help convince your readers that a tight, well-constructed thought process led you from your assertion in the issue statement to your conclusion.

You will probably not start out with a tight, well-constructed body of information when you sit down to compile a legal document. The process of creating a brief, for example, involves researching the facts and the law, thinking about the significance of the research, writing up the research, and then going back to do additional research before writing a final draft. In creating any document, research, thought, and writing are interactive — as you write, you realize that you need more research; as you do more research, you change what you have written.

How do you impose a structure on a process of this sort? Begin with the assumption that you do not want to walk your readers through the twists and turns you had to take to develop your argument. You want them to follow your reasoning along one straight path — and to think that the path you have chosen is sound and logical.

In order to create a logical structure, think about what you are trying to accomplish when you deal with a problem in law. You will often find that you are trying to establish that a specific set of facts fits within a well-settled rule of law. One way to do this logically and systematically is to use the principles of deductive reasoning to set up the skeleton of your legal analysis.

1. Deductive Reasoning in Law

You are probably familiar with the basic categorical syllogism. For example:

> MAJOR PREMISE: All men are mortal.
> MINOR PREMISE: Socrates is a man.
> CONCLUSION: Socrates is mortal.

Deductive reasoning is the thought process that occurs whenever you set out to show that a minor premise (a specific situation, event, person, or object) fits within the class covered by a major premise (an established rule, principle, or truth) and to prove that, consequently, what applies to the class covered by the major premise must necessarily apply to the specific situation. In short, deductive reasoning allows you to prove that your particular case is covered by an established rule.

Deductive reasoning is a cornerstone of legal thought. Lawyers are often called upon to decide how a rule of law applies to a given case. Since the rule is usually stated in general terms and a client's problem is generally very specific, deductive reasoning can be used to bridge the gap between the general and the specific. For example:

> *Rule of Law* (major premise): Courts have held that any agreement made in jest by one party and reasonably understood to be in jest by the other party will not be enforced as a contract.

Facts of our case (minor premise): Robert agreed to paint Lee's entire house, but both Robert and Lee understood that Robert was only joking.

Conclusion: Robert's agreement is not an enforceable contract.

These basic steps of deductive reasoning form the skeleton of a legal argument. In fact, the rule, application, conclusion sequence of IRAC forms a simple syllogism: The rule contains the major premise, the application contains the particular facts of the minor premise, and the conclusion sums up the information.

The order in which you present a syllogism may not be the order in which you accumulate the information or think through the problem. Thus, you may work in the order: conclusion, rule, application. If you do that, you begin by deciding what you want to accomplish for your client. Then you go over rules from analogous cases, statutes, or constitutions to find one that will serve as your major premise, or you propose a new rule from the information you have gathered in your research. Finally, you carefully review the facts of your case and present them in a way that fits the rule of law.

For example: What do I want to accomplish for my client? I want my client declared "not guilty." What rule or law can I use? Insanity is a defense — insane people are not guilty. What must I do to make a persuasive argument? I must demonstrate, in the way I present my facts, that my client is insane.[1]

We thought through this process as conclusion, rule, application. In a brief, however, we would present it as rule, application, conclusion: Insane people are not guilty. My client is obviously insane (because . . .). Therefore, my client cannot be considered guilty.

Another way to construct your argument is in the order: application, rule, conclusion. You begin with the facts of your case, try to find or construct a rule that accommodates the facts, and then reach the best conclusion you can for your client.

In building your case, you can work on the parts of the syllogism in any order. You work with them interactively until you achieve a logical relationship among the three parts. Moving the parts around can help you to clarify your own thinking, while keeping the basic structure of the syllogism in mind tells you what your argument should look like when you present it to the reader.

---

1. Keep in mind that you may *present* facts in a way that will best fit a rule of law and serve your purposes, but that you cannot *change* the facts of your case. It is perfectly permissible to interpret the ambiguities that exist in any factual situation in your own favor, but it is unethical to distort or to hide facts.

No matter how you got to your conclusion, you should present it as rule, application, conclusion — a syllogism. This not only helps your readers to follow your argument, it may help persuade your readers that you reached the conclusion in favor of your client only *after* following the syllogism to its logical conclusion.

2. Expanding the Syllogism into a Legal Argument

The syllogism serves as the skeleton of a legal argument. Once you have created the skeleton, you must flesh it out. For example, once you have the major premise in a particular case, you must present evidence that your specific fact situation does indeed fit within the class covered by the major premise. In the example about painting Lee's house, you would have to show that there was a promise but that both parties knew that it was made in jest, as "jest" has been interpreted by the courts.

In the rest of this section, we discuss techniques for expanding the different parts of a syllogism. We present the parts in the order of the standard syllogism, even though you may not always work in this order when you construct your argument.

a. *The Major Premise*

In most cases, your major premise will either be a given (you are told what the rule of law is and you must apply it to a set of facts), or you must extract the rule from legal authorities such as constitutions, statutes, regulations, and reported cases. You must then draw the appropriate information from these authorities and present the information so that your rule is well substantiated. In addition, you must define the abstract terms in the rule in order to clarify the rule and make it easier to apply the rule to the facts in your case.

Using legal authority effectively. In many of the legal arguments you will make, the link between your assertion and conclusion will depend upon the credibility of the authority you use in your major premise. You will argue that your assertions are valid because your authority says they are, and your authority is worth following. Legal authority can take a number of forms. It can be *enacted law*:

- A constitution or charter
- A treaty
- A statute or ordinance
- An administrative regulation
- A rule of procedure

or it can be *case law*:

- An opinion based on an enacted law
- An opinion based on common law
- An opinion based on principles of equity
- An opinion involving a combination of enacted law, common law, or equity[2]

Under certain circumstances, scholarly works and treatises can also be the legal authority that you rely on.

You will learn, in time, how much weight is usually given to a certain authority under different circumstances and how authorities relate to each other. Once you understand these principles, you must learn to build them into your documents so that your assertions are well researched and completely substantiated. Here are several guidelines to follow.

1. Make sure that the authority actually supports your position. Do not take information from an authority and use it out of context so that it appears to support a position that it really does not.
2. Quote directly out of your sources of authority if the material you are quoting is effective and well written or if the quoted material is well known. This lends authenticity and directness to your argument that you could not achieve by paraphrasing. However, if the material is poorly written, paraphrase it.[3] Also, be careful not to overquote. Don't create a document that merely repeats what others have said when you should really be presenting legal analysis.
3. Make sure that you are quoting the relevant portions of your source.

Using definitions to clarify terms. Some rules of law include abstract terms that need definition. Sometimes the key to using the authority you want to cite is to define one or more of its terms to show that your case fits into the definition.

For example, Article I §8(1) of the U.S. Constitution states that "The Congress shall have power to . . . lay and collect taxes, duties, imposts, and excises, to pay the debts and provide for the common defense and general welfare of the United States; . . ." The term "general welfare" is not de-

---

2. For more information on each of these kinds of authority, see W. Statsky & F. Wernet, Jr., Case Analysis and Fundamentals of Legal Writing 83 (1977).
3. Always paraphrase with care so that you do not distort the meaning of the material. In addition, it is seldom a good idea to paraphrase a statute or other enacted laws, since each word may be essential to the meaning of the law.

fined. It is up to Congress and the courts to determine what specific situations the term covers, and it would be up to you to define this term if you wanted to use it as part of an argument.

Let's say you want to argue that Congress's giving federal money to a private corporation, X Auto Company, serves the general welfare of the country. You might begin by constructing a syllogism for this argument.

MAJOR PREMISE:	Congress can spend money for the general welfare.
MINOR PREMISE:	Giving federal money to economically distressed corporations such as the X Auto Company serves the general welfare of the country.
CONCLUSION:	The Congress can give federal money to X Auto Company.

In order to support your case, you should define "general welfare" so that your use of it in your minor premise fits within the term as it is used in your major premise.

Because legal definitions frequently have several layers, you can use these layers to build the definition you need. For the case of X Auto Company, you might argue

1. Congress can exercise broad discretion.
2. This means that Congress can provide revenues to specific groups and individuals as long as these allocations will benefit the entire country and not just a privileged few.
3. These specific groups and individuals can include the elderly, the unemployed, local disaster victims, etc.

You can show that your definition is accurate by citing these authorities:

1. In *Helvering v. Davis,* 301 U.S. 619, 640 (1937), the Supreme Court held that "[T]he discretion [regarding what constitutes general welfare] belongs to Congress, unless the choice is clearly wrong, a display of arbitrary power, and not an exercise of judgment." The Court interpreted the phrase "general welfare" very broadly.
2. The Supreme Court has held in a number of cases that Congress's broad discretion extends to legislation affecting specific groups and individuals.
3. This legislation has included the unemployment compensation scheme created by the Social Security Act of 1935, *Steward Machine Co. v. Davis,* 301 U.S. 548 (1937), the old-age benefit provisions of the Social Security

Act, *Helvering v. Davis,* local disaster victims, and individuals with moral claims against the government.

Note that the first two layers include broad terms such as "welfare" and "discretion." You must continue to define until you have reached the level where the definition is illustrated by concrete facts. Once you have concrete examples, you must make them meaningful to your case. In the next section, we discuss how you can use analogy to tie the examples in your definition to the facts in your case.

Let's look at another example of a definition. Definitions that arise strictly from the common law rather than from a constitution or statute also frequently contain broad terms. For example, the tort of battery has been defined, in part, by the following elements:

1. An *act* by the defendant that *brings about harmful or offensive contact* to the *plaintiff's person.*
2. *Intent* on the part of the defendant to bring about harmful or offensive contact to the plaintiff's person.
3. *Lack of consent* from the plaintiff.

All of the italicized terms are in need of further explication. What behavior on the part of the defendant constitutes "an act"? What is "intent"? What is an "offensive contact"? What constitutes the "plaintiff's person"? How does the plaintiff give (or withhold) "consent"?

Let's pursue the layers of definition for "plaintiff's person."

1. The plaintiff's person has been construed to include the plaintiff's body and *anything that is connected* to the plaintiff's body.
2. In *Fisher v. Carousel Motor Hotel, Inc.,* 424 S.W.2d 627 (Tex. 1967), the plaintiff was a black man who was attending a buffet lunch at the defendant's hotel. While the plaintiff was waiting in line to be served, one of the defendant's employees snatched the plaintiff's plate and shouted that the plaintiff would not be served. The court held that the unpermitted and intentional grabbing of the plate was a battery, even though the plaintiff himself was never touched.

b. *The Minor Premise*

The most important techniques for expanding your major premise are citing authority and defining terms. The most important technique for expanding your minor premise is analogy, either to the facts of other cases or to the policies underlying other decisions.

Arguing by analogy: similarity of facts. When you argue by analogy, you reason that if two or more situations are the same in some significant respect, they are likely to be the same in other significant respects as well, so they ought to be classified together. (If you want to *distinguish* your case from others, you show that it is *not* analogous.)

You could link the major and the minor premises of the general welfare case by using the following analogy: Funding should be provided for X Auto Company because the case is similar to cases in which the Court has approved Congress's funding in the past. Here is a way you might express this.

The facts in the X Auto Company case are very similar to the facts in cases that have already established the scope of "general welfare." In all of these cases, the courts agreed that

1. Private individuals or entities may receive funds from the federal government.
2. Individuals and entities may receive money that they did not personally contribute to the government.
3. Individuals and entities may receive money from the government when it helps them continue to earn money and spend money.

Arguing by analogy: similarity of policy considerations. Another way to link the major and minor premises is to show that the facts of your case are covered by a particular rule because your case furthers the same social goals as other cases already covered by the rule. For example, in the X Auto Company case, you might argue that your case and the previously decided cases all fulfill the following goals, regardless of the similarities or differences in their facts.

1. They keep individuals from turning to the state for support.
2. They keep the economy balanced and functioning.
3. They show people that the government will intervene if a segment of the population is about to experience an economic crisis.

The first step in making a policy argument is to identify what the authors of a rule intended when they created the rule. If you are investigating legislation, try looking at and analyzing legislative history or policy statements in the legislation itself. If you are investigating an opinion, try comparing your case with other cases that have been decided under the rule and showing that your case will help to further the same goals. You can look at any language in these opinions that sheds light on the objectives of the ruling.

Once you have established the purpose of the rule, i.e., what it was intended to accomplish, you can alter your major premise to include this purpose and emphasize the specific facts in your minor premise that suit the major premise. You would then argue that the authors of the rule intended that the rule cover cases like yours and that the principles behind the rule will be dangerously eroded if the court excludes your case.

If you were arguing that by analogy to the *Steward Machine* case X Auto Company should get federal funds, you might use this analogy on policy considerations:

> The courts have found that federal payments to particular groups or individuals such as the unemployed or the elderly can serve the general welfare because, in the long run, these payments benefit the entire nation. This idea is reflected in the words of Justice Cardozo in *Steward Machine,* 301 U.S. 548, 586–587 (1937):
>
> > During the years 1929 to 1936, when the country was passing through a cyclical depression, the number of the unemployed mounted to unprecedented heights. . . . The fact developed quickly that the states were unable to give the requisite relief. The problem had become national in area and dimensions. There was need of help from the nation if the people were not to starve. It is too late today for the argument to be heard with tolerance that in a crisis so extreme the use of the moneys of the nation to relieve the unemployed and their dependents is a use for any purpose narrower than the promotion of the general welfare.
>
> X Auto Company employs hundreds of thousands of employees. In addition, there are thousands of other employees who work in industries that depend on X Auto Company. Even though the problems of X Auto Company are not on the scale of the problems of the Great Depression, the loss of part of a major U.S. industry would have devastating effects on the U.S. economy as a whole. If federal funds can help X Auto Company continue to employ its workers, then thousands of private individuals will continue to earn and spend money. This will help protect the health of the nation's economy.

On the other hand, you could counter an argument based on similarity of policy considerations by showing that giving X Auto Company federal funds would widen the scope of the rule beyond the limits intended by those who derived the rule. This widening would have all kinds of adverse effects or troublesome consequences, such as opening the courts to a flood of frivolous litigation.

Setting up an analogy. To set up an analogy between two cases, using both the facts and the policy issues, begin by making a list of similarities and differences. Here is how you might expand the general welfare example to show that one case that has already been decided involving the old-age benefit provisions of the Social Security Act is or is not analogous to the X Auto Company case.

Similarities

In both situations the recipients may receive money that they only indirectly paid into the system. For example, Social Security recipients may receive funds in excess of the amount they actually put into the fund. The X Auto Company will receive funds that it indirectly paid in the form of taxes, etc.

Many individuals who need support will benefit from the federal funds; employees in the case of X Auto Company, and older members of the population in the case of old-age benefits.

The X Auto Company funds will help keep the economy healthy because it will keep a major industry alive and will keep X's employees (and employees of other companies that depend on X) off of welfare and other forms of state subsidy. Similarly, the old-age benefits of Social Security assure citizens that they will have an opportunity to put money into a fund that they can draw on in their old age, provided they have worked the requisite amount of time to qualify. This keeps older people from having to turn to the state for support.

Differences

The recipients of old-age benefits have paid into an insurance fund over the years, while the X Auto Company would be receiving money from a nonspecific tax fund that it has not contributed to. Taxes and insurance are not the same thing.

It is quite a different thing for the federal government to provide funds to a private corporation than to provide them to individuals. The government is set up to benefit members of the general population. It is not the government's purpose to benefit a large private corporation.

Giving funds to a private business may actually unbalance the economy, disturbing the free market and fair competition.

In section B of this chapter we discuss writing techniques that emphasize favorable information and de-emphasize unfavorable information. You can use those techniques to stress either the similarities or differences between cases.

c. *The Conclusion*

After you have established and developed your major and minor premises, you are ready to reach a conclusion that follows logically from them. You may need to use a cause-and-effect argument to show *how* you came to the conclusion.

In law you will often be required to show that there is a cause-and-effect relationship between certain events or actions. For example, causation is an element of many torts and crimes. We will not go into the subtleties of causation here; however, you should know that when you set up a cause-and-effect relationship, you have to do so logically.

Here is an example of how a cause-and-effect relationship can be established within a deductive argument. First, set up the skeleton of your argument.

> *General rule* (major premise): Under the law of State *X*, the operator of a motor vehicle is liable for his or her wrongful act, neglect, or default if it causes death or injury to another person.
>
> *Specific facts* (minor premise): The plaintiff was riding in her car on the freeway when the defendant's car hit her from behind. Two days later, the plaintiff suffered severe back pains and headaches.
>
> *Conclusion:* Therefore, the defendant should be liable for the damages the plaintiff has suffered.

If you terminated your argument at this point, it would appear that you had based your conclusion on a faulty premise or assumption: "All pain that occurs within two days of an accident is necessarily caused by that accident." (For more on faulty premises, see section 3 below.) Or your conclusion may appear to result from a *post hoc* fallacy, in which you assert that because event *B* follows event *A* in time, event *A* has therefore caused event *B*. To avoid the appearance that your conclusion does not follow logically from the premises, you must articulate the causal link between events. You could do so by beginning your conclusion with the following information.

> There is a good deal of evidence that the plaintiff's injury was caused by the defendant's act of hitting the plaintiff from behind. First of all, the plaintiff's medical records show that the plaintiff did not have a history of back problems or headaches, so there is no possibility that her

injuries are part of a recurrent or chronic problem. Also, she has not engaged in any activity or suffered any other injury within the last few years that might have led to back pain or headaches. In addition, Dr. Jones, the plaintiff's physician, has examined the plaintiff and will testify that the pain the plaintiff is experiencing is the kind that the plaintiff would be likely to feel several days after a rear-end collision in an automobile.

You would finish your argument by qualifying your conclusion to reflect the evidence you have presented:

> Because the evidence from medical records and from an expert demonstrates that, in all probability, the plaintiff's injuries were caused by the defendant's conduct, the defendant is liable for the damage the plaintiff has suffered as a result of that conduct.

When you are constructing a cause-and-effect argument, keep the subject matter in mind. If you are working with causation in a complex statistical argument, you must comply with the generally accepted principles of statistical analysis. For example, you may have to adhere to a scientific definition of causation. However, if you are writing about more common types of problems, try to appeal to your readers' sense of how the world works: Present a cause-and-effect relationship that your readers will recognize from their own experience. You can appeal to your readers' common sense and to the "common wisdom of the community." Remember that judges and other attorneys are part of the community and that they will share this sense of what probably did or did not happen in a given situation.

3. Faulty Logic

Logic can be faulty in a number of ways. We end this discussion by pointing out two of the most common faults.

Faulty premise. An argument can be perfectly logical, but invalid. For example, you might have a syllogism like this, in which the major premise is false:

> MAJOR PREMISE: All witnesses are men.
> MINOR PREMISE: Lee is a witness.
> CONCLUSION: Therefore, Lee is a man.

In other words, an argument is sound only if both of its premises are true.

Undistributed middle. If your minor premise can occur outside the bounds of the major premise, it will not necessarily follow from your major premise. For example:

MAJOR PREMISE: No one has been sentenced to death for murder in California in the last two years.

MINOR PREMISE: Smith was convicted of murder last year, but he was not sentenced to death.

CONCLUSION: Therefore, Smith must have been tried in California.

The major premise in this example is not faulty. The problem is that the minor premise can occur outside the bounds of the major premise, i.e., Smith could have been tried in another state and still not have been sentenced to death.

EXERCISES

1. Under the equal protection clause of the Fourteenth Amendment, the Supreme Court has held that legislation that contains racially based classifications is subject to very strict review by the courts. However, legislation that establishes gender based classifications receives a lesser level of review. Compare and contrast the cases of women and blacks in this country in terms of their history of being discriminated against and their present need for protection. Set up your comparison with two columns, one for similarities and one for differences.

2. Read the following excerpt from an appellate opinion and pull the syllogism out of it.

> The contract for the purchase of certain machinery recited that "[n]o representations or warranties, of any sort, express or implied, except warranty of title, have been made by Seller unless specifically set forth in writing in this contract." (There were no warranties set forth elsewhere in the contract.) An action was brought on the contract by the Seller seeking recovery of the balance of the purchase price. The purchaser, in defense thereto, sought to set up the defense that the contract was unconscionable under Code §109A-2-302, which defense was disallowed by the trial judge and the verdict and judgment were rendered in favor of the plaintiff. The defendant appealed. *Held:* The provisions of the contract contended by appellant to be unconscionable under Code §109A-

2-302 are provisions which the law itself specifically permits. This contention is without merit.

B Step Two: Using Effective Writing Techniques

Now that we have discussed ways to construct a logical argument, we will discuss how to present the argument effectively. This section tells you how to assess the audience of a persuasive document, how to make the argument fit the audience's needs and expectations, and how to write to make the most of your position.

1. Assessing Your Audience

In writing a persuasive document, you must first try to find out what your audience needs to know and to believe in order to accept your argument. You can do this by putting yourself in the audience's place.

Decide how much your audience knows. When you write a persuasive document, you must decide how much the audience already knows about the subject you will be covering. If you assume too much, you will lose the reader at the outset. If you assume too little, the reader may have to read — or at least scan — extra material. However, it is far safer to explain too much than too little. Remember to assess both lay and legal audiences. A law professor or judge may not be as well acquainted with a topic as you might think.

Assess the role or position of your audience. Know what your reader must *do* with the information in your document. For example, if you are writing for a judge, determine what information he or she needs in order to decide in your favor. In general, a judge needs to know what other judges have done in cases similar to your case. Present the judge with the one reasonable solution to the problem in the case — the one your client needs — and characterize your position as one that any reasonable judge would accept.

Consider the interests of your audience. Think about the goals your audience may have. For example, is your audience interested in furthering certain social or political goals?

Consider the constraints of your audience. What constraints does your audience have? For example, judges are constrained by the previous judicial opinions that make up a body of law. Judges cannot easily deviate from earlier decisions. If you take this into account, you can state your position in a way that will make the judge feel comfortable with it. Your document should not ask the judge to make a great leap beyond an established position. Present your position as a small step in the same direction as judges have been going, or as the smallest step possible in a new but necessary direction. Justify any move you are advocating. Convince the judge that he or she will be providing continuity and certainty by deciding in your favor.

Assess the fears of your audience. Show your audience that their fears are not justified because undesirable side effects will not occur in your particular situation. Or show your audience that in your particular case, any undesirable side effects are overridden by more important considerations. For example, if you are trying to argue the advantages of a homosexual rights statute to an ultraconservative group, you may want to spend only a small amount of space on the advantages of the statute and a great deal of space allaying the group's fears about the changes the statute will bring.

2. Emphasizing Effective and Appropriate Information

You can tailor your argument to fit your purposes by emphasizing different components of the syllogism covered in section A. You might want to stress the importance of the rule you have stated as your major premise, arguing that the reader should heed the fine points of the rule and should adhere to established law. On the other hand, you might want to argue that the facts in your case are all-important or that the policy considerations in your case should take precedence over both rule and fact.

Here is an example: In *Gleitman v. Cosgrove,* 49 N.J. 22, 227 A.2d 689 (1967), the court relied on a rule in order to avoid discussing controversial policy issues. The child plaintiff in the case suffered severe birth defects because his mother had had German measles in the second month of her pregnancy. The mother testified that she had informed her doctor of her illness and that he had told her it would not harm her baby. Thus, she was denied an opportunity to decide whether she would have the child or have a legal abortion. Her lawyers sued on the basis of "wrongful birth." However, the court would not allow the child to sue for "wrongful birth" because it would be too difficult for courts to apply the normal rule for measuring damages in tort actions.

Damages are measured by comparing the condition plaintiff would have been in, had the defendants not been negligent, with plaintiff's impaired condition as a result of the negligence. The infant plaintiff would have us measure the difference between his life with defects against the utter void of nonexistence, but it is impossible to make such a determination. This Court cannot weigh the value of life with impairments against the nonexistence of life itself.

49 N.J. at 49, 227 A.2d at 703.

If your case has human appeal, then present it in human terms, especially if the law is unsettled. Focus the court's attention on a very real problem, dilemma, or hardship faced by another human being — your client. The dissent in the *Gleitman* case illustrates the point:

[Mrs. Gleitman] was told . . . that her child would not be at all affected. In reliance on that she permitted her pregnancy to proceed and gave birth to a child who is almost blind, is deaf and mute and is probably mentally retarded. While the law cannot remove the heartache or undo the harm, it can afford some reasonable measure of compensation towards alleviating the financial burdens.

While logical objection may be advanced to the child's standing and injury, logic is not the determinative factor and should not be permitted to obscure that he has to bear the frightful weight of his abnormality throughout life.

49 N.J. at 50, 227 A.2d at 704.

3. Using Appropriate Writing Techniques

Once you have assessed your audience and chosen the argument you want to make, you need to know how to present your argument in a way that will convince your audience. For your document to be effective, you must achieve the appropriate tone. You can set the tone of your document by the information you choose to present and the order in which you present it, the grammatical constructions you use, and the vocabulary you choose. We have discussed some of these features earlier in this book; they are particularly important in persuasive writing.

The first thing you must do after you have chosen your argument is to decide how you want to present yourself to your reader. When you write a research document such as an intraoffice memo, you want to come across as an individual who supports the position of the client but has not allowed this bias to cloud your reasoning or prevent you from gathering all of the facts and law in the case. You construct a balanced document for the scrutiny of a colleague — a document that presents the strengths and weaknesses of your client's case. If you are asked to make recommendations, then you should make them honestly, without allowing the tendency to favor your client influence your suggestions. It is in this way that a memo is a persuasive document: You strive to persuade your colleagues or your supervisors that you have written a document that contains scrupulous research, sound reasoning, and good judgment.

But when you are writing a brief, your major purpose is quite different: You are trying to persuade your audience that your argument is the correct one. Even so, you still want to appear as the scrupulous researcher and sound reasoner who is simply showing the judge the best way to analyze a situation or to resolve a dispute. In other words, you want to appear reasonable and logical: You want to argue your case without appearing strident or argumentative. However, because you must present information that is favorable to your client, you may need to mold the information to suit your purposes. You can accomplish much of this by emphasizing favorable information and de-emphasizing unfavorable information. There are a number of techniques that you can use to do this.

a. *Emphasizing Positive Information*

Put favorable information in a prominent place. Research shows that information that is presented either first or last tends to receive more attention than anything in between.[4] In many legal documents, you will want to put your most important or compelling information first. For example, if one of the purposes of your document is to serve as a reference, then the reader will want to get to the major issues immediately. If the purpose of your document is mainly to be persuasive, then you will want to win your reader over quickly by starting with your most impressive arguments.

Make sure that important information not only appears in a prominent place, but is properly highlighted. When you are presenting facts, for example, it may not be advisable for you to present every detail as it occurred. Often students are afraid to leave any information out, so they end up burying critical facts in a detailed chronology. It is more valuable to isolate what is important, move facts out of chronological order if they are better emphasized that way, and leave out incidental information.

4. See, Atkinson and Shiffrin, Human Memory: A Proposed System and Its Control Processes, 2 The Psychology of Learning and Motivation: Advances in Research and Theory (Spence & Spence eds. 1967); K. Fernandes & A. Rose, An Information Processing Approach to Performance Assessment: An Investigation of Encoding and Retrieval Processes in Memory, Technical Report, November 1978, American Institutes for Research, Washington, D.C.

Describe favorable information in detail. A detailed description of the contents of a law or of the facts of a particular case can attract the reader's attention and, often, sustain the reader's interest — as long as the details are important ones. The plaintiff's attorney who wrote the following fact statement wanted to emphasize the defendant railroad's negligence. Notice the narrative quality of the description of the late train, the employees' actions, the bright lights of the waiting room, and the poorly lit staircase. The reader can almost picture the scene.

> The train was running behind time. Several witnesses testified that the passengers were told by railroad employees to "hurry up." Mrs. Roberts emerged from the brightly lit waiting room, which naturally emphasized the darkness outside. Mrs. Roberts hurried down the unlighted outside staircase that leads to the train platform, missed a step, and fell beyond the narrow platform in front and down the slope beyond, incurring serious injuries. The fall aggravated Mrs. Roberts's existing health problems, which include diabetes and a thyroid condition.

Use effective sentence structures and grammatical constructions. The guidelines in Chapter 5 will help you improve your writing, and clearer writing is likely to be more persuasive. Here we will discuss a few of the guidelines that are particularly relevant to persuasive writing because they give your arguments force without making them strident.

The grammatical constructions that you use can greatly affect how persuasive your document will be. Thus, when you use the active voice, your writing will be direct and it will not be difficult to tell who did what. The passive voice will be less persuasive. For example, if your complaint on behalf of the plaintiff states that "The plaintiff was knocked to the ground and was repeatedly kicked" you have diluted the impact of the defendant's acts. However, if you rewrite this sentence in the active voice, you put life and action back into it, and you directly indict the defendant: "The *defendant knocked* the plaintiff to the ground and repeatedly *kicked* him."

You can also make your writing direct and forceful by using verb clauses and adjectives instead of nominalizations. For example, you might have stated that "The witness's *embezzlement* of company funds in 1980 is an example of his *untrustworthiness*." The terms "embezzlement" and "untrustworthiness" are abstract; it is almost as though the defendant has committed concepts and not acts. The sentence can be rewritten into a direct and forceful statement: "The witness *embezzled* funds from the company in 1980; this shows that *he cannot be trusted*."

Short sentences tend to be more forceful and hence, more persuasive than long ones. The more the reader has to remember when going through a sentence, the more likely he or she is to get bogged down. Thus, anything that makes a sentence less complicated is likely to result in a more effective sentence. Since intrusive phrases and complex conditionals tend to add length and complexity to sentences, following the guidelines for eliminating intrusive phrases and simplifying complex conditionals will help you produce more persuasive writing.

Choose your words with care. Another device that enhances persuasiveness is the use of straightforward, unqualified language. Avoid excessive use of adjectives and all-purpose intensifiers. For example, you will tip your reader off that you are trying too hard to be convincing if you write sentences such as this: "It took the plaintiff a *very, very long time* to see a doctor about his injury." You could make this same point more effectively by stating the dates of the injury and the doctor's visit and by emphasizing the amount of time between the two.

Intensifiers or qualifiers such as *quite, rather, extremely,* and *very* can also dilute the forcefulness or persuasiveness of a sentence. Psycholinguistic research has shown that readers regard unqualified sentences as being much more forceful than sentences with adverbial qualifiers.[5] You are better off avoiding these qualifiers when you can, using instead appropriately strong nouns or verbs that don't need qualifiers. For example, you can replace *run very fast* with the much stronger *dash*. If you cannot eliminate qualifiers entirely, be sure to choose them carefully and use them sparingly.

Similarly, it is often a mistake to speak in absolutes. The law is seldom absolute. Most of your legal writing will consist of arguments or recommendations to apply established principles to new facts. Therefore, avoid words and phrases such as *clearly, without a doubt, undeniably,* and *obviously.* In addition, these words and phrases have been so overused and misused that they have lost their punch; they are usually little more than excess baggage.

On the other hand, be careful not to let the natural uncertainty of legal analysis force you into using a hesitant or tentative style. You should also avoid words like *somewhat, occasionally,* and *possibly.* Don't say: "We think this is possibly the answer that the court is looking for in cases of this kind." You want to write forcefully and convincingly and make straightforward, affirmative or negative statements: "We think this is the answer that the court is looking for" or better still "This is the answer that the court seeks."

5. Feezel, A Qualified Certainty: Verbal Probability in Arguments, 41 Speech Monographs 348 (1974).

Use active, descriptive words. You can choose words that add persuasiveness to your writing by being aware of connotations and subtle shades of meaning. In the example below, the italicized words render the description flat and lifeless.

> The defendant *ran* down the street *toward* the plaintiff and *collided with* the plaintiff. The plaintiff *fell* to the ground. The defendant *picked up* the plaintiff's handbag, *opened* it, and *placed* the contents of the bag on the sidewalk. He *sorted through* the *contents* until he came upon the plaintiff's wallet. He then *picked up* the wallet and ran.

This example can be rewritten to be more effective. Although the words that are italicized in this rewrite are close in meaning to the words in the original example, they convey action and some emotional impact.[6]

> The defendant *charged* down the street *at* the plaintiff and *knocked* the plaintiff to the ground. The defendant then *grabbed* the plaintiff's handbag and *spilled* the contents on the sidewalk. He *rummaged* through the plaintiff's *belongings* until he found her wallet, then he *grabbed* the wallet and ran.

However, when you are trying to add life and emotional impact to your writing, do not go overboard. If you choose cliches or words that are emotionally overloaded, you risk tipping off your reader that you are struggling to convince. For example, an attorney wrote in a brief:

> It is *difficult to conceive of a more graphic example* of the term "abandon" than that which is presented here, where *mere infants* were *rendered pitifully vulnerable* to the *dangers of the night* as a result of the preoccupation of a mother with her *personal pleasures*.

The attorney could have created a more convincing, forceful description if she had eliminated the italicized words and phrases and had presented more details. The facts tell the story; they do not need embellishing.

> In this case, the mother was preoccupied with her own plans to attend a party that evening. She left her two infants, aged five and three, alone in

---

6. Research by Loftus and Palmer, Reconstruction of Automobile Destruction: An Example of the Interaction Between Language and Memory, 13 J. Verbal Ed. 585 (1974), showed that when the experimenter varied the verb in the question "How fast was the blue car going when it (contacted/collided with/smashed into) the red car?" different subjects who had seen the *same* film of the accident gave estimates of speed that increased significantly from "contacted" to "smashed into."

her apartment, locked in the bedroom, until morning. No one else was in the apartment when the fire broke out. None of the neighbors could reach the children because their mother had bolted the front door. The children could not get out of the bedroom because their mother had wedged a chair under the outside of the bedroom door to keep the children from leaving.

b. *De-emphasizing Negative Information*

Your natural inclination in writing a persuasive document will be to present only those facts that are most favorable to your own side. However, legal documents are generally not one-sided accounts. You must deal with negative or damaging information for two reasons.

1. Your opponent will probably introduce the information. If you have not discussed damaging information, you will look, at best, careless and uninformed, and, at worst, dishonest. If your audience thinks that you have told only part of the story, they may doubt your entire analysis.
2. You may have an ethical obligation to inform the court.[7]

You can help give your document a more balanced, "scholarly" tone if you present negative as well as positive information. But do not state the negative information so well that you make your opponents' arguments for them. If your document seems too balanced, your readers will not know which side you are on. To avoid this, try to minimize the importance of negative information. Acknowledge the information, but arrange your analysis so that the points in your favor appear crucial, while the damaging information appears to be merely peripheral. There are several ways to accomplish this.

Put negative information in an obscure place. Place damaging or unfavorable content in the middle of your document, where it is less likely to attract attention. If possible, bury negative information in the middle of paragraphs or sentences. If you are enumerating items or issues, place the least favorable information in the middle of the list.

You can also bury negative information by putting it in a subordinate clause. This will emphasize the information in the main clause and de-emphasize the information in the subordinate clause. In addition, you can bury negative or controversial material by juxtaposing it with neutral material.

---

7. Ordinarily there is no ethical duty to volunteer harmful facts. However, there is an exception: In an *ex parte* proceeding, where the adversary is not present, an attorney must inform the court of *all* facts necessary to an informed decision. ABA Model Rule of Professional Conduct §3.30. There is always a duty to inform the court of all relevant *law* whether it is harmful or not.

Present negative facts broadly or in summary. You can gloss over negative information by presenting it broadly or as a summary, leaving out the details that might capture and hold your reader's attention. If you look back at the example of the fact statement from the railroad station case discussed in the section on emphasizing favorable information (p. 154), you will remember that details were used to highlight the negligence of the railroad. In the fact statement from the defendant's brief, the defendant emphasizes different facts and glosses over details about the railroad station. The reader will barely be able to picture the station, but will probably have a very good idea of what Mrs. Roberts looks like and how she behaved before she was injured.

> Mrs. Roberts, a corpulent woman weighing two hundred and fifty pounds, left the railway waiting room to catch her train. Witnesses testified that she was walking quickly and wearing shoes with very high heels. She apparently rushed onto the outside staircase without giving her eyes a chance to adjust to the light and tripped on one of the steps.

Use "ineffective" sentence structures and grammatical constructions. You can also obscure negative information by reversing the language guidelines; that is, by using passives, nominalizations, embedded phrases and clauses, and "fuzzy" or ambiguous terms. However, be extremely careful when violating the guidelines. The sections you have selected to de-emphasize may stand out so much that you end up drawing attention to them instead.

Following is an example of how one attorney presented the facts in a memorandum of points and authorities in a way that emphasized certain facts and de-emphasized others. Notice how the attorney describes the petitioner's activities during the time the will was being probated.

FACTS

Luanne Cox died on April 3, 1976, leaving a last will and testament which she executed in New York as a resident of the Borough of Manhattan, City, County and State of New York on December 7, 1971. Arnold Squire, the executor nominated under the will, filed a petition for probate in Surrogate's Court, County of New York, on May 8, 1976. Petitioner John Cox, a son of the decedent, signed a waiver of citation and a consent to have the will admitted to probate, after consulting with his personal attorney. The probate court admitted the will to probate on June 16, 1976, without objection. The will was probated as a will of a New York domiciliary. Petitioner, as a beneficiary under the will, subsequently was paid a $10,000 bequest. On March 3, 1978, nearly two years after Squire offered the will for probate, John Cox filed a petition to (a) vacate his waiver of citation and the consent to admit the will to probate, and (b) vacate the decree admitting the will to probate.

Petitioner alleges that he executed the waiver believing that the will, although being probated in New York, would be probated as that of a Louisiana resident and that Louisiana law would apply. This would have allowed the petitioner to elect against the will and receive one quarter of the estate.

Notice how the author presents certain dates and activities with precision: Luanne Cox died on April 3, 1976; Arnold Squire, the executor, filed a petition for probate on May 8, 1976; and the probate court admitted the will to probate on June 16, 1976.

However, the dates on which John Cox supposedly found out certain information are very vague. We are not told *when* Cox signed the waiver and consent, except that it was sometime after consulting with his personal attorney. We are also not told when Cox received his bequest, except that it was sometime after the will was probated. However, the author suddenly becomes precise again: On March 3, 1978, John Cox filed a petition to vacate his waiver and consent. Note how the author emphasizes the fact that the date John Cox filed his petition was nearly two years after Squire offered the will for probate. The author argues later in the memo that the petitioner in this case was well informed about how his mother's will was being probated and that he failed to establish grounds to vacate the probate decree and set aside the waiver of citation and consent to probate.

The fact statement appears to present a precise chronology. Few readers would realize that the author has not told us in which order certain events occurred or how they relate to each other in time. The author has created the impression that the petitioner was greedy and filed the petition only when he became dissatisfied with the $10,000 bequest and found out that he could receive more under Louisiana law.

EXERCISE

Read through the facts presented below (based on *In Re Hawley*, 67 Cal. 2d 824, 433 P.2d 919 (1967)). Imagine that you are the attorney representing the defendant at his murder trial. Write a fact statement for a brief. Then write a fact statement from the perspective of the prosecuting attorney. Be prepared to identify the differences in your approach to each.

The defendant is 29 years old. He had been drinking almost continuously from March 7, 1966, until the date of the homicide on March 19, 1966. On that day he met a woman in Sacramento's West End. They spent the morning drinking wine and in the evening decided to have intercourse. The defendant remembered seeing a mattress in an abandoned hotel. They entered the hotel and went into a small, dark room where decedent, Alejandro Lopez, also under the influence of liquor, was sleeping on the mattress. Defendant woke Lopez and asked him to leave. Lopez got up, said something in Spanish and tried to kick defendant, who knocked Lopez down with his fist. The defendant then had intercourse with his lady friend. Afterwards, Lopez made a remark that the defendant did not understand. The defendant grabbed a stick and hit Lopez with it until he stopped talking. He then dragged the still-alive Lopez into another room 50 feet away. He gathered papers and small sticks together around Lopez and lit them. The defendant says that he does not remember any of the details, nor does he remember dragging Lopez or lighting the fire. The defendant then went out of the building, his lady friend left him, and he met and started to drink with a male friend. The defendant noticed there was no fire in the building he had vacated and took his friend inside. The friend saw the body, and called the police. The two men waited until the officers arrived. The defendant then related some of these facts to the officers and signed a statement. An autopsy revealed that the fire caused Lopez's death. The only damage to the building was a charring of the floor by the body. The defendant was later indicted for murder and arson. He was represented by the public defender, who requested Dr. S. Green to prepare a psychiatric study of the defendant. In his report, Dr. Green reviewed the defendant's background. It showed that the defendant's mother, father, and girlfriend had all been killed in separate automobile accidents while they were intoxicated. The defendant had only completed the tenth grade in school. Since 1954 he spent about ten months of every year in prison, each incident resulting in his incarceration occurring while he was intoxicated. Dr. Green found physical deterioration and dilapidation with consequential impairment of retention, memory, and vocabulary. The defendant expressed no guilt about his actions and little concern over his fate. Dr. Green found him to be presently sane and responsible, but concluded as to his condition at the time of the crimes: "At the time of the alleged crime of arson, the effect of prolonged alcoholism would be so severe it would contaminate any intent he may have had. Furthermore, the amount of wilfulness and maliciousness would be severely restricted and he would be unable to comprehend such an action or govern himself."

7

Reviewing
and
Editing

A Writing as a Process

Throughout this text we have characterized writing as a step-by-step process. If you approach writing as a process, you can build your documents in a careful and systematic way and still have the flexibility to accommodate different situations. For example, when you write a memorandum you need to be flexible in the way you order the tasks of doing research and writing. You would probably first do some research, then compile and write up your research; but once you have seen what you have accumulated, you might want to do more research and then revise what you have written.

Even though you may have to be flexible in the way you carry out various parts of the writing process, it is valuable to begin any writing task by articulating the steps you plan to take. It is also worthwhile to place the steps in a workable order, even if you end up moving the steps around or omitting some of them as you create the document. Look again at the writing plan we suggest on page 162.

B Reviewing, Revising, and Editing

Reviewing and revising appear in the diagram as post-writing steps, and indeed you should review and revise extensively and carefully once you have completed a draft of a document. However, you should also try to review and revise throughout the writing process. You can check what you have already written at any stage by looking at the legal sufficiency of the content

FIGURE 7-1

Prewriting Steps

Define *Purpose.*
Why do you need the document?

- Define *Audience.*
  Who will use the document?

- Determine *Constraints.*
  What limits do you have on how you can write?

Writing Steps

- *Organize* the document.
  What is the most logical and effective order for the material?

- Use the *language guidelines* for effective prose. What do you need to do to make your writing as clear as possible?

- Use *persuasive techniques* where necessary. Which persuasive strategies make your writing most effective?

Decide on *Content.*
What should go into the document?

Post-Writing Steps

- Use *graphics techniques.*
  Which techniques will show your organization to your readers and make your document more readable?

Review, revise, and edit.
How can you improve each draft of a document?

162

of your writing and the quality of the writing itself. In this chapter, we discuss a few techniques for reviewing and editing your writing for appropriateness, effectiveness, and correctness.

The techniques presented below are useful not only for your own writing, but for reviewing and editing the writing of others. For example, you may find, if you serve on a law journal, that you are in a position to edit the work of other students and of legal scholars who submit articles to the journal. Eventually, when you are working as a lawyer, you will probably edit the work of your colleagues or of junior associates.

1. Checking for Appropriateness

Correctness is an important dimension of the reader's expectations, but it is not the only one. The reader also expects to be able to follow the writing. The assumptions underlying the two dimensions — correctness and appropriateness — are quite different. The reader's expectations about *correctness* are based on the assumption that professional writing should follow the rules of a dialect often called Standard American English. Structures and word forms that follow the rules of Standard American English are considered correct; those that do not are considered incorrect in professional writing.

The reader's expectations about *appropriateness* are based on the assumption that the pieces of information relate to one another in an orderly and comprehensible way. When a reader encounters pieces of information that do not seem to relate to what has come before, they violate the reader's expectation of what is appropriate. The violation can occur at any level from that of a single word within a sentence to that of an entire argument within a brief. At whatever level the violation occurs, the reader pauses to try to make sense of what has been said — to try to create a relationship among the pieces of information that he or she has encountered. This relationship can be thought of as a link between what the reader already knows or has been told — *given* information — and the *new* information that the writer is introducing.

How the given-new concept works. To understand the basic assumption that a reader expects to be able to relate pieces of information in a text, first look at these examples.

> The plaintiff had delivered a package just before lunch.
>
> The plaintiff had delivered a lecture just before lunch.
>
> The plaintiff had delivered a calf just before lunch.

Although your picture of the plaintiff changes from sentence to sentence (perhaps from the plaintiff's being a delivery person to a professor to a veterinarian or farmer), you can still easily make sense of each sentence. It is possible to relate the person (plaintiff) to the action (delivered) and the object.

When a reader cannot relate the pieces of information to one another, the writer has seriously violated the reader's expectations. Look at this example:

The plaintiff had delivered a store just before lunch.

A sentence like this is a complete stopper. The new information (store) simply does not fit into the given, the context of the sentence (plaintiff delivered). A reader cannot make sense of the sentence without assuming that words have been omitted (e.g., "delivered *for* a store," or "delivered *something to* a store").

Although these sentences about the plaintiff delivering something are simple, they demonstrate the concept that underlies the dimension of appropriateness — readers expect pieces of information to relate to one another. More specifically, readers assume

1. That what appears first provides a context (is the given)
2. That what follows (new information) relates to the given (i.e., can be easily assimilated into the context)
3. That any special relationship between the given information and new information will be made explicit by the writer

These three assumptions form the basis of the reader's expectation of appropriateness. In this section, we will deal with the way the given-new concept works with regard to words within sentences.

How the given-new concept functions at the level of the word. When a person is reading a sentence, each word in the sentence immediately becomes part of the reader's short-term memory and sets up expectations about what will follow. To see how strong the expectation for individual words can be, read the passage below. Fill in the three blanks in the last sentence. Put only *one* word in each blank.

A. Statutory Entitlement to Homemaker Services Is Created by Federal and State Regulations
To have a statutory entitlement, more than a unilateral expectation of benefit is required. *Board of Regents of State College v. Roth,* 408 U.S.

564 (1972) (nontenured professor does not have statutory entitlement to position in absence of statute or contract). Instead, the property interest is both created and defined by "existing rules or understandings that stem from an independent source." *Id* at 577. Plaintiff Clark has a statutorily created property interest in the homemaker services. This property _____ is conferred on her _____ Title XX of the _____ Security Act.

The correct words are *interest, by,* and *Social.* Each of these illustrates a type of appropriate information. You used information you had from the previous sentence, the other words in the sentence with the blanks, and your knowledge of English and law to fill in the blanks. As a reader, you would feel jarred by another word in any of these positions — your expectations would be violated by words such as these:

This property (concern/issue/matter) is conferred on her (at/in/for) Title XX of the (Law/Tax/Compensation) Security Act.

Your expectation of the word *interest* (rather than *issue* or *matter*) comes from the information in the beginning of the passage that the legal issue here is "property interest." Your expectation of the word *by* comes from your knowledge about the English language (e.g., things are conferred *on* people *by* other people, *by* statutes, etc.). Your expectation of the word *Social* in "Social Security Act" may come from the context of the case, perhaps from your knowledge of Title XX and homemaker services, or perhaps from your general knowledge that the primary "Security Act" is the "*Social* Security Act."

There is another language expectation about words that the entitlement passage did not illustrate: the use of the right word. A writer violates that expectation by using the wrong word, as in the following example with the wrong word italicized.

This is the only Maryland case where the court *intravened* with the distribution of property at the end of a meretricious relationship.

A wrong word like *intravened,* though close to the appropriate word *(intervened),* will jar the reader. Following is a list of several frequently confused words, with examples of their proper use.

imply/infer: By denying John's accusation, you *implied* that John is a liar. From that, the police *inferred* that John was the culprit.

affect/effect: The new ruling will not *affect* your ability to appeal. I expect our motion will have the desired *effect* on the defendant.

moral/morale: Alice is a very *moral* person. Her *morale* is low because she lost the case.

deter/defer: We attempted to *deter* him from pursuing the lawsuit, but he would not *defer* to our wishes.

ensure/assure: There was no way to *ensure* that they would win the case, but their lawyer *assured* them that she would do her best.

then/than: I said *then,* as I say now, that Dr. Smith was harder to cross-examine *than* Dr. Jones.

There are many other frequently confused words. Whenever you are uncertain of the spelling or meaning of a word, look it up before using it.

EXERCISES

Each sentence contains at least one word that is inappropriate. Circle the inappropriate or wrong words in each passage and correct them. To correct an error, you may substitute another word or rewrite part of a sentence.

1. Statistics have been made to show the yearly cost of raising a child from infancy to 18 years of age. If the court will accept the speculative computations, expectancy measures should be given.
2. We should also be able to establish a cause of action for breach of contract, if you can insure me that the following statements were made by Dr. Cooper on January 10, 1978.
3. To prove medical malpractice, several steps must be followed. Dr. Cooper must have done something in his treatment on Mrs. Tall.
4. It was foreseeable that a breach of Dr. Cooper's promise of performance would result with your becoming pregnant.
5. Recovery in your case is predicated by a proven economic detriment borne by your family as a result of the new addition.
6. Recovery under a restitution remedy merely compensates you for the medical expenses that were conferred upon Dr. Cooper.
7. The carpet was put in the downstairs store, presumably for business reasons. A concrete floor would be somewhat out of decorum for a men's fashion boutique.

8. Title XX of the Social Security Act allows states much discretion in deciding what type of services they must offer, but requires that the state provide at least one service directed at each of the five goals set forth at 42 U.S.C. §1399c(2)(B) (1976).

2. Checking for Effectiveness

There are two major ways that you can check a document for effectiveness: by assessing the overall organization of the document and by assessing the style of the prose in the document.

You can examine the organization to make sure that it is logical and complete by making an outline of the headings and subheadings in a finished draft. This will help you determine whether the headings are parallel, whether sections are missing in the overall structure, or whether the document jumps from one topic to another without the proper transitions.

If you still cannot tell whether the structure of the document is sound, do a more detailed outline. Write a five- or six-word precis or summary of each paragraph in the document and arrange these units in order. This should help you determine whether the parts of the document fit together logically. For other organization problems, use the checklist in the next section. Pay particular attention to item 15.

Once you have assessed the organization of the document, you should scrutinize the language and sentence structure. You can do this by using the language guidelines. We have provided a checklist that you can use to quickly ascertain whether the writer has followed the guidelines. Each item in the checklist has a number or letter that you can use as a code when referring to a problem you find in your own or another writer's work.

In general, when using this or any other editing system, keep in mind the following points.

1. *Praise* as well as criticize. A critique that is totally negative can dishearten or anger the writer. The writer might even shrug off the criticism, contending that the critic's comments are simply a difference of opinion. Try to avoid corrections that merely reflect a difference in taste.
2. *Describe,* don't judge. Instead of writing "poor organization" or "weak," describe the problems you encountered in reading the document. For example, "There is no transition between points three and four; therefore, I could not follow your argument."
3. *Be specific* regarding where the problems occur.

Editing Checklist

1. Are the sentences *too long*?
2. Are the parts of sentences in an *illogical order*?
3. Do the sentences in the document contain *intrusive phrases* or *clauses*?
4. Are there tangled *complex conditionals*?
5. Is the *passive* voice used inappropriately?
6. Are *nominalizations* used inappropriately?
7. Are there too many *negatives* or *multiple negatives*?
8. Is the *structure nonparallel*?
9. Is there unnecessary *ambiguity*?
   a. at the *word* level
   b. at the *sentence* level
10. Is the *vocabulary* inappropriate?
    a. word or term needs definition
    b. word or term needs replacement
    c. archaic word
    d. inflated language
    e. incorrect use of legal terms
    f. wrong word
    g. jargon
11. Are there unwieldy *noun strings*?
12. a. Is there *redundancy*?
    b. Are there *extraneous* words?
    c. Is there *overspecificity*?
13. Is the *style* inappropriate?
    a. incorrect point of view
    b. parties, individuals, etc., labelled incorrectly
    c. incorrect use of pronouns
    d. incorrect tense
    e. language too colloquial
    f. language too pompous
    g. too much like a term paper
    h. too many cliches
14. Has the writer failed to write within his or her *constraints*?
    a. formal rules not followed
    b. informal rules not followed
    c. document is too long
    d. document is too short
    e. wrong content or information

15. Is the document *poorly organized?*
    a. no coherent organizing principle
    b. steps for a basic expository document missing
    c. steps for a complex legal document missing
    d. no context at the beginning of the document
    e. no "roadmap" section
    f. no table of contents in a long document
    g. appropriate headings or subheadings missing
    h. headings or subheadings not informative
    i. organization of the document not made apparent
    j. document not broken down into manageable sections
    k. sections not parallel
    l. good transitions needed
16. Does the writer need to rethink his or her *persuasive strategies?*
    a. document is too one-sided
    b. too much prominence given to damaging material
    c. information not ordered so that positive information stands out
    d. information not ordered so that negative information is de-emphasized
    e. more convincing vocabulary needed

EXERCISE

Use the language guidelines to edit the memo below. Also be prepared to make suggestions for improving the organization of the memo.

TO:	Senior Partner
FROM:	Associate
RE:	Liability of Homeowner in Regard to Drowning of Minor
DATE:	October 30, 1984

QUESTION PRESENTED

Whether a parent of a minor is entitled to recover against a private homeowner for the drowning death of a minor, when the homeowner is in compliance with local building codes.

BRIEF ANSWER

In pursuance to the state of Kentucky, the landowner would be liable for injuries as result of any injury or death that are incurred.

In regards to the above situation, Kentucky state law has recognized in certain situations like the above, from the finding that possessor of land is liable for physical harm if he creates or maintains an artificial condition which he realizes or should have realized will involve an unreasonable risk or serious bodily harm to children who would not have comprehend the risk of danger involved. Under Kentucky law a swimming pool is considered an artificial construction. Thus a landowner would be liable upon the finding that the Doctrine of Attractive Nuisance exists.

STATEMENT OF ALLEGATIONS

Harry Winston constructed a swimming pool. Winston enclosed his entire backyard with a six-foot high fence in compliance with the local building code. Melvin, who lives across the street, and is nine years old, climbed into Winston's yard. Melvin jumped into the pool, panicked and drowned.

ANALYSIS

There is no question but that the parents of the minor has a valid cause of action, if it can be shown that the doctrine of attractive nuisance is applicable.

"The Attractive Nuisance Doctrine provides that one who maintains upon his premises a condition, instrumentality, or other agency which are dangerous to children of tender years by reason of their inability to appreciate the peril therein, and which may reasonably be expected to attract children of tender years to the premises, is under a duty to exercise reasonable care to protect them against the dangers of the attraction." The Restatement of this principle has been applied to numerous cases involving actions for death of or injury to a child which was caused by a private residential swimming pool.

The evidence indicates that the minor was on a homeowner's property. However, the Attractive Nuisance Doctrine governs the liability of landowners to minors. Whether a minor is classified as a trespasser, licensee, or invitee is not a controlling consideration in the application of the Attractive Nuisance Doctrine. It could be argued that the Attractive Nuisance Doctrine is inapplicable, since the homeowner was in compliance with local building code requirements for maintaining an artificial structure in his backyard. That the homeowner is released of liability from injuries incurred to trespassing minors, because he had taken all necessary precautionary measures by erecting a six-foot fence. In the following case the Attractive Nuisance Doctrine is inapplicable *Hanners v. City of Ashland,* 331 S.W.2d 729 (Ky. 1960). The case involved a child eight years old who drowned while swimming on private property. The court held that Attractive Nuisance Doctrine did not extend to city's reservoir, which was filled with water, the city was not held liable for the death of the eight-year-old child drowned while swimming in the reservoir. The court's rationale behind its decision was that a reservoir is not considered the same as an artificial structure as in the case of a swimming pool. The principle of law is controlled by the decision and reasoning in *Schaufs' Admr. v. City of Paducah,* 106 Ky. 228, 50 S.W. 42 (1954). The principle of law was also controlled out of *Von Almen's Admr. v. City of Louisville,* 180 Ky. 441, 202 S.W. 880 (1918) and has not been departed from in this state. The facts from the above case are substantially similar to the facts in our present situation. Although in the above case the court denied the plaintiff the right to recover, the same underlining principle is applicable. *The City of Ashland* case further establish the rule that ordinarily the landowner is liable for the action of minor, when physical harm results from artificial structures which the homeowner may anticipate constitutes unreasonable risk of serious injury to children who would not realize such danger.

It was also established in the leading case of *Louisville Trust Co. v. Nutting,* 437 S.W.2d 484 (Ky. 1968). Here, the court held that a homeowner is liable for the harm of trespassing minors, if he creates or maintains artificial condition which realize or should realize will involve unreasonable harm to children, and the instrumentality is one that would reasonably attract a child's attention to come on his premises.

While it appears to be a valid cause of action. It is important to take into consideration that the view is moderately restricting the application of the Doctrine of Attractive Nuisance theory. *Bentley v. South-East Coal Co.* 334 S.W.2d 349 (Ky. 1960) considering the fact that the homeowner was in compliance with the local building codes will be our strongest contention. However, the theory behind the Doctrine of Attractive Nuisance is in our favor. Because of a child's immaturity and want of judgment, the "minor is presumed incapable of understanding and appreciating all of the possible dangers which he may encounter entering upon the land of another, or making his own decisions as to the chances he will take. Since it is not practical for the parents to chain to a bedpost. Thus if a child is to be protected at all, it will be the one upon whose land the child strays," Prosser fourth edition *Torts*. This view is the traditional social interest in the safety and welfare of children. The general rule is in our favor. Therefore it is a possibility of recovery under the Kentucky state Wrongful Death Statute 411-130:

> In a wrongful death action in which the decedent was a minor child, the surviving parent or parents may recover for loss of affection and companionship that would have derived from such child during its minority in addition to all other elements of damage usually recoverable in a wrongful death action, in negligence.

3. Checking for Correctness

After you have checked a document for appropriateness and effectiveness, you should also check it for correctness. This means that you should proofread your document for mechanical errors.

Proofreading is necessary, first because humans make mistakes and second because we are not especially tolerant of the mistakes that others make. When you write, you will probably make careless mistakes. Your readers will not overlook these mistakes and may not forgive you for them. Educated readers such as law professors, senior partners, and judges expect correctness. If your final copy contains frequent errors, even seemingly trivial ones, you jeopardize your credibility as a professional. Errors — either frequent small ones or occasional serious ones — can cause a reader to make negative inferences about you. Because of errors in a document, a reader may conclude that you are lazy, uninterested in your work, illiterate, illogical, or incompetent.

As a professional, you cannot afford this "halo" effect of errors. Yet, if you simply reread one of your documents from top to bottom, you will probably not catch all the errors. The content is so familiar to you that you see what you expect to see or what you intended to put on the page. You may also have difficulty catching errors because you are reading word groups as quickly as you can comprehend them. Experienced readers do not read letter by letter or even word by word.

Good proofreaders do read slowly, often letter by letter, to be sure they are seeing each word as a word and not as a component of a thought. There are several ways to shift your focus away from the ideas to the words and letters. For most people, the trick is to slow down normal reading speed. Here are a few ways to do this.

1. Read your document out loud to someone who is proofreading a duplicate copy. The listener can concentrate on checking the accuracy of each word he or she hears rather than on absorbing the ideas.
2. Read your document backwards from the last sentence to the first, or, alternatively, read each page from the bottom to the top. These approaches slow down your reading considerably because you have to hunt for the beginning of each sentence.
3. Proofread each page line by line, placing a ruler under the line you are reading to keep your eyes from automatically moving ahead to the next word group.
4. Proofread each page line by line from *right to left* to maximize your review of each word. This method works particularly well as a final check for standard typographical errors such as dropped letters or transposed letters — provided that earlier readings have ensured that no words or punctuation are missing and that the overall flow is good.

Once you have selected a method and started proofreading, you will undoubtedly encounter errors that need to be marked for correction. If you plan to make all the corrections yourself, any mark will do. If, however, there is clerical staff available, it is good to know the accepted proofreading marks. Every dictionary has a page on proofreading marks; however, we have included the more common ones here for your convenience (see Figure 7-2). You will be able to use them with the exercises that follow.

The proofreaders' marks are designed to communicate virtually any change with ease. To guarantee a perfect final product, be sure you use the correct mark, position it properly, and write it legibly.

If your document has been prepared with ample space between the lines, you can make corrections and insertions directly above the word or spot in question. If you don't have enough room there, however, you will need to treat your page and your corrections differently.

Draw an imaginary line down the center of the page. Any corrections needed to the left of that line will be written in the lefthand margin; any corrections to the right, in the righthand margin. A caret (∧) will mark the spot in the line where each correction is to be made. Use the margin space immediately to the left or right of the line to write the correction. Separate

Figure 7-2 Proofreaders' Marks

ℐ	delete: the ~~the~~ court
⌒	close up: law maker
⌐⌐	delete and close up: statutory
∧	insert: the bill passed
#	add space: S. Ct.
eq. #	space evenly ✓ where ✓ indicated
Stet	let it ~~stand~~
tr.	transpose: justice
⌐	move right
⌐	move left
⌐⌐	center
⌐	move up
⌐	move down
¶	begin new paragraph
sp.	spell out: U.S. United States
caps	set in capitals: CAPITALS
sc	set in small capitals: SMALL CAPITALS
lc	set in lowercase: lowercase
ital.	set in italic: *italic*
rom.	set in roman: roman
bf	set in boldface: **boldface**
=	insert hyphen: landlord-tenant
1/M	insert em dash: — 463 U.S. — (1985)
∨	superscript: footnote[1]
∧	subscript: H_2O
∧	comma
∨	apostrophe
⊙	period
∧	semicolon
∧	colon
∨ ∨ or ∨ ∨	quotation marks
(/)	parentheses
/	used to separate two or more changes or at the end of an insertion

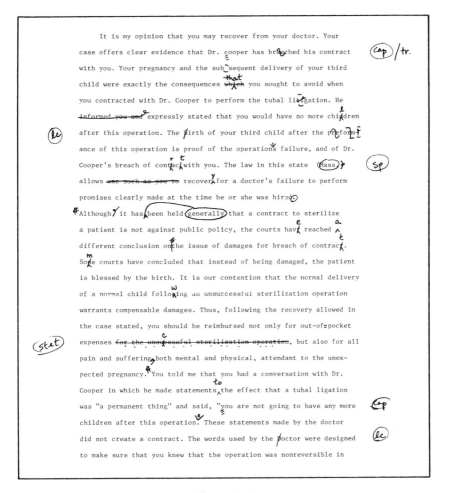

It is my opinion that you may recover from your doctor. Your case offers clear evidence that Dr. cooper has breached his contract with you. Your pregnancy and the subsequent delivery of your third child were exactly the consequences which you sought to avoid when you contracted with Dr. Cooper to perform the tubal ligation. He informed you and expressly stated that you would have no more children after this operation. The birth of your third child after the preform ance of this operation is proof of the operations failure, and of Dr. Cooper's breach of contact with you. The law in this state (Mass.) allows one such as you to recover for a doctor's failure to perform promises clearly made at the time he or she was hired. Although it has been held generally that a contract to sterilize a patient is not against public policy, the courts have reached a different conclusion on the issue of damages for breach of contract. Some courts have concluded that instead of being damaged, the patient is blessed by the birth. It is our contention that the normal delivery of a normal child following an unsuccessful sterilization operation warrants compensable damages. Thus, following the recovery allowed in the case stated, you should be reimbursed not only for out-of-pocket expenses for the unsuccessful sterilization operation, but also for all pain and suffering both mental and physical, attendant to the unexpected pregnancy. You told me that you had a conversation with Dr. Cooper in which he made statements to the effect that a tubal ligation was "a permanent thing" and said, "you are not going to have any more children after this operation. These statements made by the doctor did not create a contract. The words used by the doctor were designed to make sure that you knew that the operation was nonreversible in

Figure 7-3

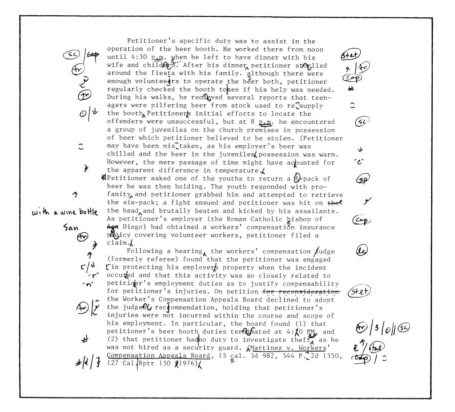

Figure 7-4

corrections with a vertical line. (See the examples of corrected pages, Figure 7-3 and Figure 7-4.)

EXERCISES

To test your ability as a proofreader, proofread these exercises. The exercises contain a total of 20 careless errors. The errors include mistakes like transposed letters (*raed* for *read* or *form* for *from*), omitted words or letters, substituted letters (*test* for *text*), wrong words (*then* for *than*), and omitted or unnecessary punctuation marks.

1. Brooks converted the store into a mens clothing store and converted the second floor into an apartment. He removed the original radiators and

installed and electric heating system to heat both floors. A new carpet was placed on a wooden flame which was bolted to the first floor, and an air conditioner was placed in a frist floor window. On the second floor he replaced the plumbing fixtures and installed a new toilet and shower.

2. Mr. Brooks may remove and sell the air conditioner. Since the unit is a window type, it is only tenuously annexed to the building an may be removed without damage. It is not particularly adapted use in that location; that is, the unit would fit equally well in countless other window. Also, the vhoice of such a model indicates Mr. Brooks intention to remove it later. Other jurisdictions have decided this point.

3. These two bojects—the forced-air heat pump, including duct work, and the upstairs plumbing fixtures—can be consider together since they all under the same legal theory. The law that covers these two object is that of replacements, since the forced-air system and the newly-installed bathroom replace systems of the same type that were in existence when our client moved in. A fixture substituted for one that was on the premises at the time of the lease is generally not removable if the original has been damaged or permanently removed, since the effect of such action would be to leave the premises in a worse condition then when the lessee took the lease.

4. In that case the tenant, Jensen, took out a broken toilet, substituting a working toilet for the duration of his lease. On leaving the premises, Jensen remove the toilet he had installed and re-installed the original broken toilet, leaving the property in in substantially the same state in which he received it. The court ruled that the lessee has a right to remove the improvemnets and additions that he has made to the leased property, provided he leaves it in the state which it was received. It follows form that decision that if our client still has the old toiler, me may reconnect it and remove the new toilet as personal property.

8

Using
Graphic
Techniques

The Components of Graphic Design

If you compare the two insurance policies in Chapter 3, you can see the effect that graphic design — type size, typeface, and layout — can have on a document. In this chapter, you will learn more about the ingredients of a well-formatted document. You should not overlook the importance of physical appearance: The way a document looks can help determine whether the reader will have a positive or negative impression of its content.

A well-formatted document will be easier to read, easier to absorb, and easier to use. The content of a poorly formatted document may be perfectly polished but still fail to present information in an easily accessible fashion. Proper use of graphic techniques will result in a document that carries its message to the reader simply and effectively.

The main components of graphic design are:

1. *Structure:* the headings that divide the document into manageable topics.
2. *Type:* the size of the type and the type style — roman, boldface, or italic.
3. *White space:* the margins and the space surrounding text, quotes, footnotes, etc.
4. *Special treatments:* the various ways of highlighting particular points or sections of a document (lists, block indention, etc.).
5. *Paper:* the size, color, finish, and weight of text and cover.

Before you can begin using these graphic elements, you need to know what your constraints are.

- Are there preexisting format restrictions?
- Has your document been prepared to reach a particular audience (such as the elderly, the general public, the Supreme Court)?
- Is length (total number of pages) a constraint?
- What are your resources (time, budget, accessibility of staff and equipment)?

If there is a predetermined formula for presenting the material to your audience (such as the restrictions on Supreme Court documents), you may have very few decisions to make. If, however, there are no preexisting parameters, you will need to think about your graphic options carefully. Once you know your audience and your constraints, you can use appropriate graphic techniques in the final product.

The only graphic component in the bulleted list above that you may have to deal with initially is length. If length is a constraint, you probably have been monitoring it through each draft and should now have a general idea of how long your document is. Knowing *exactly* how long the document will be in its final form is important in helping you decide on the best way of presenting it.

For example, if your document is a warranty that will be included in the packaging of a small product, you will not be able to fit ten pages of typed copy on an enclosure card. If you have written three pages of copy instead of the ideal two pages, however, you may be able to change the typeface (the term for an individually designed alphabet that has an identifiable look, such as **Helvetica**, Baskerville, or Melior) and the type size to accommodate the full three pages. You may, of course, be sacrificing legibility to some extent, but it may be worth the trade-off. Be sure you know your priorities, and compromise for best overall effect once you have satisfied your top priorities.

B Determining Length

To obtain an accurate estimate of length, you need to go through two steps.

1. Find out how much material, or copy, you have in its current form (handwritten, typed, word processed); and
2. Convert the results from Step 1 into figures for how much copy you will

have in the document's final form (typewritten, word processed, or formally typeset).

The simplest example is a conversion from handwritten text to typed manuscript. If all you need is a rough figure, it is fairly easy to estimate length going from handwritten material to typed material. The average double-spaced typewritten page has 250 words on it. To find the length of your handwritten copy count the words. Your total count will be the most accurate if you count every word, but to speed the process, you can work with averages. Count the words in 10 lines and divide the total number of words by 10 to get the average number of words per line. Multiply this average by the number of lines in the document to determine the total number of words. You can then divide that number by 250 to find approximately how many typed pages you will get from your handwritten copy.

The most precise length estimate requires counting every single "character" in your document — this means counting every letter, every figure, every punctuation mark, and every space between words occurring on one line.

For example, there are 67 characters in this line of typeset copy.[1]

This is called a "character count," and it is very time-consuming. It is a useful technique only if space constraints are crucial. But again, you can work with averages. The "average" word is said to have six characters, therefore you can multiply the total number of words by six to find total characters. The character count can then be converted either to typewritten copy or typeset copy.

If your final document is to be typewritten, and you need a very accurate estimate of how long it will be, get a 10-line sample of the type from the typewriter or word processor you will be using. Be sure the margins in this sample match, or at least approximate, the margins you will use in your final product. Then, count the characters in all 10 lines of the sample and divide the total by 10 to get the average number of characters per line. Divide the total characters from your handwritten version by the average characters per line in the sample to find out how many lines you will have in the final version. Once you have determined how many lines per page the final document will have (see section D, which discusses margins, p. 188), you can divide the total number of lines by the lines per page to see how many pages there will be in the final version.

1. The optimal line length for reading ease is between 40 and 70 characters.

1. The Typewriter

What if the final figure is more (or less) than your length requirement? If you are working with a typewriter, you can adjust your margins to increase (or decrease) the number of characters per line. The more sophisticated typewriters also permit you to

1. Shift from *pica* type to *elite* type (pica type = 10 characters per inch, elite type = 12 characters per inch)
2. Increase the spacing between letters for fewer characters per line
3. Switch type fonts (e.g., the type balls of an IBM Selectric) to alter the look of the final product
4. Use half spaces between lines (e.g., $1\frac{1}{2}$ spaces) rather than single or double spacing
5. "Justify" the copy at the right margin rather than using a ragged right-hand margin

Any one of these adjustments, or a combination of them, may help you to meet your length requirements. Each will have a measurable effect on the final appearance and readability of the document, so you should carefully weigh the decision to make an adjustment. Single-spaced copy with narrow margins in elite type will give you the maximum amount of text per page — but it will also cause the maximum amount of eyestrain for your reader.

If the more mechanical ways to modify your document to fit space requirements are not sufficient, you will simply have to decrease the amount of copy. Once you have finished editing the draft you can then recount the number of words and choose the best format for your document.

2. The Word Processor

All of the changes listed above require completely retyping the document — unless your draft was originally prepared on a word processor. Since their introduction in 1964, these specialized computers have become standard equipment in most law firms. They can accomplish any of the tasks listed above simply and quickly, without retyping.

Because the word processor separates the act of typing from the mechanical process of printing, you can type continuously, without ever hitting the carriage return. The characters you have typed are stored in the machine's memory until you are satisfied with the copy and are ready to instruct the machine to print out the document. As long as the copy is stored, you can correct and refine it repeatedly.

The early word processors performed only the few specific functions that were built into the hardware (the machine itself). The current models are actually small microcomputers with greater capabilities, because they can use many different software packages (computer programs). Software is available for an increasing number of functions.

Word processors have four major advantages over typewriters for preparing documents. With a word processor you can

- Store your text for revision or updating later
- Edit quickly, easily, and heavily
- Format for a neat, consistent final product
- Produce multiple originals quickly

Thus, at the writing stage you can

- Correct an error without using an eraser or opaquing fluid by simply retyping the letter or letters
- Insert or delete letters, words, phrases, paragraphs, headings, or entire pages
- Easily move even large portions of an existing draft from one place to another

At the formatting stage you can select the particular characteristics of physical appearance you want (such as line length, number of lines per page, or spacing). If you don't like the way the final document looks, you can alter one or all of the characteristics by typing in a few instructions.

At the printout stage you can produce multiple originals without retyping and are guaranteed a perfect, consistent original each time.

C Structure

Once the copy is ready, the first step you must take in formatting the final document is to quickly review the structure and organization of the draft. Focus on the signposts — the headings.

If you have organized your document well during your pre-writing and writing stages, you should have a visible structure that will provide a good roadmap for your reader. Your document should have headings that signal changes in subject matter and that clearly lay out the progression of your thoughts from introduction to conclusion.

1. Headings

Before determining what each heading should look like, be sure your headings are working the way you want them to. Double-check your document.

- Are there enough headings? Can the reader move about in the document quickly and easily? Is the structure clear?
- Are the headings informative? Are they too long? Are they parallel in construction?
- Are lower level headings introducing material that belongs under a main or primary heading?

After you are satisfied with the content of your headings, you must then decide how they should appear. To work most effectively, the more important headings should have more visual impact than the less important ones. The physical appearance of each heading should reflect its position in the hierarchy of headings. As you go through this section, notice the various techniques — capitalization, spacing, position, and underlining — that can establish this hierarchy.

The headings in your document — their precision, clarity, and informativeness — will create the first impression of the content of your document. Your options for headings will be determined by the equipment you use to generate the final product. Typewriters only have four options for distinguishing heads: use of capitals, spacing, position, and underlining. The more sophisticated word processors add the options of different type styles: italic and boldface. Having your documents typeset gives you a full range of choices: capitals, spacing, position, and type style, as well as different typefaces and type sizes.

2. Capitals

Using capital letters is the usual way to add weight to a heading. For short, primary headings, you can use all capital letters. However, capitals are more difficult to read than lowercase letters and should be used sparingly. In fact, anything more than four or five words in all capitals slows down reading speed significantly. Don't put large blocks of text into capital letters unless you are required to.

FACTS OF THE CASE

SUMMARY

For longer primary headings or any secondary heading, you can use capitals and lowercase letters, capitalizing the first letter of all words except prepositions and articles.

DEFENSES IN DEFAMATION CASES

Privileges in the Public Sphere

For lower level headings, you can use an initial capital and then lowercase, so that you capitalize the first letter of the first word only.

DEFENSES IN DEFAMATION CASES

Privileges in the Public Sphere

Legal proceedings and reports

3. Spacing

The importance of a heading can also be changed by varying the space around it. To set off any dominant heading, you can make it "freestanding," i.e., give it a line of its own with space above and below. A primary heading might have two lines of space above and one line of space below.

> . . . otherwise lawful private activities, and otherwise permissible uses of private property, on whatever grounds such private bodies deem appropriate — including grounds that would clearly be forbidden to the state itself.

Summary of Argument

Conferring upon church leaders the uncontrolled power, within a 500-foot radius, to decide who may serve or sell liquor to whom invests ecclesiastical officials with governmental . . .

To set off a secondary heading, you can leave one line of space above and below *or* one line of space above and no space below.

. . . otherwise lawful private activities, and otherwise permissible uses of private property, on whatever grounds such private bodies deem appropriate — including grounds that would clearly be forbidden to the state itself.

Summary of Argument

Conferring upon church leaders the uncontrolled power, within a 500-foot radius, to decide who may serve or sell liquor to whom invests ecclesiastical officials with governmental . . .

or

. . . otherwise lawful private activities, and otherwise permissible uses of private property, on whatever grounds such private bodies deem appropriate — including grounds that would clearly be forbidden to the state itself.

Summary of Argument
Conferring upon church leaders the uncontrolled power, within a 500-foot radius, to decide who may serve or sell liquor to whom invests ecclesiastical officials with governmental . . .

To set off a lower level heading, you can use a run-in heading. Start with a paragraph indent. Use any variation of capitalization listed above. End the heading with a period. Continue with the text immediately, i.e., run the heading into the text. For extra impact, you can leave a line of space above the paragraph *or* underline each word of the heading.

. . . otherwise lawful private activities, and otherwise permissible uses of private property, on whatever grounds such private bodies deem appropriate — including grounds that would clearly be forbidden to the state itself.

Summary of Argument. Conferring upon church leaders the uncontrolled power, within a 500-foot radius, to decide who may serve or sell liquor to whom invests ecclesiastical officials with governmental . . .

or

. . . otherwise lawful private activities, and otherwise permissible uses of private property, on whatever grounds such private bodies deem appropriate — including grounds that would clearly be forbidden to the state itself.

Summary of Argument. Conferring upon church leaders the uncontrolled power, within a 500-foot radius, to decide who may serve or sell liquor to whom invests ecclesiastical officials with governmental . . .

4. Position

Another choice that you must make is where to position the headings. You can

1. Center all headings between the margins
2. Place all headings at the left-hand margin
3. Put primary headings in the center and put lower level headings at the left-hand margin
4. "Hang" lower level headings in the margins, outside the text area, as illustrated below

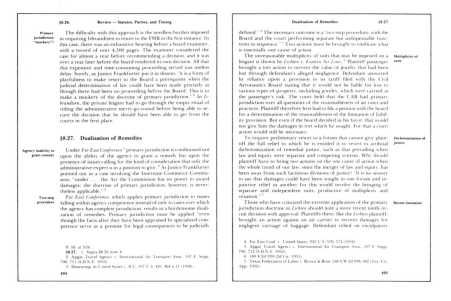

Headings should be predictable. Headings that are the same level should look the same and be in the same position. If you have only a couple of levels of headings — for example, primary headings and one level of subheading — you can select either of the first two options and use capitals and spacing to distinguish the headings. If you have numerous levels of heading, you may need to use the third option, putting the more important headings in the center and the less important ones at the margin.

Headings "hung" in the margins (marginal heads) can be used most effectively in typeset material. They are particularly helpful to the reader if you have multiple levels of headings, space constraints, and numerous lower level headings (of equal importance). These marginal headings can be signposts for quick reference in the document because they are highly visible.

5. Underlining

You can use underlining with either freestanding or run-in headings. This device is not necessary if you only have a couple of levels of headings.

It is best used

- When you need to add more visibility to an upper level heading
- When you want to further distinguish a centered heading from a heading at the margin
- When you want to add weight to a run-in heading

As with capital letters, too much underlining makes difficult reading. Use it with restraint.

6. Type Styles

Some of the newer word processors can create the look of italics or boldface type. Italic type is a slanted roman type and boldface is "doublestruck," i.e., the words are printed twice and therefore look darker.

In your hierarchy of headings you should use boldface for higher level headings because it dominates a page. Italic type works well for lower, freestanding headings or for run-in headings. Type styles can be graded, as follows, from the most to the least visible.

Most — **Boldface**

Italic

Least — Roman

If your document has only one or two heading levels, you may prefer the more subtle effect of italic type. Remember, however, that your headings are signposts and should be easy to spot on the page. The reader will never notice roman run-in headings that are not underlined, for instance.

7. Type Size

As we noted above, if you are using a typewriter or a word processor, your only choice of type size will be between pica and elite type. However, if you have your document typeset, you will have a large range of type sizes from which to choose. Type size is measured in *points*. Here are examples of

6 point type

8 point type

10 point type

12 point type

Any point size from 9 to 11 points is comfortable to read; try to keep anything you have typeset within those bounds. The "fine print" that you may have seen in some legal documents is usually 6 points or less.

D White Space

White space makes an important contribution to the final appearance of your document. Small changes in the white space surrounding the text, headings, quoted items, and footnotes can totally transform the look and the readability of your document. If you fill your pages to the edge with type and squeeze headings into the text, your document will look dense and be difficult to read. Your reader may not even want to read it.

Adequate margins open up the page and give it a less formidable appearance. Ample space around headings and special items such as quotations or lists sets them off from the text and allows them to be identified quickly. The page breaks up visually into smaller, more manageable units, which improves reading speed and comprehension.

Wide margins, however, mean shorter lines of type and fewer characters per page, and this means increased length. Your use of white space and wide margins must be tempered by length constraints. Balance your decisions against your goals and constraints for the best overall effect. If you have many headings, for example, you can use their surrounding white space to compensate for smaller margins and more characters per line. The same is true if your document contains numerous text items that call for special treatment. If you open up space around these items, you can draw attention away from relatively narrow margins.

E Special Treatments

Your document may consist of continuous text with headings and footnotes as the only unusual items. Many documents, however, contain elements that could benefit from special treatment: quotations, lists, tabular material, charts, figures, etc. Using special treatments for these elements adds to the visual interest of your document. A special treatment should stand out from the text, but not so much as to disrupt the flow of the text and the reader's concentration. Overusing these highlighting tricks can result in choppy text that distracts the reader.

1. Quotations

Excerpts from outside sources frequently are candidates for special treatment. Quotations that run less than six lines usually should be left inside quotation marks within the body of the text. An exception would be if the quotation is particularly important or if the quotation is the shortest of a series of excerpts of equal importance. To maintain its status within the series, the shortest should also be set off from the text.

The most common device for highlighting a quotation is the block indent. Leave one line of space above and below the quotation and indent either the left-hand margin only (for maximum line length) or the left-hand and right-hand margins (for maximum emphasis).

> We are of course aware that, if possible, statutes are to be construed to avoid constitutional defects. But no reasonable reading by us of "church," when expressly defined as "a church or synagogue building dedicated to divine worship," can transform section 16C into a religiously neutral law . . .

It is not necessary to use quotation marks for excerpts set up as block indents, because the format signals that the material is quoted.

Remember that more than half a page of indented copy becomes ineffective because the reader loses the contrast between the longer and shorter lines and begins to consider the shorter lines normal.

2. Key Points

If you want to highlight a key point in your argument, you can use a different type style (italic or boldface) to make it stand out from the text. For even greater impact, you could use the block indentation described above to physically separate your point from the text and focus attention on it. If you combine these options, using indention and italic or boldface type, you will further emphasize the key point.

3. Lists

Lists are an excellent way to make collections of thoughts or questions more manageable and more visible. They work best if the items are similar in nature and importance and if the items are parallel in structure. Lists are the perfect way to synthesize information into the most usable format. They focus the reader and add some visual interest to the page.

Lists can be set up in any number of ways — with numbers, letters, bullets, etc. Double-check your draft to be sure that there are no lists embedded in the body of the text that would be more effective if given some special treatment. The main options for distinguishing a list from text are:

1. *Space:* Use a line of space above and below your list, or even between the items of a list, to make it a visually identifiable unit.
2. *Indention:* As with quotations, you can indent your list only at the left or at both the left and right to set it off.
3. *Special characters:* Numbers and letters are most commonly used to label the items in a list. However, if the quantity of items is unimportant and the items are not mentioned later, you can lead off with

   • *Bullets.* Bullets (a lowercase "o" on a typewriter) are useful for short lists consisting of items that are short phrases.

   — *Dashes.* These are useful for introducing longer lists composed of sentences or paragraphs.

☐ *Boxes*. These work best for checklists or when there would be an advantage to literally or figuratively ticking off the item.

4. *Double-column format:* In circumstances where you have a long list of short items, it may be helpful to break it in half and use two columns.

F Paper

Paper can have a noticeable impact on the overall appearance of your document. The care you have taken at the earlier stages of preparation should be reflected in your choice of paper. The reader's impression of the professionalism of the final product will be influenced positively by appropriate quality paper.

If your document must meet preexisting standards, the paper size, bulk (thickness of each sheet), finish (dull or glossy surface), and color may be dictated for your text and for your cover, if one is required. Appellate courts, for example, frequently require that briefs of the plaintiff and defendant have covers of different colors to distinguish them from each other.

When the choice is yours, pick the best quality paper available. Use a standard size and color for your type of document. Be sure you get sufficient weight and opacity (density) so that the document will be comfortable to handle and pleasing to read (no "show-through" from page to page). Onionskin, for example, is both difficult to hold and to read. Its flimsiness detracts from even topnotch content.

Another factor in readability is finish. Text is easier to read when the paper has a dull surface. Pictures are more appealing and sharper if printed on paper with a glossy finish. (Think of the paper used in a novel as opposed to the paper used in a magazine.)

Documents that will be duplicated to generate the final product should be typed or word processed on the whitest paper available. This will maximize the contrast between the type image and the paper and produce the best possible copies. Also check the quality of the copying paper — good quality paper makes for better reproduction.

Commercial duplication services usually carry a variety of weights and colors of paper. They can advise you on the best choice for your document. Various weights of paper are also available for office duplicating equipment, but you may have to special order it. Plan ahead if you have special needs.

IV

9

Writing a

Legal

Memorandum

A   What Is a Memorandum?

A memorandum (memo) is an informative document that summarizes the research on the points of law or the facts of a particular case. The memo is an internal office document[1] that is usually requested by, and addressed to, another lawyer — often a colleague or supervisor in the writer's firm. The writer may be asked to resolve a predefined issue or set of issues or to first identify all of the issues in a problem and then to resolve them. In practice, a memo may be used for many purposes: to alert the reader that more information is needed either from the client or through discovery, to inform the reader about the status of the law, or to present the reader with recommendations on how to proceed with a case.

A memo is a research tool rather than a document advocating a particular point of view. It should provide the reader with a complete picture of the facts and law in a case, including both positive and negative information, so that the reader can use the memo to anticipate counterarguments and to make sound decisions about the case. Thus, while the writer of the memo should indicate which side he or she is on, the writer should also present both the strengths and weaknesses of the client's position.

This chapter consists of two parts: The first part is an outline of the structure of a memo with explanations of each section of the memo. The second part of the chapter is made up of two sample memos.

Keep in mind that this outline is only a basic structure: Memo formats vary widely, depending upon the preferences of a particular law professor, law

---

1. There are also external or advocacy memos that resemble briefs. We will not discuss advocacy memos in this text. Many of the rules that apply to appellate briefs apply to advocacy memos.

firm, or agency. The writers of the sample memos, for instance, have organized their memos in their own way, following already established conventions. With our outline, however, we show you one useful way of organizing a memo when you have had little or no experience in writing one. Our outline will not only help you to organize your first attempts at writing a memo, it will also help you think about the kinds of information, arguments, and supporting evidence that should go into your memo. Remember that the order in which you present the information in a memo may not be the order in which you research, think about, or write that information.

B The Structure of a Memo

1. Outline

Heading

Background and Purpose of the Memorandum
Statement of the Issues
      Question 1   (There may be one or several questions. These ques-
      Question 2   tions are sometimes called issues.)
Short Answer
Statement of the Facts
Applicable Statutes
Discussion
      Analysis of Question 1
      Analysis of Question 2
Conclusion

2. Explanation of the Parts of a Memo

a. *Heading*

Most memos begin with a heading in caps, MEMORANDUM OF LAW, and a heading that includes an identification of the case (use your client's name or the names of the parties if you know who they are), the name of the person who requested the memo, the name of the person submitting the memo, and the date the memo will be submitted. It should look something like this.

MEMORANDUM OF LAW

TITLE: Smith v. Jones
REQUESTED BY: Professor Freedman
SUBMITTED BY: H. Monroe
DATE SUBMITTED: November 12, 1984

A memo may require a more informative title. The title above can be replaced by a description of the subject of the memo. This description helps the reader to identify a memo quickly and will also be helpful to anyone who uses the memo in the future. Here is one way to provide this information.

MEMORANDUM OF LAW

TO: Professor Freedman
FROM: H. Monroe
DATE: November 12, 1984
RE: Liability of an employer for an assault committed by an employee in *Tibits v. Northern Industrial Suppliers, Inc.*

b. *Background and Purpose*

Some memos open with a discussion of why the writer has been asked to produce the memo or with some background information. This kind of introduction can quickly orient the reader to the topic of the memo. This section may not have a formal title. Here is an example:

> You have asked me to develop arguments in support of a motion for summary judgment in *Smith v. Jones* on the grounds that the plaintiff's claim is barred by the statute of limitations. This memo discusses several ways in which we can move for summary judgment.

c. *Statement of the Issues*

This section may also be called *Questions Presented*. It lists the legal questions that are presented in the memo. A writer must analyze the problem carefully so that all of the questions or major issues in the problem are dealt with.

According to convention each question should consist of one sentence, and one sentence only. This makes these questions very difficult to write. If a question comes out too long, is structurally very complex, and doesn't inspire the reader to agree with the writer's position, then it needs to be rewritten. The question may need to be restated or broken down into several separate issues. Here is an example of a statement of the issues.

Statement of the Issues

1. When a lease gives a lessee the power to renew the lease for "additional terms," how many renewals is the lessee entitled to?
2. When a lessee attaches personal property to the leasehold and later wants to remove it, what test will the court use to determine whether the property has become a fixture and thus belongs to the lessor?

However, if the issues in a memo are complex or if there are many issues, this section may contain only a summary of those issues. Each specific issue statement or question then appears at the beginning of the section in which the issue is actually analyzed.

Summary of the Issues

This memorandum discusses the contract doctrines of mutuality of obligation and mutuality of remedy. The memo focuses in particular upon scholarly treatment of these principles and how the courts have recently applied these principles. The memo also analyzes how courts have applied contract law in deciding cases arising under 42 U.S.C. §1981, which prohibits racial discrimination when contracts are created or enforced.

d. Short Answer

This section contains a short answer to the questions presented in the statement of the issues. For example:

Short Answer

Our client should be entitled to an equitable increase in its fixed fee based on the cost of the eight-month extension of management and support services that it provided as a result of the government's change in orders. In addition, the costs that our client incurred for 22 months of extended management and support services as a result of the government's delays provide a basis for an increase in fee. This increase is warranted because the contract establishes time of performance as a crucial element in defining the scope of work.

e. Statement of the Facts

This section contains a clear and concise statement of the pertinent facts of the case. These are the facts upon which the discussion and conclusion are based. The statement of facts should include both favorable and unfavorable facts, since the writer must analyze the legal significance of each. Here is an example from a memo written by a firm representing the defendant, John Deboe. The issue in this case is whether the plaintiff, Long, can collect directly from Deboe's insurance company that part of a judgment against Deboe that exceeds Deboe's insurance coverage. There is evidence that the insurer acted in bad faith by refusing to settle with Long.

Statement of Facts

On October 10, 1984, John Deboe was involved in a traffic accident in which Lillian Long and her daughter were injured. Long sued Deboe in a Minnesota court for property damage and personal injuries to herself and her daughter. Long obtained a judgment against Deboe in the amount of $63,000. Deboe had automobile insurance with Good Group Insurance Company in the amount of $23,000, $40,00C less than the judgment against him. Good Group has paid the full amount of its coverage under the policy to Long, but Long has not yet collected any of the judgment in excess of the $23,000 policy amount.

Good Group had several opportunities, before trial, to settle with Long for an amount within the limits of Deboe's policy. Good Group refused on each occasion.

f. *Applicable Statutes*

Some memos will include a section that lists citations for all of the statutes and regulations that have been used in the memo. Some agencies or firms may also want the applicable portion of the law reproduced along with these citations.

g. *Discussion*

The *discussion* is the core of the memo. It restates each of the questions that are presented in the memo. Each question is followed by a discussion or analysis in which the writer shows how the law (pertinent cases, statutes, etc.) can be applied to the facts in the case to answer the question.

For a sample discussion, see the memos in Section C below.

h. *Conclusion*

A memo might include a *conclusion* that briefly summarizes the conclusions the writer has drawn from the discussion and that recommends actions that the reader might want to take, based upon the analyses in the discussion.

C Writing a Memo: Two Examples

Now let's look at two memos to see how all of these sections go together. The first memo was written by a practicing lawyer. It has been adapted somewhat, and the names have been changed. The second memo was written by a student and has been edited slightly.

MEMORANDUM

TO: Jack Armstrong
FROM: Harvey Gold
DATE: March 4, 1986
RE: Disqualification of Norris Carter, Plaintiffs' Counsel *Parkman et al. v. Doberman, Inc.,* Civil No. 84-156 WAI (Del., filed January 3, 1985)

Introduction

This memorandum examines whether we should move to disqualify plaintiffs' counsel, Mr. Carter, from participating in litigation pending against our client, Doberman, Inc., in the United States District Court, Delaware.

As more fully outlined below, plaintiffs, a group of Delaware businessmen, instituted an action for breach of contract against Doberman, Inc. Plaintiffs are represented by Norris Carter, a local attorney and entrepreneur. You have asked me to evaluate the possibility of disqualifying Carter because of his intimate involvement in the contract negotiations that gave rise to the pending litigation. Because of that involvement it is likely that either plaintiffs or defendant will call Carter as a witness. Carter is also an individual plaintiff in the action. This complicates the analysis and may make it difficult, under the "advocate-witness" rule, to completely disqualify him from participating in the litigation.

On July 17, 1985, plaintiffs, six businessmen from Dover, Delaware, approached our client, a New Jersey Corporation whose business is waste management disposal, and offered to sell our client their interest in certain waste disposal sites situated in the northeast corridor of the United States. Because of the magnitude of the transaction, negotiations were complex and lengthy. Numerous issues were involved, including the safety of the facilities, the nature of the waste products stored at the various sites, and the price to be paid. As part of the negotiations, the parties agreed that they needed to commission an environmental study to determine the amount of various chemicals that each of the sites could safely accommodate. They would then use the results of the studies to fix the fair market value of each of the sites. The parties agreed that the cost of the studies would be borne by Doberman, if it purchased the sites.

Soon after that, the plaintiffs arranged to have the studies undertaken at a cost of $75,000. After the studies were completed, Doberman offered to purchase the sites for $250,000, an amount significantly less than the $2.5 million that the plaintiffs had hoped to receive. Plaintiffs rejected the offer and asked to be reimbursed for the cost of the studies. Doberman refused, arguing that it was only obligated to reimburse plaintiffs if it purchased the sites, and because plaintiffs had rejected its offer, it was not obligated to reimburse them. Plaintiffs maintain that during the course of the negotiations, Doberman indicated that if the results of the studies were satisfactory it would make a good faith offer. Plaintiffs also maintain that although the results of the studies were satisfactory, Doberman did not make an offer in good faith. Doberman rejects the contention that it reached such an understanding with plaintiffs during the negotiations and adheres to its position that its obligation to pay for the studies was contingent on its actually purchasing the sites.

Norris Carter, one of the plaintiffs, was present along with the other plaintiffs during the negotiations, and he actively participated in them. It is our understanding that the plaintiffs will corroborate each other. It is also our understanding that the corporation that conducted the environmental studies is owned by Carter and two of the other plaintiffs, and it is possible that the cost of the studies may have been artificially inflated.

Issues

1. What standards should be used in determining whether an attorney who is also a potential witness should be disqualified from participating in the trial?
2. If an attorney ought to be disqualified, would the attorney's pro se status affect the disqualification?
3. Can a client waive the disqualification rule?

Legal Standard

The applicable provisions of the American Bar Association's Model Code of Professional Responsibility state:

DR 5-101 Refusing Employment When the Interests of the Lawyer May Impair His Independent Professional Judgment. . . .

(B) A lawyer shall not accept employment in contemplated or pending litigation if he knows or it is obvious that he or a lawyer in his firm ought to be called as a witness, except that he or a lawyer in his firm may testify:
(1) If the testimony will relate solely to an uncontested matter.
(2) If the testimony will relate solely to a matter of formality and there is no reason to believe that substantial evidence will be offered in opposition to the testimony.
(3) If the testimony will relate solely to the nature and value of legal services rendered in the case by the lawyer or his firm to the client.
(4) As to any matter, if refusal would work a substantial hardship on the client because of the distinctive value of the lawyer or his firm as counsel in the particular case.

DR 5-102 Withdrawal as Counsel When the Lawyer Becomes a Witness.

(A) If, after undertaking employment in contemplated or pending litigation, a lawyer learns or it is obvious that he or a lawyer in his firm ought to be called as a witness on behalf of his client, he shall withdraw from the conduct of the trial and his firm, if any, shall not continue representation in the trial, except that he may continue the representation and he or a lawyer in his firm may testify in the circumstances enumerated in DR 5-101(B)(1) through (4).
(B) If, after undertaking employment in contemplated or pending litigation, a lawyer learns or it is obvious that he or a lawyer in his firm may be called as a witness other than on behalf of his client, he may continue the representation until it is apparent that his testimony is or may be prejudicial to his client.

Discussion

I. AN ATTORNEY MUST BE DISQUALIFIED IF (1) THE ATTORNEY OUGHT TO BE CALLED AS A WITNESS ON BEHALF OF HIS OR HER CLIENT OR (2) THE ATTORNEY'S TESTIMONY WOULD PREJUDICE HIS OR HER CLIENT.

The Model Code of Professional Responsibility (Code) delineates two situations in which an attorney is obligated to withdraw from pending litigation. First, the attorney is obligated to withdraw from conducting a trial if the attorney "ought" to be called as a witness on behalf of his or her client. See DR 5-102(A). Second, the attorney is obligated to withdraw if the attorney learns, or it is obvious, that he or she will be called as a witness by another party and that the attorney's testimony may prejudice his or her client. See DR 5-102(B). Although DR 5-102 addresses situations in which the attorney has already been retained, a parallel provision, DR 5-101, addresses the case in which the attorney has not as yet been retained. Note that the two disciplinary rules differ slightly. Under DR 5-101(B), an attorney is counseled to refuse to represent a client in contemplated or pending litigation if the attorney "ought to be called as a witness." In contrast, under DR 5-102(A) the attorney should withdraw only if the attorney "ought to be called as a witness on *behalf of his client*." (Emphasis supplied.) This distinction between the two disciplinary rules, although of theoretical interest, is of no real significance. As a practical matter all reported cases have involved attorneys who were already representing the client. Courts have uniformly relied on the language of DR 5-102 in deciding whether an attorney should be disqualified, ignoring the broader language of DR 5-101.

A. Standards for Ascertaining When an Attorney "Ought" to Be Called to Testify on Behalf of His or Her Client.

Before we move to disqualify Carter, we must determine whether he "ought" to be called to testify on behalf of his clients. Courts in various jurisdictions have formulated a variety of different tests for deciding whether an attorney ought to be called as a witness. Unfortunately, the Third Circuit has adopted the most restrictive test. In *Universal Athletic Sales Co. v. American Gym, Recreational & Athletic Corp.*, 546 F.2d 530, 539 n.21 (3d Cir. 1976), cert. denied, 430 U.S. 984 (1977), the court declared that an attorney ought to be called as a witness only when the attorney has "crucial information in his possession which must be divulged."

Other courts have given the word "ought" a broader meaning. The most liberal expression of the rule appears in *MacArthur v. Bank of New York*, 524 F. Supp. 1205 (S.D.N.Y. 1981). There Judge Sofaer stated: "defendant's argument that McNicol's testimony would merely corroborate other testimony, even if accurate, is unavailing. The test is whether the attorney's testimony could be *significantly useful* to his client; if so, he ought to be called." Id. at 1208-1209 (emphasis added). Judge Sofaer went on to conclude that, since "independent counsel would seem likely to call McNicol, both to supply his own account of the events in question (even if corroborative) and to prevent the jury from speculating about his absence," he was a witness who ought to be called. Id. The Sixth Circuit has also looked to what independent counsel would do to answer the question of whether a witness ought to be called. In *General Mill Supply Co. v. SCA Services,* 697 F.2d 704, 708 (6th Cir. 1982), the court stated, "we do not think it at all likely that any independent counsel for General Mill would feel safe in letting the case go to submission, without use of the material divulged in the affidavit [of General Mill's attorney]."

The Second Circuit also does not require testimony to be "crucial" in order to conclude that a witness ought to be called. In *J.P. Foley & Co. v. Vanderbilt,* 523 F.2d 1357 (2d Cir. 1975), the court ruled that because the attorney's testimony was "necessary" to his client's case he "ought" to appear as a witness.

Finally, the California Supreme Court has established what appears to be the only test that balances a number of factors to determine whether an attorney ought to be called as a witness.

Whether an attorney ought to testify ordinarily is a discretionary determination based on the court's considered evaluation of all pertinent factors including, inter alia, the significance of the matters to which he might testify, the weight his testimony might have in resolving such matters, and the availability of other witnesses or documentary evidence by which these matters may be independently established.

Comden v. Superior Court, 20 Cal. 3d 906, 913, 576 P.2d 571, 974, 145 Cal. Rptr. 9, 12 (1978).

Assuming that the court would apply the *Universal Athletic Sales* test, which requires testimony to be crucial in order for the court to conclude that a witness ought to be called, it is important to focus on the possible nature of Carter's testimony. On the issue of liability, Carter's testimony would probably be only corroborative. Each of the other five plaintiffs is in a position to testify about the course of the negotiations and to provide the finder of fact with pertinent evidence bearing on plaintiffs' claim. Because Carter's testimony would be only corroborative, it is unlikely that a court following the Third Circuit rule would find his testimony crucial to his client's case.

Indeed, even under the more liberal tests discussed above, a court might be reluctant to disqualify Carter. For instance, under the so-called independent counsel test used by the court in *MacArthur,* the court focuses on the significance of the attorney's testimony and on what a "detached" attorney would do under similar circumstances. Carter's testimony would merely corroborate that of five other witnesses, therefore it is unlikely that it would prove significant, and hence, it is unlikely that a detached attorney would call him as a witness. Five friendly witnesses testifying about the same events are more than enough. Indeed, it is perilous to call too many witnesses to testify about the same set of events. As most attorneys well know, the more eye witnesses that are called the more likely it is that discrepancies will arise. In short, the optimum trial strategy develops a sound and credible case while minimizing the likelihood of contradiction. Under such a strategy a detached attorney would probably call two or three plaintiffs to testify in their case in chief and reserve the others, excluding Carter, to testify in rebuttal.

Even if it develops in the course of litigation that Carter ought to testify and therefore could be disqualified under the "ought" rule, it is doubtful that a district court in the Third Circuit actually would disqualify him. As a practical matter, some courts defer to the attorney's judgment regarding whether he or she should in fact testify. The Third Circuit is a leader in deferring to an attorney's judgment about whether he or she is a necessary witness. See *Kroungold v. Triester,* 521 F.2d 763, 766 (3d Cir. 1975); *Beaver Falls Thrift Corp. v. Commercial Credit Business Loans,* 563 F. Supp. 68, 71 (W.D. Pa. 1983) ("It is not the job of this Court to second-guess the decision of plaintiff's counsel where, as here, it is not obvious that [the attorney] ought to be called as a witness and there is no indication that the decision not to call him will result in prejudice to the client"); *Zions First National Bank, N.A. v. United Health Clubs,* 503 F. Supp. 138, 141 (E.D. Pa. 1981) ("United is certainly in the best position to know whether [its attorney's] testimony is necessary to its case, and Zions has not made any specific allegations which cast doubt on United's position that it will have no need for his testimony"); *J. D. Pflaumer, Inc. v. United States Department of Justice,* 465 F. Supp. 746, 748 (E.D. Pa. 1979) ("[The] attorney and his client are in the best position to determine whether his testimony is in fact indispensable"). See also *Borman v. Borman,* 393 N.E.2d 847 (Mass. 1979) (court should defer to the counsel's decision that he not testify unless it is "obviously contrary" to the client's best interest).

Despite these precedents calling for trial judges to defer to the attorney's judgment regarding whether he or she should testify, one Third Circuit district court appears to be less restrained. "I harbor sincere doubts, however, whether the strictures of DR 5-102(A) may be avoided by the assertion that an attorney will not and need not testify on behalf of his client. This rule calls for disqualification where the attorney ought to testify, not where he will testify." *Commercial Credit Business Loans v. Martin,* No. 76-812, slip op. at 2 n.2 (E.D. Pa. June 11, 1984).

There is a great deal of law to support the court's doubts, though it is not from the Third Circuit. Numerous cases state that it is inappropriate to defer to the attorney's judgment in deciding the issue of disqualification under DR 5-101(B) or DR 5-102(A). See, e.g., *General Mill Supply Co. v. MacArthur Services,* 637 F.2d 704, 708 (6th Cir. 1982); *MacArthur v. Bank of New York,* 524 F. Supp. 1205, 1208 (S.D.N.Y. 1981) ("attorneys anxious to participate in the litigation might fail to step aside and testify even if their testimony could help the client; other attorneys might fail to step aside and testify because the client insists upon their continued representation"). See also ABA Model Code of Professional Responsibility, Ethical Consideration 5-10 ("Doubts should be resolved in favor of the lawyer testifying and against his becoming or continuing as an advocate").

In conclusion, it is unlikely that a motion to disqualify Carter on the grounds that he ought to testify would be successful. First, as a matter of law, the "ought" test cannot be satisfied because Carter's testimony would be merely corroborative of the testimony of five other witnesses. Second, courts in the Third Circuit have been reluctant to vigorously apply the disciplinary rule and instead have most often relied on the attorney's judgment about whether he or she should testify.

B. *Standards to Be Used in Ascertaining Whether an Attorney's Testimony Would Be Prejudicial to His or Her Clients.*

Carter could also be disqualified from acting as attorney for other plaintiffs under the standards of DR 5-102(B). If it is likely that the defendants would call him to the stand and elicit testimony that "is or may be prejudicial" to Carter's clients, DR 5-102(B) requires that he be disqualified. Although there is relatively little case law under this rule, the law that does exist uniformly places a heavy burden on the movant. See, e.g., *Kroungold v. Triester,* 521 F.2d 763, 766 (3d Cir. 1975); *Zions First National Bank, N.A. v. United Health Clubs,* 565 F. Supp. 138, 140 (E.D. Pa. 1981). Courts are loath to allow counsel to disqualify opponents by calling them as witnesses.

Nevertheless, when it has been demonstrated that an attorney's testimony would be likely to be prejudicial to his or her client, courts have been quick to disqualify the attorney. *Freeman v.*

Kulicke & Soffa Industries, 449 F. Supp. 974, 978 (E.D. Pa. 1978). One factor that courts have used in deciding whether an attorney's testimony would prove prejudicial is the likelihood that the attorney's credibility will be questioned during the examination. Courts have also focused on whether the attorney's testimony would contradict the testimony of other favorable witnesses or undercut the client's case. Id.

Here, there is a possibility that Carter's testimony, at least on the issue of damages, would prove prejudicial to his client's case. As noted above, Carter is part owner of the company that performed the favorable environmental studies. Although the accuracy of those studies is not in dispute, defendant is prepared to prove that the costs of those studies were unreasonably high and even inflated. Defendant may well call Carter to testify about the company's pricing policies and its profit margins. If the costs of those studies were in fact inflated, and Carter were to testify truthfully, then his testimony would prejudice his clients' damage claim. Moreover, his testimony, especially if it is developed through depositions, could also open him to suit by some of his current clients. If Carter is to be disqualified, the possibility that his testimony would be prejudicial to his clients appears to provide the only viable theory. Before this can be fully evaluated, however, we must have additional information about his potential testimony.

II. An attorney's pro se status may not necessarily bar him from being disqualified.

Even if Carter ought to be called, or if his testimony might prejudice his clients, there still exists a major roadblock in moving to disqualify him. Carter is a plaintiff in this action and under normal circumstances would be entitled at least to represent himself. In *O'Neil v. Bergan,* 452 A.2d 337, 344-345 (D.C. 1982), the court stated that when an attorney and the attorney's firm represent themselves, they have "not accepted 'employment' within the meaning of DR 5-101(B)," and hence, the disciplinary rule is not applicable. The rule does, however, still apply to Carter's representation of the other clients. In *Bottarc v. Hatton Associates,* 680 F.2d 895 (2d Cir. 1982), the court was slightly more restrained in outlining the permissible conduct of an attorney-litigant who ought to be called as a witness. *Bottarc* allowed the attorney to testify, to have his law firm represent him, and to assist in pretrial proceedings, so long as he was not the "advocate" from his firm.

Thus, even under this restrictive approach, Carter's firm could remain in the case so long as Carter did not participate as an advocate. See also *Norman Norell, Inc. v. Federated Department Stores,* 450 F. Supp. 127 (S.D.N.Y. 1978) (attorney-witness allowed to participate in pretrial preparation).

We might argue against even this type of limited participation, however, based on *General Mill Supply Co. v. SCA Services,* 697 F.2d 704, 712 (6th Cir. 1982). In that case the court disqualified an advocate-witness who was also "in a realistic and not just a figurative sense, a party in interest."

> In these days of crowded dockets, settlement of civil suits, like plea bargains in criminal cases, are much desired by courts, which cannot force them. It is part of the duty an attorney owes the court to consider carefully all opportunities of settlement and report on them objectively to the client, with a fair and objective recommendation whether acceptance would be in the client's interest. This duty, an attorney in Mr. Garratt's situation would have extraordinary difficulty in performing.
>
> Courts likewise hope the counsel in civil cases will cooperate in discovery so it can proceed without day to day supervision by the court. . . . Hope for this from an attorney in Mr. Garratt's position would be a faint hope indeed.

These same settlement and discovery arguments can be made regarding Carter as advocate, witness, and litigant.

In short, courts appear to be split on how an attorney's pro se status affects his or her ability to participate in litigation when under normal circumstances the attorney would have been disqualified. As noted above, one court has held that pro se status insulates an attorney from DR 5-102, but the majority of courts have held that the disciplinary rule is applicable even when an attorney is a party to the proceedings. Even those courts have split on the issue of whether total disqualification is warranted.

Although the uncertainty in the law makes a definitive conclusion difficult, it appears that Carter's pro se status would insulate him from being totally disqualified. It is likely that Carter would be precluded from actively participating in the trial or from representing the other plaintiffs, but he would be permitted to assist in preparing for trial. (This assumes that he would have otherwise been totally disqualified.)

III. Client may not waive the disqualification rule.

Finally, the question remains whether a client may consent to his or her attorney's being both an advocate and a witness. There is limited authority for the proposition that a client should be able to consent to such a potential conflict of interest. See, e.g., Note, The Advocate-Witness Rule: If Z, then X, but Why?, 53 N.Y.U.L. Rev. 1365 (1977). However, courts have uniformly rejected this proposition. In *Rosen v. NLRB,* 735 F.2d 564, 574-575 (D.C. Cir. 1984), the court stated:

> DR 5-102(A), unlike other rules in the Code of Professional Responsibility, . . . makes no provision for client waiver of its application. Moreover, part of the underlying rationale for the rule, namely that a lawyer's serving in a dual role of witness and advocate is unseemly, is directed at the *protection of the public interest in continued respect for the legal profession rather than any waivable private interest.* (Emphasis added.)

See also *MacArthur v. Bank of New York,* 524 F. Supp. 1205, 1209 (S.D.N.Y. 1981) ("Nor may the client waive the rule's protection by promising not to call the attorney as a witness. The ostensible paternalism of disregarding such waivers is justified by the circumstances in which the problem arises"); *Freeman v. Kulicke & Soffa Industries,* 449 F. Supp. 974, 978 (E.D. Pa. 1978) ("where a movant demonstrates that a lawyer's (or a firm member's) testimony will or is substantially likely to prejudice his or her client's case, the disciplinary rule is breached and our rules of court, which are concerned directly with the standards of the bar and only indirectly with the interests of litigants, are violated").

In short, the purpose of the rule is to preserve the distinction between advocacy, which is based on reason and is subject to objective evaluation and testimony, which is based on the witness's moral qualities and is evaluated in terms of individual credibility. Therefore, client consent is irrelevant.[1]

---

1. None of the exceptions to DR 5-101(B) or DR 5-102(A) are applicable to this situation. The first three exceptions: uncontested matters, matters of formality, and the nature and value of legal services are clearly inapposite. A quick review of the case law under the fourth "substantial hardship" exception shows similar inapplicability as it relates to the "distinctive value" of Carter's services. See, e.g., *General Mill Supply Co. v. SCA Services,* 697 F.2d 704, 713-715 (6th Cir. 1982) ("The hardship situation covered by subparagraph (4) is one where the lawyer-client team come unexpectedly upon a disqualification situation, against which they neither actually did nor could have safeguarded themselves. We do not think it was meant for a case where a possible dilemma was visible years before it arose, yet the parties went right on increasing the helpless dependence of client upon lawyer"); *MacArthur v. Bank of New York,* 524 F. Supp. at 1210 ("familiarity . . . with the client's case is not sufficient to permit an exception to the rule"); American Bar Foundation, Annotated Code of Professional Responsibility 218 (Maru ed. 1979) and cases discussed therein.

Conclusion

A motion to disqualify counsel under the advocate-witness rule is dependent on the facts, and thus Carter's probable testimony must be flushed out. Based on current information, it is unlikely that a Third Circuit court would find that Carter ought to testify. Our ability to successfully move to disqualify appears significantly greater under the prejudice test. If Carter ought to testify on behalf of his clients or might testify prejudicially to his clients, it might still be possible to move to limit his participation to pro se representation. Moreover, it is possible that even his pro se representation could be barred, if not totally, then at least from trial advocacy.

MEMORANDUM OF LAW

TO: Maureen Kaplan
FROM: Anthony I. Colasurdo
DATE: December 12, 1985
RE: Brian Morgan and Pam Carleton — application of the guest statute to a possible action against Paul McElroy.

Questions Presented

I. WHETHER PASSENGERS WHO HAVE A BUSINESS RELATIONSHIP WITH THE DRIVER OF AN AUTOMOBILE AND HAVE GIVEN HIM INEXPENSIVE CHRISTMAS GIFTS TO THANK HIM FOR DRIVING ARE CONSIDERED PAYING PASSENGERS UNDER THE DELAWARE AUTOMOBILE GUEST STATUTE, WHICH PRECLUDES NONPAYING PASSENGERS IN AN AUTOMOBILE FROM SUING THE DRIVER FOR ORDINARY NEGLIGENCE IN AN ACCIDENT.

II. WHETHER PASSENGERS IN AN AUTOMOBILE HAVE A CAUSE OF ACTION FOR DAMAGES AGAINST THE DRIVER, UNDER THE DELAWARE AUTOMOBILE GUEST STATUTE, FOR INJURIES RESULTING FROM AN ACCIDENT THAT WAS EITHER INTENTIONAL ON THE PART OF THE DRIVER OR CAUSED BY HIS WILLFUL OR WANTON DISREGARD OF THE RIGHTS OF OTHERS BECAUSE THE DRIVER, UNDER CONDITIONS THAT MADE DRIVING HAZARDOUS, DISREGARDED THE WARNING OF A FELLOW MOTORIST THAT THERE WAS DANGER AHEAD.

Brief Answer

Neither the Christmas gifts nor the business relationship provide a benefit to the driver sufficient to qualify as payment within the meaning of the guest statute.

Although the driver's conduct was neither intentional nor in willful disregard of the rights of others, his failure to heed the warning of a fellow motorist that there was danger ahead, under conditions that made driving hazardous, demonstrated a wanton disregard of the rights of his passengers.

Statement of Facts

Brian Morgan and Pam Carleton were passengers in an automobile driven by Paul McElroy. The three friends were returning home from the September meeting of a service organization of business people. McElroy always drives Morgan and Carleton to the meetings, unless his car is in the shop. In previous years, Morgan and Carleton have chipped in together on inexpensive Christmas gifts for McElroy to thank him for driving. The three also have a business relationship. McElroy insures property for both Morgan and Carleton, and he and Carleton refer clients to each other.

Before the night of the meeting it had rained steadily for several days. Driving conditions were very hazardous. When the trio left the meeting, about 11:00 P.M., it was raining heavily. As McElroy's auto neared an approach to the Meannder River Bridge, it was stopped by a fellow motorist, Charlie Wilson. Wilson, who saw rising flood waters when he approached the bridge and was turning to an alternate route, told McElroy that the bridge might be unsafe. McElroy insisted that he traveled over the bridge every day and had done so earlier that night. He turned his car onto the approach which, having been undermined by flood-level waters, collapsed under the weight of the car. The car slid down an embankment, ending up in a wreck at the bottom of the bridge approach. Morgan and Carleton seek to recover for the injuries they sustained in the accident.

Discussion

I. WHETHER PASSENGERS WHO HAVE A BUSINESS RELATIONSHIP WITH THE DRIVER OF AN AUTOMOBILE AND HAVE GIVEN HIM INEXPENSIVE CHRISTMAS GIFTS TO THANK

HIM FOR DRIVING ARE CONSIDERED PAYING PASSENGERS
UNDER THE DELAWARE AUTOMOBILE GUEST STATUTE,
WHICH PRECLUDES NONPAYING PASSENGERS IN AN
AUTOMOBILE FROM SUING THE DRIVER FOR ORDINARY
NEGLIGENCE RESULTING IN AN ACCIDENT.

The guest statute will probably be applied in deciding this case.
Morgan and Carleton appear to be "guests without payment" as
contemplated by the statute. The Delaware Automobile Guest
Statute, Del. Code Ann. tit. 21, sec. 6101(a) (1979), provides that
"No person transported by the . . . operator of a motor vehicle . . . as his guest without payment for such transportation
shall have a cause of action for damages against such . . . operator for injury" suffered in an accident, unless the accident was
intentional on the part of the operator or was caused by the driver's
willful or wanton disregard of the rights of others. The effect of the
statute is to preclude nonpaying passengers from suing automobile
operators for ordinary negligence. *Gallegher v. Davis*, 183 A. 620,
622 (Del. Super. Ct. 1936). The purpose of the statute is to protect
one who, without receiving any benefit, transports another in his
or her vehicle. *Engle v. Poland*, 91 A.2d 326, 328 (Del. Super. Ct.
1952). The determination of who is to be categorized as nonpaying
passengers or "guests without payment" has been left open to
interpretation by the courts. The language used by the statute is
indefinite and does not specify what constitutes "payment."

As a general rule, the courts have defined payment as a benefit
accruing to the driver. *Foster v. Shropshire*, 375 A.2d 458 (Del.
1977); *Grossi v. Antonelli*, 408 A.2d 293 (Del. Super. Ct. 1979);
Engle v. Poland, 91 A.2d 326 (Del. Super. Ct. 1952). It is not
required that the benefit be material to prevent the guest statute
from applying. However, the benefit to the operator cannot be the
mere pleasure of having the companionship of the passenger during
the trip. *Foster v. Shropshire*, 375 A.2d at 460 (Del. 1977).

In *Engle v. Poland*, 91 A.2d 326 (Del. Super. Ct. 1952), the court
held that a passenger was outside the scope of the automobile guest
statute if there was a reasonable expectation of benefit to the
vehicle operator. The passenger was therefore entitled to recover
damages from the vehicle operator for injuries sustained in an auto
accident caused by the operator's negligence. In that case, the
driver agreed to transport the plaintiff to the plaintiff's mother's
home to spend the night. The following morning, the driver was to
introduce the plaintiff, a salesman, to a prospective buyer in a
nearby town. The plaintiff and the driver agreed that if the plaintiff

made the sale, he would pay the defendant 25 percent of the commission earned. While driving the plaintiff to his mother's house that night, the driver was in an auto accident. The Superior Court reasoned that the transportation was sufficiently connected to the possibility of the driver's earning a commission. The trip had the potential of being financially beneficial to both parties.

In *Grossi v. Antonelli*, 408 A.2d 293 (Del. Super. Ct. 1979), the driver and passenger had been riding around in an automobile for three hours, discussing, in a broad and speculative manner, the possibility of working together on several projects. The passenger argued that the guest statute did not apply because he had a business relationship with the driver. The court disagreed, stating that "the driver could not reasonably expect to receive clearly defined benefit from the passenger's presence." Id. at 294. *Engle* was distinguished on the basis of the agreement between the driver and passenger, made prior to the transportation, that the driver would introduce the passenger to a prospective customer in exchange for a commission if a sale was made. The important factors in *Engle* that prevented the application of the guest statute were: (1) that the agreement was reached before the transportation was provided; and (2) that the agreement was definite in terms of the benefit the driver could expect to derive from providing the transportation. In *Grossi*, the driver and passenger had no agreement before the automobile ride that defined the benefits the driver could expect to receive.

In *Foster v. Shropshire*, 375 A.2d 458 (Del. 1977), the driver and the passenger were friends who occasionally went out together. They alternated in providing transportation, and the passenger for the evening did not contribute toward transportation expenses. The trial judge found that receiving free transportation at a later date was payment and a benefit to the driver. Thus the passenger was entitled to recover damages by proving ordinary negligence. The Delaware Supreme Court reversed, holding that the benefit to the driver was social companionship, which did not constitute payment. The court pointed out that in *Mumford v. Robinson*, 231 A.2d 477 (Del. 1967), upon which the trial court had relied, the benefit to the driver was not only the social companionship of the passenger. The driver also received free sewing instructions, a benefit that people usually pay for. In refusing to extend the concept of benefit to the driver to the *Foster* case, the Supreme Court referred to its decision in *Justice v. Gatchell*, 325 A.2d 97 (Del. 1974), where the court expressed its disapproval of the judicial creation of exceptions to the guest statute.

The cited cases provide ample support for application of the guest statute to this case. McElroy did not derive any benefit from driving Morgan and Carleton to the meetings, other than having the pleasure of their company during the trip. The only possible arguments that he did derive any benefit are: (1) that the Christmas gifts given to McElroy by Morgan and Carleton constitute payment for driving them to the meetings; and (2) that McElroy benefited from the business relationship he had with Morgan and Carleton.

The Christmas gifts do not satisfy the criteria of a benefit to the driver established by the cases. McElroy had no reasonable expectation of receiving the gifts, which were inexpensive in any case. There was no agreement between the parties before the transportation was provided that stipulated that McElroy would receive Christmas gifts or any other form of payment from Morgan and Carleton. Indeed, the gifts were intended by the passengers as a small token of their appreciation for the free transportation they had received. The gifts were given to McElroy after the transportation had already been provided and were not an incentive to McElroy to provide rides to future meetings. Further, Christmas gifts are not benefits that people usually pay for. There is little doubt that McElroy would have continued providing transportation to the meetings even if he had not received the gifts from Morgan and Carleton.

Likewise, the business relationship McElroy had with Morgan and Carleton was not sufficient to warrant the finding of a benefit to McElroy that would preclude the guest statute from applying. McElroy insures properties of both Morgan and Carleton. However, there is no indication that either of the passengers do business with McElroy only because he provides them with transportation to the business meetings. There is also no reason to believe that they would insure their properties elsewhere if McElroy stopped driving to the meetings. In addition to having her property insured by McElroy, Carleton refers clients to McElroy, and he refers clients to her. Again, however, there is no reason for McElroy to expect Carleton to refer clients to him because he provides her with transportation to the meetings. This reciprocal referral of client arises out of a relationship between McElroy and Carleton that is wholly independent of their relationship as driver and passenger. Finally, it might be argued that McElroy could benefit, in the form of a commission, if either Morgan or Carleton makes a business contact at one of the meetings. However, such an argument would be pure speculation. There is no agreement between the parties that provides for any commission to be paid.

II. WHETHER PASSENGERS IN AN AUTOMOBILE HAVE A CAUSE
OF ACTION FOR DAMAGES AGAINST THE DRIVER UNDER
THE DELAWARE AUTOMOBILE GUEST STATUTE FOR
INJURIES RESULTING FROM AN ACCIDENT THAT WAS
INTENTIONAL ON THE PART OF THE DRIVER OR THAT WAS
CAUSED BY HIS WILLFUL OR WANTON DISREGARD OF THE
RIGHTS OF OTHERS WHERE THE DRIVER, UNDER
CONDITIONS THAT MADE DRIVING HAZARDOUS,
DISREGARDED THE WARNING OF A FELLOW MOTORIST
THAT THERE WAS DANGER AHEAD.

Morgan and Carleton will probably be able to sustain their
action for damages for injuries they suffered in the auto accident.
The guest statute will probably apply to the present situation,
thereby precluding the plaintiffs from recovering for ordinary negligence on the part of the driver, McElroy. However, the passengers may be able to argue successfully that McElroy acted in
wanton disregard of their rights.

Once the court finds that the guest statute applies to a situation,
the passengers can only recover damages if the accident was intentional on the part of the driver or was caused by the driver's "willful
or wanton disregard of the rights of others." Delaware Automobile
Guest Statute, Del. Code Ann. tit. 21, sec. 6101(a) (1979). Judging
from the facts of this case, it appears that the driver's conduct was
neither intentional nor in willful disregard of the rights of others.
An intentional accident is a happening or event purposely brought
about. *Gallegher v. Davis,* 183 A. 620, 622 (Del. Super. Ct. 1936).
Similarly, willfulness is characterized by purpose or design. It includes the actual intent to cause injury. Id. There is no indication
here that McElroy purposely caused the accident or that he intended to cause injury to his passengers. It is quite possible, however, that he acted in wanton disregard of the rights of his
passengers.

The elements of a wanton act include consciousness of one's
conduct, realization of the probability of injury to another, and
disregard of the consequences. *Gallegher v. Davis,* 183 A. 620, 622
(Del. Super. Ct. 1936). Thus, the court in *Gallegher* refused to find
that the driver's conduct was in wanton disregard of the rights of
others. The only allegation of wantonness was that the driver
operated his vehicle at a very high rate of speed. The court pointed
out that excessive speed in itself does not constitute wanton conduct. Many drivers may not realize that there is a high probability
that their conduct will result in injury to their passengers. These
drivers are not deliberately acting in disregard of the safety of

others, they are merely unaware of the consequences of their actions.

When the supreme court took up the case of *Gallegher* on appeal, it framed a definition of wanton conduct. Wanton conduct is "such conduct as exhibits a conscious indifference to consequences in circumstances where probability of harm to another . . . is reasonably apparent, although harm to such other is not intended." *Law v. Gallegher,* 39 Del. 189, 194-195; 197 A. 479, 482 (1938).

In *Wilson v. Tweed,* 209 A.2d 899 (Del. 1965), the supreme court adopted the rule stated in *Wagner v. Shanks,* 194 A.2d 701, 706 (Del. 1963), which described conscious indifference as being evidenced by performance of "an act which is so unreasonable and dangerous" that the actor "either knows or should know that there is an eminent likelihood of harm which can result." 209 A.2d at 901. On that basis, the *Wilson* court reversed a summary judgment granted in favor of the defendant-driver by the Superior Court. It held that an issue of fact existed regarding whether the driver's conduct constituted wanton disregard of the rights of his passenger. In that case, the driver made a left-hand turn, intending to cross the oncoming lanes of a four-lane highway. When the driver began making his turn, an oncoming vehicle was only 50 to 60 feet away and was approaching at 50 miles per hour. The driver thought he had a chance to get across, but either did not hear or did not heed a warning against turning that his wife shouted to him. The driver turned his vehicle directly into the path of the oncoming automobile and was struck broadside. Based on these facts, the Court reasoned that the jury could reasonably conclude that the driver's conduct was unreasonable and dangerous and that he knew or should have known of a likelihood of harm to his passengers. Such a finding by the jury would indicate a conscious indifference or "I don't care" attitude to consequences on the part of the driver and would render his conduct to be wanton. See *McHugh v. Brown,* 125 A.2d 583, 586 (Del. 1956).

In *Wilson v. Tweed,* 209 A.2d 899 (Del. 1965), the Court did not indicate that the warning shouted by the driver's wife was the particular factor that influenced its determination in the case. However, the importance of the warning to the *Wilson* court's finding is revealed in the reasoning of the supreme court in *Foster v. Shropshire,* 375 A.2d 458 (Del. 1977). In *Foster,* the defendant-driver was attempting to pass a tractor trailer when her car began to shake and swerve. Nevertheless, her foot remained on the accelerator. She lost control of the vehicle, it left the highway and overturned. The driver had had three drinks prior to the accident, but there was nothing to support a conclusion that she was intoxicated. The court held that these facts did not indicate the conscious indifference to the consequences that is characteristic of wanton conduct. The passenger contended, however, that the evidence was sufficient to submit the issue of wantonness to the jury, based on the supreme court's decision in *Wilson*. The *Foster* court disagreed and distinguished *Wilson,* stating, "In *Wilson,* the defendant-driver chose to turn into the path of an oncoming car *despite an explicit warning*" and that "such action manifested a conscious indifference to consequences." 375 A.2d at 461 (emphasis added). No similar disregard was found to exist on the part of the driver in *Foster.* It is evident, then, that the supreme court relied heavily in its opinion in the *Wilson* case on the warning given to the driver by his wife prior to the accident.

In the present case, McElroy's conduct was probably in wanton disregard of the rights of his passengers. His actions demonstrated a conscious indifference to consequences in circumstances where it was reasonably apparent that probability of harm existed.

McElroy's failure to heed the warning of a fellow motorist that the bridge might be unsafe reflects a conscious indifference to consequences or an "I don't care" attitude. In light of the weather conditions, he was already taking part in an activity that could be considered dangerous. The hazardous driving conditions dictated a need for caution on the part of the driver. Thus, in the face of the need for such caution, McElroy's disregard of the warning he received concerning the bridge was unreasonable. The warning should have made McElroy aware of the consequences of going further. McElroy proceeded, acting in disregard of possible harmful consequences. The supreme court has previously recognized such conduct as being in wanton disregard of the rights of others.

McElroy may argue that he did not demonstrate a conscious indifference to consequences by ignoring the warning of a fellow motorist. McElroy had no reason to rely on the warning. The fellow motorist was not a figure of authority — a police officer or bridge operator. There was no road block set up or warning signs posted. Besides, McElroy had encountered no problems when he had traveled over the bridge earlier that night. This argument might be persuasive had it not been for the poor weather conditions. When driving conditions are hazardous, as was the case here, the driver must exercise a high degree of caution. In exercising such caution, a driver must be sensitive to any indication that danger may lie ahead. Thus, McElroy may have been justified in ignoring a warning by a fellow motorist under normal conditions. However, under the circumstances of the present case, McElroy should have given the fellow motorist the benefit of the doubt and taken heed of his warning.

Conclusion

The guest statute will be applied to the present situation, thereby precluding an action by the passengers against the driver for ordinary negligence. However, the passengers will be able to sustain a cause of action under the statute for the driver's wanton disregard of their rights. The statute applies because the passengers were nonpaying guests in the driver's automobile. The driver did not receive any benefit from the passengers' presence which would usually be paid for. Nor did the driver have a reasonable expectation of receiving a clearly defined benefit.

The guest statute does allow recovery when a driver acts in wanton disregard of the rights of a nonpaying passenger. The driver's conduct here was wanton because he ignored a warning of impending danger under conditions that dictated a need for caution. Thus, he demonstrated a conscious indifference to consequences when it was reasonably apparent that probability of harm existed.

10

Writing an Appellate Brief

A What Is an Appellate Brief?

An appellate brief is a written argument designed to persuade an appellate court that your position on the case on appeal is the correct one. If you are the appellant, your brief argues that the lower court made errors in its decision on a particular case and that these errors were prejudicial. If you are the appellee, you argue that there were no prejudicial errors and that the lower court's decision should stand. A brief states the facts of the case, identifies the relevant issues, and presents an argument that is supported by statutes, regulations, and precedent. Every section of a brief is written to persuade: The facts of the case are written so that they present the writer's position in the best light, the issues are drafted so that they optimize the writer's argument, and so on. The entire brief must convince the court that the analysis of facts and law and the conclusions in the brief are sound and should be adopted. In addition, a brief serves as a reference for the court. It should contain a list of relevant cases and statutes and a well-documented analysis of the pertinent issues.

There is no rigid formula for the format of a brief. Courts in each jurisdiction usually have their own rules, and these rules range from requiring a highly structured and specific brief to requiring a brief whose structure is fairly discretionary. You will see some variation in both the labels and formats of the examples in this chapter, since the examples are from real documents.

This chapter is divided into two parts. The first part is an outline for a brief, followed by explanations of each section of the brief; the second part consists of two sample briefs. The first brief was actually submitted to the

Supreme Court: You may recognize the case. The second brief was prepared by a student for Moot Court Competition. Keep in mind that there are entire texts written on the subject of brief-writing and that there are many schools of thought on how an appellate case should be presented to a tribunal. The strategies used in brief-writing are as varied and complex as the strategies used in presenting a trial. Thus, you should regard this outline as a useful, but not necessarily universal, conceptual framework for a brief.

B The Structure of a Brief

1. Outline

Cover page
Table of Contents
Table of Authorities
Opinions Below
Jurisdictional Statement
Questions presented
      Question 1
      Question 2
Statement of the Facts
Argument
      Analysis of Question 1
      Analysis of Question 2
Conclusion

2. Explanation of the Parts of a Brief

a. *Cover Page*

The *cover page* should include the name of the appellate court, the number assigned to the appeal, the parties' names, the name of the lower court that rendered the decision that is being appealed, a description of the kind of brief that is being submitted (appellee's or appellant's brief), and a list of the attorneys who are submitting the brief. See Figure 10-1 for an example of a cover page from a brief that was submitted to the United States Supreme Court:

FIGURE 10-1

No. 79-121

In the
Supreme Court of the United States

OCTOBER TERM, 1979

UNITED STATES OF AMERICA,
PETITIONER

v.

BILLY GALE HENRY,
RESPONDENT

ON WRIT OF CERTIORARI TO THE UNITED STATES COURT OF
APPEALS FOR THE FOURTH CIRCUIT

BRIEF FOR THE UNITED STATES (PETITIONER)

WADE H. MCCREE, JR.
Solicitor General
PHILIP B. HEYMAN
Assistant Attorney General
ANDREW L. FREY
Assistant Attorney General
EDWIN S. KNEEDLER
Assistant to the Solicitor General
DAVID B. SMITH
Attorney
Department of Justice
Washington, D.C. 20530

b. *Table of Contents*

The *table of contents* lists the major parts of the brief and shows the page number on which each part can be found. The list includes all of the section divisions of the brief, as well as the headings and subheadings of the writer's argument.

Not only does the table of contents serve as a reference tool for quickly finding information within the brief, but informative headings and subheadings provide the reader with an overview of the writer's argument. Well constructed headings can do a great deal to persuade the reader, since they present a logical map of the steps in the writer's reasoning. Here is a sample table of contents from a brief written for the Supreme Court:

Table of Contents

c. *Table of Authorities*

The *table of authorities* lists, in separate categories, all of the cases, statutes, regulations, and miscellaneous sources (such as law review articles and treatises) used to support the attorney's arguments. These are listed with full citations and references to every page in the brief on which they appear. Some courts may require that the most important citations be starred. Here is an example of part of a table of authorities. A full table of authorities may be considerably longer.

Table of Authorities

Cases

*Aguilar v. Texas, 378 U.S. 108 (1964)	5
Barnes v. State, 25 Wis. 2d 116, 130 N.W.2d 264 (1964)	5
*Katz v. United States, 389 U.S. 347 (1967)	5, 6
*Terry v. Ohio, 392 U.S. 1 (1968)	7
United States v. Robinson, 414 U.S. 218 (1973)	8

U.S. Constitution

Fourth Amendment	2, 4, 5, 7, 8
Article VI	10

Statutes

26 U.S.C. 174	2, 9

Miscellaneous

Tribe, *American Constitutional Law* 20 (1978)	11

d. *Opinions Below*

A brief may include a section that tells the reader where to find any published lower court opinions on the case. Here is an example from a Supreme Court brief.

Opinions Below

The opinion of the court of appeals is reported at 590 F.2d 544. The memorandum order of the district court is not reported.

e. *Jurisdictional Statement*

Briefs sometimes include a separate section for general information about the case. This section can include one or more of the following:

1. The statutory basis or the rule under which the court can hear the case
2. The judicial history of the case (any rulings below that are now being appealed, dates of any judgments, etc.)
3. The general nature of the case or summary of the dispute
4. How the case has come before the present court
5. Who the parties are

Here is a sample of a jurisdictional statement.

Jurisdiction

The judgment of the court of appeals was entered on December 26, 1981. The government's petition for rehearing was denied on March 30, 1982. On June 14, 1979, the Chief Justice extended the time within which to file a petition for a writ of certiorari to and including July 28, 1982. The petition was filed on July 25, 1982, and was granted on October 1, 1982. The jurisdiction of this Court is invoked under 28 U.S.C. §1254(1).

f. *Questions Presented*

This section may also be called *Legal Issues* or *Issues Presented*. It focuses on the issues of the case that the writer wants the court to consider. The issues are framed as questions. The questions should be one sentence, and they should be concise and worded in a way that presents the writer's argument in the most favorable light. (See Chapter 6 for information on how to do this.) Here is an example of this section.

Questions Presented

1. Does a search warrant that particularly describes the premises to be searched and the occupant of those premises also cover a visitor's purse?
2. Do the circumstances of the petitioner's presence in an apartment where narcotics had been sold provide a basis to search her purse incident to her arrest or in order to prevent her from destroying evidence?

g. *Statement of Facts*

The *statement of facts* may include the information that would otherwise be included in the jurisdictional statement if the format does not require that jurisdictional information be placed in its own separate section. In addition, this section must state the facts of the case. Some attorneys consider this the most important section of a brief, since it can set the tenor for the rest of the document.

The facts should be presented thoroughly and accurately but concisely. The statement should include everything that is relevant but should emphasize favorable information and de-emphasize unfavorable information in order to present the facts in the light most favorable to the writer's position.

Here are examples of fact statements from opposing appellate briefs. The first version was written by the respondent, who is claiming that the petitioner's sentence is constitutional. The second version was written by the petitioner, who is claiming that the petitioner's sentence violates the Eighth Amendment prohibition against cruel and unusual punishment.

Respondent's
Statement of Facts

In January of 1973, a Texas grand jury indicted the petitioner for the felony offense of obtaining money under false pretenses. The indictment alleged that the petitioner had twice before been convicted of similar felonies. The petitioner pled not guilty to obtaining the money under false pretenses, but a jury of his peers found him guilty as charged. After the state proved his two prior convictions, the petitioner received an enhanced sentence of "life imprisonment" under the Texas habitual criminal statute then in force, Texas Penal Code Ann. §12.42(d) (Vernon 1974), a statute designed specifically for repeat offenders.

Petitioner's
Statement of Facts

In 1964, the petitioner was convicted of using a credit card with the intent to defraud in the amount of approximately $80. The petitioner served time for this offense. In 1969, a full five years later, the petitioner was convicted of passing a forged instrument worth $28.36. Again, the petitioner served time for the offense. Finally, in January of 1973, four years after the second offense, the petitioner was indicted for the offense of obtaining $120.75 under false pretenses. The petitioner pled not guilty, but was convicted by a jury. For sentencing purposes, the state proved the two prior convictions. In spite of the nonviolent nature of the crimes, the insubstantial amounts of money involved in each, and the fact that the crimes were substantially separated in time, the three offenses were considered felonies under Texas law in 1979. As a result, the petitioner received a sentence of life imprisonment under the Texas habitual criminal statute that was in effect at the time. Tex. Penal Code Ann. §12.42(d) (Vernon 1974).

Notice the difference in emphasis in the two versions. In the respondent's fact statement, the author begins with the most immediate offense, providing few details about it, but pointing out that it was a felony offense. The author immediately ties the present offense to the petitioner's past offenses. These are not described in detail either, but the author points out that they were also felonies. The emphasis on the similarity of the felonies suggests that the petitioner is incorrigible and that he will continue periodically to commit the same kind of felony if he is not finally stopped by a new, specially designed penalty that will keep him away from society. Finally, the author mentions that the statute under which the petitioner received the life sentence was designed specifically for repeat offenders. The respondent's fact statement focuses on the conditions for applying a rule and on how the petitioner's actions fit the conditions for applying the rule — almost an abstract exercise.

The petitioner's fact statement, on the other hand, presents information about the offenses in a chronological order — as though the author is telling the petitioner's story. The story stresses many of the details of each offense: that the amounts involved in all three amounted to little more than $250, that in nine years the petitioner committed only three offenses, and that the offenses were nonviolent. The author also points out that the plaintiff has already served time for two of the offenses, implying that this new sentence may, in a way, cause the petitioner to be penalized twice. In total, the fact statement paints a picture of the petitioner as a "small timer" who periodically commits minor offenses that happen to be classified as felonies. The petitioner's fact statement focuses on the specifics of the case to help the reader see that an attempt to fit the petitioner's actions to the conditions for applying the rule will lead to an unjust result.

h. *Argument*

The *argument* is the heart of the appellate brief and contains the writer's analysis of the issues that the writer identified in the questions presented. The argument is broken into sections, with each section devoted to a single legal issue. The sections are identified by headings or subheadings that present the writer's conclusions or assert an answer (either positive or negative) to the questions that were presented earlier in the brief. For example, the sample question presented in the Questions Presented section:

> Does a search warrant that particularly describes the premises to be searched and the occupant of those premises also cover a visitor's purse?

would be rephrased as follows:

> A search warrant that particularly describes the premises to be searched and the occupant of those premises would also cover a visitor's purse.

It would be difficult to present an example of an argument section of a brief in this outline. Be sure to look at that section in the sample briefs at the end of this chapter. In addition, refer to Chapter 6 for information on how to construct a convincing legal argument.

i. *Conclusion*

The writer's analysis of each legal issue should be followed by a brief summary of the analysis, a conclusion, and a description of the action the court should take on the basis of the analysis. At the end of the brief, the writer should present a final conclusion that does not summarize the arguments under each issue, but asks the court to take certain actions. For example:

> For the foregoing reasons, the respondent respectfully requests that the judgment of the Supreme Court of Virginia be affirmed.

C Writing an Appellate Brief: Two Examples

Following are two sample briefs. *Larkin v. Grendel's Den, Inc.*, which was actually submitted to the Supreme Court, has not been edited at all. We chose this brief because its organization and reasoning are excellent. However, some of the sentence structures and other grammatical constructions in it are highly complex. Only a skilled writer like Professor Tribe, writing for a sophisticated audience such as the Supreme Court, can carry off this style of writing.

National Audubon Society v. Clark, a very good brief prepared by a student for moot court, has been lightly edited in a few places. The page numbers in the tables of both briefs have been changed to refer to the page numbers of this book.

No. 81-878

In the
Supreme Court of the United States

OCTOBER TERM, 1981

JOHN P. LARKIN, ET AL.,

v. *Appellants,*

GRENDEL'S DEN, INC.,

Appellee.

ON APPEAL FROM AN *en banc* JUDGMENT OF THE
UNITED STATES COURT OF APPEALS FOR THE FIRST
CIRCUIT

BRIEF OF APPELLEE

LAURENCE H. TRIBE,
1525 Massachusetts Avenue,
Cambridge, Massachusetts 02138.
(617) 495-4621
Counsel of Record.

IRA KARASICK,
206 Fifth Avenue,
New York, New York
DAVID ROSENBERG,
1525 Massachusetts Avenue,
Cambridge, Massachusetts 02138.
Counsel for Appellee.

Question Presented

May a state delegate to each "church or synagogue . . . dedicated to divine worship" an unfettered governmental power to decide which restaurants, liquor stores, and bars may be licensed to serve or sell alcoholic beverages within a 500-foot radius of the religious body's premises?

Table of Contents

Table of Authorities Cited

CASES

CONSTITUTIONAL AND STATUTORY PROVISIONS

MISCELLANEOUS

N. Sykes, Church and State in England in the Eighteenth
Century 188 (1934)   249

W. Walker, The Creeds and Platforms of Congregationalism (1893)   244

S. & B. Webb, The History of Liquor Licensing, Principally
From 1700 to 1830, Vol. 11 of English Local Government 34-39, 64, 69-74, 80-81 (1903)   246

Webster's Third New International Dictionary of the English Language, Unabridged 663 (1981)   247

Roger Williams, "The Bloody Tenet of Persecution"
(1647)   245

17 C. Wright, A. Miller & E. Cooper, Federal Practice and
Procedure 40 (1978)   251

No. 81-878

In the
Supreme Court of the United States

OCTOBER TERM, 1981

JOHN P. LARKIN, ET AL.,

v.   *Appellants,*

GRENDEL'S DEN, INC.,

Appellee.

ON APPEAL FROM AN *en banc* JUDGMENT OF THE
UNITED STATES COURT OF APPEALS FOR THE FIRST
CIRCUIT

BRIEF OF APPELLEE

Statement of the Case

At issue in this case is the validity of Massachusetts General Laws
c. 138, §16C (Section 16C), Brief of State Appellants (State Br.)
2a-3a, which delegates to certain churches and synagogues —
those that, in the statute's terms, are "dedicated to divine worship," id. 2a — an ad hoc and absolute veto power over the
approval of each liquor license within a 500-foot radius of the

church or synagogue.[1] Because it is providently located near the intersection of Mt. Auburn and Boylston Streets in Cambridge, and is invested by the State with an unreviewable veto power under Section 16C, the Holy Cross Armenian Catholic Parish Church (Holy Cross Church) can and does exercise absolute regulatory authority over the acquisition of liquor licenses in virtually the entire Harvard Square area.[2]

The relevant facts have been stipulated. J.A. 48-52. In May 1977, after purchasing an existing liquor license, appellee Grendel's Den, Inc. (Grendel's) applied to appellant Cambridge License Commission (CLC) for permission to transfer the license to its Harvard Square restaurant. In a letter sent to the CLC on May 25, Father Luke Arakelian of the Holy Cross Church entered a written objection to Grendel's application, J.A. 53, and on September 8 the State's Alcoholic Beverages Control Commission (ABCC) upheld the CLC's May 31 denial of the license because "the governing body of the church objected to the license of the premises under provisions of Chapter 138, Section 16C and *this represents an absolute veto.*" J.A. 24-25 (emphasis added). The ABCC expressly found "that the church's objection under Section 16C was

---

1. Section 16C also delegates such veto power to public and private schools, including parochial schools. On the prior versions of Section 16C, see n.29, infra. Selling liquor once the veto has been exercised — and one's license accordingly disapproved — is a crime punishable by a fine of up to $1,000 and/or up to 1 year's imprisonment. Mass. G.L. c. 138, §2.

2. Indeed, the absolutely unchecked nature of the regulatory power granted the Church under §16C, as authoritatively construed by the state's highest court, Arno v. Alcoholic Beverages Control Commission, 377 Mass. 83, 90, 384 N.E.2d 1223, 1228 (Mass. 1979), is made painfully obvious by appellants' answers to appellee's interrogatories 11 and 12. J.A. 32-38. Asked whether §16C would allow a church to bar issuance of a license on the basis of the applicant's race, sex, religious affiliation, or political persuasion; on the basis of the applicant's failure to furnish a suitable "donation" to the church; or on the basis of "a pay-off by a competitor of the license applicant," the state appellants themselves, and the Attorney General's office, responded that §16C "does not require the governing body of a church to state *any* reason for its objection to the issuance of a license to sell alcoholic beverages. . . ." J.A. 35, 37-38 (emphasis added).

   At the hearing before the Massachusetts Alcoholic Beverages Control Commission (ABCC), the only commissioners who spoke both agreed that no limits exist on a church's power to veto licenses under §16C. They thus stated that no evidence Grendel's might produce could alter the result, since "it really doesn't make any difference *what* the circumstances are, it [Section 16C] *always* applies when [a church] opposes [an application]." J.A. 63 (emphasis added).

   ABCC Chairman Goodwin succinctly advised Grendel's: "the law mandates their [the Cambridge License Commission's] refusal, and I assume we are in the same position, because we are not going to declare a statute unconstitutional at this level." J.A. 60-61.

the *only* basis on which the transfer was denied." Id. 25 (emphasis added).[3]

Grendel's then brought this action against the state and city appellants in the district court, challenging the validity of Section 16C under the Due Process and Equal Protection Clauses of the Fourteenth Amendment, the Establishment Clause of the First Amendment, and the Sherman Act, 15 U.S.C. §§1, 2, as made controlling by the Supremacy Clause of Article VI. On August 14, 1980, the district court held that Section 16C on its face violated the Due Process and Establishment Clauses, J.S.A. 101A-133A, and further held that the state action exemption to the Sherman Act would provide no bar to a judicial declaration that defendants cannot deny a license under Section 16C where, as Grendel's offered to prove had been the case here, Section 16C's veto had in

---

3. What basis the Church *itself* uses for deciding whether and when to object to the issuance of any given liquor license is less than clear on this record. But see Grendel's Amended Complaint, ¶12, in State's Appendix in Court of Appeals at 5 (alleging that Church requires monetary "contributions" from potential licensees as a prerequisite to not exercising its absolute veto power).

Proximity to the church is clearly *not* the dispositive variable. As was pointed out at the ABCC hearing, Holy Cross Church has opposed liquor licenses for premises located further from the church than others which it has not contested. For example, the church opposed a liquor license for the Swiss Alps Restaurant located at the outer edge of the 500-foot circle, but made no objection to licensing Casa Mexico, right across the street from the Church. J.A. 62-63.

Nor does it seem likely that "abuse" from Grendel's patrons was the touchstone for the church's decision. It is hard to imagine that the quiche-and-salad crowd which frequents Grendel's was a greater threat to the tranquility of church members than the denizens of Whitney's Bar and Grill or Jonathan Swift's Pub, or the clientele of the Harvard Provision Company's package liquor store on the same street (Mt. Auburn), less than one block away. See J.A. 69-72.

To be sure, Grendel's and the Holy Cross Church occupy visually similar brick buildings located on premises sharing a common rear property line. But the ten-foot distance between the two, stressed by appellants, State Br. 14, is wholly illusory, since it describes nothing but the distance between two blank (and quite solid) brick walls, each of which forms the rear of the building involved. Far more than a few drinks would be required to allow any patron of Grendel's to approach the Holy Cross Church by *that* route! Indeed, the sidewalk distance from the *door* of the Church, which is its only public entrance and faces north onto Mt. Auburn Street near its intersection with Boylston Street (one of the busiest motor and pedestrian crossings in Cambridge), to the *entrance* of Grendel's, which faces south on Winthrop Street (a one-block alley), is roughly 400 feet, which greatly exceeds the distance from the church door to several other licensed establishments along Boylston Street, as even a cursory look at the map appended to the back cover of appellant CLC's brief reveals. See also J.A. 69-72.

fact been used by the Church as part of an anti-competitive scheme. Id. 138A-142A.[4]

The First Circuit reversed. *Grendel's I,* J.S.A. 31A-100A. Upon Grendel's petition, however, the court granted rehearing en banc, J.S.A. 149A, and then affirmed the district court's judgment. *Grendel's II,* J.S.A. 1A-30A. The court of appeals recalled that "consistent judicial tradition [holds] that legislation conditioning the receipt of any significant benefit, power, or privilege on the commitment of the members of the recipient group or institution to a religious faith is inherently a 'law respecting an establishment of religion,'" and is therefore void under the Constitution of the United States. Id. 21A. The court reasoned that Section 16C's "non-generalized grant to churches of . . . absolute discretion to confer or withhold an important commercial privilege . . ." squarely violates this long-settled maxim because it "distributes benefits on an *explicitly religious basis.*" Id. 14A-15A (emphasis in original). The grant of "specialized political power" on this basis, id. 12A, the court held, has a "'primary' or 'principal' effect of advancing religion." Id. 23A.[5]

The court also noted that Section 16C would allow its church beneficiaries to "bargain over the sale of . . . an indulgence" with each neighbor who seeks a liquor license. Id. 12A. Whether or not such bargains have been struck, see n.3 supra, it is undisputed that they *might* be; that there are at least twenty-six establishments possessing Massachusetts liquor licenses within the 500-foot circle

---

4. Grendel's argued in the district court that the "state action exemption" to the Sherman Act, announced by this Court in Parker v. Brown, 317 U.S. 341 (1942), did not apply in cases where, as here, the only state action involved routine ratification and implementation of entirely private anti-competitive choices. The district court agreed that, for this reason, the state-action exemption had no application here. J.S.A. 138A-142A. The court of appeals unanimously upheld that conclusion, id. 86A-89A, and appellants have not contested it since. See State Br. 13 n.11. If this case were to proceed to trial, Grendel's antitrust and other "as applied claims [would] remain open for further litigation." Id. 9 n.6.

5. The court was unable to find any possible interpretation of the statute which would *not* violate the Establishment Clause. As the majority put it:

> We are of course aware that, if possible, statutes are to be construed to avoid constitutional defects. But no reasonable reading by us of "church," when expressly defined as "a church or synagogue building dedicated to divine worship," can transform section 16C into a religiously neutral law. . . . We consequently are forced to the conclusion that section 16C's language at the very least distinguishes between religious and nonreligious groups by granting significant rights to the former that it withholds from the latter.

Id. 15A-17A. The court of appeals found it unnecessary, on its en banc rehearing, to reach the due process or antitrust arguments, since the establishment clause flaw in Section 16C was found to be fatal. Id. 9A.

controlled by the Holy Cross Church, J.A. 49; and that at least fourteen of these licenses have been established in the last ten years — the decade throughout which the Holy Cross Church has consistently opposed Grendel's attempt to acquire such a license.[6] Although appellants describe the veto power through which the Church has achieved this result as "a less restrictive alternative to a broad ban on the sale of liquor," State Br. 38; id. 18, it is plain that the challenged delegation of ad hoc veto power establishes a dependence of each applicant upon the holder of such power that a mandatory ban, and even an all-or-nothing ban imposable at the holder's option, would not. In fact, insofar as a selective ban unequally disables Grendel's and unequally aids its nearby competitors, the economic impact of such capricious power upon a restaurant such as Grendel's makes Section 16C far *more* "restrictive" than a uniform ban could possibly be.

Finally, whatever values of tranquility and temperance might be associated with a genuine liquor-free area, any virtue claimed for Section 16C must necessarily be very different: not in living memory has this or any other "million square feet" of Harvard Square, J.S.A. 13A, been the serene and sober retreat that appellants describe Section 16C as designed to secure for those churches and schools that seek to shield their members from "noise and distractions," State Br. 17; *id.* 45, 48, "while they [attend] as well as while they go to and from such facilities." Id. 53, 60; CLC Br. 34.

The precise question posed by this case, therefore, is *not* whether a state may "accommodate the diverse interests of its citizens," State Br. (Question Presented), by directing a public agency to give due weight to their needs and desires to be shielded "from the disturbances associated with the [nearby] distribution and consumption of liquor." Id. The question is whether a state may do so by conferring upon selected private bodies, defined in

---

6. The 500-foot circle that centers upon the objecting church in this case encompasses not only appellee's restaurant but virtually the entire area known as Harvard Square, the celebrated business and entertainment center of Cambridge. Curiously, even the initial First Circuit decision reversing the district court's judgment, see J.S.A. 31A, seems to have acknowledged that the Constitution would bar giving churches "power to 'veto' licensing within an excessively broad radius such as five miles." Id. 79A n.9. But if five miles is "excessively broad," it is a mystery why a radius sufficient to engulf nearly all of Harvard Square is not. Indeed, the present law has the very effect the First Circuit initially condemned, since virtually every major commercial and entertainment area in Massachusetts is within 500 feet of *some* church. At all events, the gist of Grendel's challenge to Section 16C is that it entrusts governmental power to churches. The particular *radius* of the sphere of influence thereby ceded to religious bodies — whether ten feet or ten miles — is constitutionally immaterial: the First and Fourteenth Amendments were not, after all, written with straightedge and compass.

terms of their religious aim and character, an ultimate and unreviewable governmental power to forbid otherwise lawful private activities, and otherwise permissible uses of private property, on whatever grounds such private bodies deem appropriate — including grounds that would clearly be forbidden to the state itself.

Summary of Argument

Conferring upon church leaders the uncontrolled power, within a 500-foot radius, to decide who may serve or sell liquor to whom invests ecclesiastical officials with governmental authority in clear contravention of the ban on state establishment of religion under the First and Fourteenth Amendments.

This violation is aggravated by the narrow, discriminatory, and content-based definition of the religious bodies to whom such political power is entrusted: only those devoted to the worship of God are eligible.

Nor would this delegation of veto power have been constitutional even if the favored class had included all religious groups, or even all private bodies arguably in need of nearby tranquility. For the submission of personal liberty and private property to the standardless and unreviewable control of *any* private body independently violates due process.

Finally, it is beside the point to ground the state's delegation of such control in the Tenth Amendment or in the Twenty-first. Neither of these sources of state authority confers upon any state a license to ignore the First and Fourteenth Amendments, or to delegate governmental power in derogation of these constitutional protections.

I. By Investing Selected Church Officials with Coercive Civil Authority, Section 16C Restores the Ill-Fated "Fusion of Governmental and Religious Functions"[7] That the Establishment Clause was Specifically Designed to Forbid.

Despite appellants' repeated insistence that Section 16C involves none of the evils against which the Establishment Clause was directed, State Br. 19, 47, 49; CLC Br. 28, 33, 39-40, or that its violation of the Establishment Clause is at worst de minimis, State Br. 54, 57; CLC Br. 39, it is hard to imagine a law more precisely or completely embodying *the* central evil of establishment: "religious . . . control over our democratic processes," *Wolman* v.

7. Abington School District v. Schempp, 374 U.S. 203, 222 (1963).

Walter, 433 U.S. 229, 263 (1977) (Powell, J., concurring and dissenting), in which a "concert or union" of "Church and State," *Zorach* v. *Clauson,* 343 U.S. 306, 312 (1952), links "priesthood and magistracy in arbitrary rule." B. Bailyn, Ideological Origins of the American Revolution 98-99 n.3 (1967) (discussing Americans' "[f]ear of the conjunction of civil and ecclesiastical tyrannies").[8] As

8. Eighteenth-century Americans tended to associate the concept of an "established" church with the danger of *political oppression,* not simply with a denial of *religious freedom.* Indeed, to many Americans in the years immediately preceding the Revolution, "the only use of an established church and clergy in society . . . [was] to enforce obedience to civil sanctions." Bailyn 253 (quoting Patrick Henry). For these people, like the famous Boston clergyman Jonathan Mayhew, English churchmen and the whole established church itself were merely instruments for "establishing a tyranny over the bodies and souls of men." Jonathan Mayhew, quoted in Bailyn 97. As the philosopher David Hume had expressed it, established churchmen were "enemies to liberty" and mere tools of "despotic power." D. Hume, Of the Parties of Great Britain, reprinted in C. Hendel, ed., David Hume's Political Essays 86-87 (1953 ed.).

Because Americans of the Revolutionary period were so profoundly distrustful of both political and religious authority, the most awful oppression for them would combine both. To John Adams and others, the conjoining of "temporal and spiritual tyranny" spelled a fate totally "calamitous to human liberty." J. Adams, Works III, 450-451 (1851). And by far "the worst possible calamity a people could suffer would be the fusing of the canon law and feudal (aristocratic) law into [what Adams called] 'a wicked confederacy'" which would lead to "'civil and political slavery.'" C. Bridenbaugh, Mitre and Sceptre 237 (1962), quoting John Adams, Works III, at 449-450, 462. It was "a hatred, a dread, a horror, of the infernal confederacy [between civil and ecclesiastical law] . . . that [originally] projected, conducted, and accomplished the settlement of America." J. Adams, A Dissertation on the Feudal and Canon Law, in Works III, at 451. This confederacy, after all, was the same one that had created the "oppressions" that drove Americans out of England in the seventeenth century; now, in the 1760s and 1770s, the same confederacy was seeking "to enslave all America." John Adams, quoted in Bailyn 98 n.3; Bridenbaugh 245, 280.

Perhaps the most obvious symbol to Americans of the dreaded combination of civil and church authority was the proposal circulated throughout the colonies that an Anglican Bishop be appointed for America. In the early 1760s, there were "profound fears" and "growing anxiety" "that an American episcopate was about to be established." Bailyn 96, 255. Americans could still remember the virtually absolute power commanded by Anglican Archbishop Laud in the early seventeenth century through his political influence, his persecutions, and his ecclesiastical courts; they had come to "dread the Establishment of Bishops [sic] Courts" in America that would place their "civil liberties . . . in eminent [sic] danger," and they noted how seldom Bishops in general had "been favourable either to the religious or civil rights of mankind." Letters of John Rodgers and Micajah Towgood to Jonathan Mayhew, quoted in Bridenbaugh 243, 281.

Americans in fact came to view the episcopacy proposal as part of England's overall political and economic plan for subjugating the colonies, linking the proposal in their minds to the economic Stamp Tax placed on various commercial items. To them, "the Stamping and Episcopizing [of] our Colonies were . . . only different Branches of the same Plan of Power." *St. James Chronicle,* March 22, 1766. Ultimately, "[r]eligion and politics could never again be distinguished one from another after the uproar created in the colonies by the Stamp Act." Bridenbaugh 260.

the Revolutionary crisis progressed, Americans viewed every attempt to place governmental power at the disposal of a church as a dangerous consolidation of civil and ecclesiastical authority and as the very worst sort of "establishment" of religion. The *crucial* evil in creating such an established church, as far as the colonists were concerned, was not necessarily that people would be forced to submit to its *theological* beliefs, but that *governmental power*— the power of the state — would be placed at the church's service and command. See n.8 supra. In the Quebec Act of 1774, for example, the primary purpose of the British Government was "to accord some privileges to the Catholic Church, principally the right to sue for the collection of tithes." L. Pfeffer, Church, State, and Freedom 157 (1967). The Catholics were not granted monopoly status, nor was anyone required to submit to their beliefs; in fact, Protestantism "still retained principal government favor." Id. 158. Yet Americans were quick to attack the Act, claiming that its effect was to " '*establish* the Popish religion.' " Id. (emphasis added). In its list of grievances against Parliament in 1774, the Continental Congress gave a prominent place to the Act " 'for *establishing* the Roman Catholic religion in the province of Quebec.' " Id. (emphasis added). The historical evidence thus makes plain that late eighteenth century Americans treated as objectionable "establishments" those legal arrangements that placed government power in church hands or provided for government enforcement of church decisions.

The legislative history of the Establishment Clause likewise confirms that, in prohibiting establishments of religion, the Framers sought more than merely to safeguard freedom of conscience. The following two alternative versions of the First Amendment were proposed in the Senate but rejected:

Congress shall make no law establishing one Religious Sect or society in preference to others, or prohibiting the free exercise thereof, nor shall the rights of conscience be infringed;

and

Congress shall make no law establishing any particular denomination or religion in preference to another, or prohibiting the free exercise thereof, nor shall the right of conscience be infringed.

Journal of the First Session of the United States Senate, p. 70 (September 3, 1789). If preferential treatment of one religion over another, and invasion of religious freedom of choice, were the only evils the Framers wanted to prohibit, either of these versions would have sufficed, and each indeed seems to convey this limited meaning far more clearly and explicitly than does the broad version which the Framers ultimately adopted.

Thus, the very use of the term "establishment of religion," as opposed to either of the narrower options, corroborates what the record of the Revolution and its concerns compellingly suggests — namely, that the First Amendment was intended to do more than simply protect Americans from direct or indirect compulsion to worship at, or contribute to, churches not of their choosing; it was designed as well, and indeed centrally, to prevent precisely the type of oppression, resulting from a combination of church and state authority, that they had feared and fought so long. Its "object . . . was to create a complete and permanent separation of the spheres of religious activity and civil authority," *Abington,* 374 U.S. at 217, quoting from the dissent of Justices Rutledge, Frankfurter, Jackson, and Burton in *Everson* v. *Board of Education,* 330 U.S. 1, 31-32 (1947).

Indeed, even the Massachusetts Bay Colony, which had perhaps the strongest established church in America during the colonial and Revolutionary periods, insisted from its earliest days on separating the secular tools of civil power from the spiritual authority of the church.[9] What is most significant for present purposes is that

---

9. The colonists in early Massachusetts, as well as the other colonies, deliberately and overtly separated the powers available to their civil and church authorities. In fact, most colonies created a "double jurisdiction" of church and state, so that any given misdeed would be dealt with separately by each institution. Thus, Anne Hutchinson was tried twice — once by the church and once by the colonial government — for her supposed blasphemy. G. L. Haskins, Law and Authority in Early Massachusetts 89 (1960). The church could *censure* Robert Keayne for "making excessive profits on the sale of goods," id. 90, but at the same time "[n]o church censure" could "degrad [sic] or depose any man from any Civill dignitie, office, or Authoritie he shall have in the Commonwealth." Liberties of the Massachusetts Colony ¶60 (1641). And while the "civill Authoritie hath power and libertie to see the peace, ordinances, and Rules of Christ observed in every church," it could do so only *"in a Civill and not in an Ecclesiastical way."* Liberties of the Massachusetts Colony ¶58 (emphasis added).

The Massachusetts church leadership clearly recognized this concept of "double jurisdiction" in its synods and official doctrines. The Cambridge Synod and Platform of 1648, for example, stated categorically that "Church-government stands in no opposition to civil government of comon-welths, nor any intrencheth upon the authority of Civil Magistrates in their jurisdictions." It was "unlawfull for church-officers to meddle with the sword of the Magistrate," or for the Magistrates to intrude upon the domain of the churchmen or "to compell their subjects to become church-members." The Cambridge Synod and Platform (1648), reprinted in W. Walker, The Creeds and Platforms of Congregationalism 235-236 (1893).

Virginia had a similar system of separating the exercise of civil and church power. The first meeting of the General Assembly in 1619, for example, passed a law which provided that if an individual were found drunk "for the first time he is

the despotic "fusion of governmental and religious functions," *Abington*, 374 U.S. at 222, from which the Framers and their forebears fled was in fact exemplified in significant part by *practices in England that were nearly identical to those reenacted on American soil by Section 16C*, although such practices had been rejected even in the American colonies that harbored established churches around the time of the Revolution. These practices involved legal arrangements which gave Anglican church officials direct control over the occupational liberty of groups as diverse as doctors and alehouse-keepers,[10] specifically delegating to selected churchmen the absolute power to veto individual liquor licenses in their vicinities whenever they might choose to do so. See 26 George II c. 31,

---

to be reprooved *privately by the Minister*, and second time, *publiquely*, the third time to lye in boltes 12 houres in the House of the Provost Marshall & to paye his fees, and if he still continue in that vice, to undergo such severe *punishment, as the Governor & Councell of Estate shall think fitt* to be inflicted on him." Laws Bearing Upon Religion and Moral Conduct, And Concerning The Indians Adopted at The First Meeting of the General Assembly in 1619, reprinted in G. M. Brydon, 1 Virginia's Mother Church and the Political Conditions Under Which it Grew 422 (1947) (emphasis added). Thus, ministers played a role in maintaining discipline throughout society, but when the instruments of civil power — most specifically, severe punishments — were involved, the civil authorities had to make the final determination.

Even Roger Williams, as a dissenter in Massachusetts and then as founder of Rhode Island, where there was no established church, believed in a rigid separation between the tools and tactics available to magistrates and ministers. To Williams, "the *conscience* of the *Civill Magistrate* . . . bound [him] to preserve the *civill* peace and quiet of the *place* and people under him," but "[t]o batter downe *Idolatry, false worship, heresie, schisme, blindnesse, hardnesse* . . . [those] *spirituall strong holds* in the soules of men, *Spirituall Artillery* and *weapons* are proper . . . [and] civill *weapons* are improper . . . and never able to effect ought in the *soule*." Roger Williams, The Bloody Tenet of Persecution (1647), reprinted in 1 P. Miller and T. Johnson, The Puritans 222-223 (1963) (emphasis in original). See also n.12 infra.

10. Church officials in England appear to have exerted extensive control over various occupations since the early sixteenth century. A law of 1511, for example, provided that "no person within the city of London" could hold the position of physician or surgeon "except he be first examined, approved, and admitted by the Bishop of London, or by the Dean of St. Paul's for the time being." Meanwhile, any individual wishing to practice medicine outside London was required to "be first examined and approved by the bishop of the same diocese, or . . . by his vicar general." 3 Henry VII c.11 (1511).

By the early seventeenth century, church officials had already been granted certain regulatory and policing powers specifically over the *liquor trade* and over *liquor use*. A 1623 law charged churchwardens, among several other groups, with reporting unlicensed liquor sellers and with prosecuting those licensed alehouse-keepers who served drunken persons within their establishments. 21 James I c.7 (1623). In 1627, churchwardens were assigned the responsibility, along with local constables, of enforcing "An act for the better suppressing of unlicensed alehouse-keepers" and were entrusted with the authority of levying the fines that the Act provided. 3 Charles I c.3 (1627).

Sec. 2 (1753).[11] Thus Section 16C reestablished in modern America a power characteristically conferred in England upon the Established Church but carefully withheld in our colonies even from the churches that had been "established" here. It is difficult to imagine a more direct or dramatic historical demonstration that the "establishments of religion" which the Framers meant to ban did indeed encompass the delegation to churches of power to veto nearby liquor licenses.

But the point would be analytically plain even if the history were less clear. For such veto power entails striking a balance among relevant land-use and other considerations and then enforcing that balance through law upon the entire community. Appellants necessarily concede that this is an inherently legislative task. State Br. 18, 29; CLC Br. 32. Yet, as is plain on the law's face, this legislative task is entrusted by Section 16C not to a body chosen by and accountable to the community but to schools and to those "church[es] or synagogue[s] [that are] dedicated to divine worship." In itself, such a delegation of governmental power to churches inescapably "establishes" religion.[12]

---

11. If ever a page of history could erase whatever doubts logic alone might leave, that page was surely written by England's experience, from the 1750's through the 1790's, in vesting the established clergy with discretionary authority to withhold the certificates of approval required by law whenever local applicants sought licenses to serve liquor. See generally S. & B. Webb, The History of Liquor Licensing, Principally From 1700 To 1830, Vol. 11 of English Local Government 34-39, 64, 69-74, 80-81 (1903). Predictably, "licenses were frequently restricted, in practice to adherents of the dominant sect." Id. 10 n.1; 38 n.1 ("Roman Catholics" denied licenses). The process was one in which the clergy often worked hand-in-hand with Justices of the Peace who were, as one contemporary described them, "men of profligate lives, needy, mean, ignorant, and rapacious." Id. 45; 50 n.1; 117. This "proved corruption of the Justices," id. 95, combined with the Free Trade movement to create strong support for total reform of the liquor licensing process, and the ultimate passage of the perhaps *overly* laissez-faire Beer Act of 1830: "The local veto exercised by the squire, the clergyman, and the principal inhabitants was ruthlessly broken down." Id. 126. It is noteworthy that such power, a major incident of "establishment" for the Church of England, was not resurrected in the colonies. See n.9 supra; n.16 infra.

12. See pp. 9-11 supra; see also Part II infra. In conferring upon churches and synagogues the inherently governmental role of vetoing proposed land uses and effectively confiscating investments in liquor licenses, cf. Jackson v. Metropolitan Edison Co., 419 U.S. 345, 353 (1974) (taking private property is a function "traditionally associated with sovereignty"), Section 16C entrusts "'to religious societies as such a legal agency in carrying into effect a public and civil duty.'" Walz v. Tax Commission, 397 U.S. 664, 712 (1970) (Douglas, J., dissenting) (quoting James Madison). That the decision by a religious body is made conclusive by Section 16C only when the body *exercises* its veto, see J.S.A. 121A-122A (absence of church veto does not guarantee issuance of license), by no means shows that the power delegated is any the less governmental. After all, the veto power of the President under Article I, Section 7, Clause 2, is hardly rendered

Worse, this delegation of power reinforces the classic evils of forbidden establishment by bestowing the state's political bounty on a favored few religious bodies. It is true, as the state appellants observe, that those who gather at the religious institutions favored by Section 16C might play secular music or talk party politics as well as pray. State Br. 51-52, 81. But it is only the "governing bod[ies]" of entities "primarily devoted" to the "worship" of God[13] — a set of institutions defined expressly by the *content* of

---

"non-governmental" in character by the fact that the provision allows the President unilaterally to *doom* legislation that cannot command two-thirds support in the House and Senate, but creates no analogous presidential power to *enact* legislation. If anything, the case with respect to Section 16C is even more compelling, since a church's veto cannot be overridden even by a unanimous vote of all the city and state officials involved in the licensing process.

Although religious bodies have the right, under this Court's decisions protecting church autonomy, see Serbian Eastern Orthodox Diocese v. Milivojevich, 426 U.S. 696 (1976), to make at least some binding decisions as to *their own members and officials*, some Justices have perceived even in that context a danger that blind enforcement of church decisions by government "can easily [make civil authorities] into handmaidens of arbitrary lawlessness." Id. at 727 (Rehnquist, J., joined by Stevens, J., dissenting). Indeed, as the Court recognized in the seminal case of Watson v. Jones, 80 U.S. (13 Wall.) 679 (1871), the First Amendment in no way confirms for churches a plenary authority to exercise civil justice even over their own members. As the Court there observed,

if the General Assembly of the Presbyterian Church should undertake to try one of its members for murder, and punish him with death or imprisonment, its sentence would be of no validity in a civil court or anywhere else. Or if it should at the instance of one of its members entertain jurisdiction as between him and another member as to their individual right to property, real or personal, the right in no sense depending on ecclesiastical questions, its decision would be utterly disregarded by any civil court where it might be set up.

Id. 733. The *Watson* Court concluded that "[t]he structure of our government has, for the preservation of civil liberty, rescued the temporal institutions from religious interference," and therefore that, "when a civil right depends upon an ecclesiastical matter, it is the civil court . . . which is to decide." Id. 730-731. See also n.9 supra.

A fortiori, when church decisions reach out to the broader public and dispose of the personal or pecuniary interests of non-members, it seems an understatement to say that making "available the coercive powers of civil [bodies] to rubber-stamp ecclesiastical decisions of . . . religious associations, when such deference is not accorded similar acts of secular voluntary associations, would . . . create . . . serious problems under the Establishment Clause." *Serbian Orthodox Diocese*, supra, at 734 (Rehnquist, J., joined by Stevens, J.).

13. State Br. 2a. Section 16C delegates a veto power over liquor licenses only to those churches and synagogues "dedicated to divine worship." Id. Webster's Third New International Dictionary defines the word "divine" as (1) "of or relating to God: proceeding from God"; (2) "of or relating to a god . . . proceeding from a god"; or (3) "devoted or addressed to God." Webster's Third New International Dictionary of the English Language, Unabridged 663 (1981). Any applicable definition of the term "divine worship" would seem to preclude religions that do not teach a belief in the existence of God, including "Buddhism, Taoism, Ethical Culture, Secular Humanism, and others," Torcaso v. Watkins, 367 U.S. 488, 495 n.11 (1961), and it would surely preclude atheism or any other direct denial of God's existence.

their discourse and beliefs — that enjoy the special status and power conferred by Section 16C. The content-based discrimination could hardly be more blatant: thus, the governing bodies of a meditation center, a branch of Alcoholics Anonymous, a hospital or library, a home for the aged or a day care center, an historical commission, a Secular Humanism society, a Buddhist temple, or an atheists' club, do not share Section 16C's benefits or occupy the position of privilege Section 16C creates. While all such groups and their leaders may express their views about various nearby liquor establishments and are entitled to have their members' needs and wishes regarding tranquility and temperance weighed by the appropriate public licensing authorities,[14] *not one of them* is given what the city appellants aptly describe as the "right" conferred by Section 16C on places of "divine worship," CLC Br. 39; and *not one of them* receives what the state appellants correctly call the "guaranteed" ability ceded to certain churches and synagogues under Section 16C to veto any given liquor license within a 500-foot radius, State Br. 91, whenever they choose to do so.[15]

14. Compare p. 36 & n.34, infra.
15. Thus Section 16C violates the Religion Clauses not only in delegating inherently governmental power to churches as such but also in favoring "those religions based on a belief in the existence of God as against those religions founded on different beliefs." Torcaso v. Watkins, 367 U.S. at 495 (citations omitted). For similar reasons, Section 16C also violates the First Amendment's Free Speech Clause inasmuch as it distributes public privileges to groups defined in terms of the ideas they hold or advocate, thus "violat[ing] the fundamental principle that a state regulation of speech should be content-neutral." Widmar v. Vincent, 102 S. Ct. 269, 278 (1981) (holding unconstitutional a "content-based exclusion of religious speech" from state college facilities). Finally, as the *Widmar* Court also noted, any law such as Section 16C creates an *impermissible entanglement* of church and state insofar as it requires the latter "to determine which words and activities fall within [the term] 'religious worship,'" id. 275 n.11 — or, in this case, "divine worship," an even more elusive category to identify without entangling intrusion. See id. 274 n.6.

The suggestion of the state appellants that appellee Grendel's, which has undisputedly suffered direct economic injury by virtue of Section 16C's delegation of power to certain church bodies, lacks standing to complain of Section 16C's narrowly content-based designation of the churches and synagogues that may wield a veto, State Br. 76, betrays a basic misunderstanding of the law of standing. Valley Forge Christian College v. Americans United, 102 S. Ct. 752 (1982), cited in State Br. 77 n.69, is plainly inapposite, since plaintiffs there had "alleged [no] *injury* of *any* kind, economic or otherwise, sufficient to confer standing." 102 S. Ct. at 766 (footnote omitted) (emphasis in original). Moreover, the question in this case is *not* the protected or unprotected status of Grendel's *activities* as compared with those of third parties whose rights Grendel's might wish to champion in an overbreadth attack, cf. Village of Schaumburg v. Citizens for a Better Environment, 444 U.S. 620 (1980); the only question is the validity of Section 16C, which is the cause of Grendel's injury. Here, as in Cabell v. Chavez-Salido, 102 S. Ct. 735 (1982), appellee does not claim to be "asserting the constitutional rights of others; rather, [it] claim[s] that

Finally, the fact that such a veto can indisputably be withheld by a church or synagogue favored by the would-be licensee with a suitably timed and sufficiently generous contribution obviously *aggravates* the Establishment Clause violation. It does so *first*, by illustrating the "worldly corruptions" to which Roger Williams feared that establishment would lead, see CLC Br. 16, and to which it apparently *did* lead, in the very field of liquor licensing, at least in England;[16] and *second*, by creating a mechanism through which religious bodies might clandestinely cajole and even coerce members and non-members alike into filling church coffers as a precondition of engaging in a lawful occupation or making lawful use of their property. Cf. *Thomas* v. *Review Board*, 450 U.S. 707, 717-718 (1981) (indirect pressure to compromise one's religious convictions in order to enjoy public benefit may violate Free Exer-

---

[Massachusetts] denies [it] the . . . protection of the [First and Fourteenth Amendments, in part] because [Section 16C] is so [under] inclusive that it destroys the State's asserted justification," id. 741 n.8, and creates further problems under the First Amendment. It is, of course, settled that there need be no particular "nexus," outside the context of taxpayers' suits, between the injury caused by a challenged state action and the constitutional norms said to be transgressed by that action. Duke Power Co. v. Carolina Environmental Study Group, Inc., 438 U.S. 59, 78-81 (1978).

16. See n.11 supra. Williams' fears about the "worldly corruptions" and temptations that would engulf the clergy and church if they became too involved in political matters were, if anything, more apt for the eighteenth century than they had been for the seventeenth. By the end of the eighteenth century, many churchmen were using their positions to accumulate great wealth. N. Sykes, Church and State in England in the Eighteenth Century 188 (1934). Over all, the eighteenth-century British clergy were known for their "episcopal opulence and nepotism" and their "secular association . . . with affairs of state." Id. 41, 408.

James Madison may have been drawing upon this background in 1785 when he wrote in his "Memorial and Remonstrance Against Religious Assessments" that "[e]xperience shows that ecclesiastical establishments, instead of maintaining the purity and efficacy of Religion have resulted in pride and indolence in the Clergy." James Madison, "Memorial and Remonstrance Against Religious Assessments," excerpted in Pfeffer 112-113.

Ultimately, Americans of the eighteenth century came to believe, as Williams had, that churches would be spiritually purer and less politically oppressive if they maintained their separation from the state and from the internal workings of the political process. As James Iredell, a future Justice of this Court, stated in the North Carolina Convention for ratifying the Constitution of 1787 on July 30, 1788, "It would be happy for mankind if religion were permitted to take its own course, and maintain itself by the excellence of its own doctrines. The Divine Author of our religion never wished for support by worldly authority." 4 J. Elliot, The Debates in the Several State Conventions on the Adoption of the Federal Constitution 194 (1836). And, as another North Carolina delegate pointed out, the decision that "no one particular religion should be established . . . leaves religion on a solid foundation of its own inherent validity, without any connection with temporal authority; and no kind of oppression can take place." Id. 200.

cise Clause); *Engel* v. *Vitale,* 370 U.S. 421, 430-431 (1962) (indirect coercive pressure to take part in "voluntary" prayer may exacerbate violation of Establishment Clause). In this sense, Section 16C places at the disposal of selected religious institutions an informal but highly effective "taxing" capacity, making the provision objectionable not only as an explicitly religious and indeed discriminatory establishment of *regulatory* power, but also as an unusually direct assault on the familiar Establishment Clause injunction against *exacting tribute* from citizens for theological purposes that may not be their own.[17]

Given the state appellants' concession that what counts is the *nature* of the benefit a challenged measure confers upon religious

17. Use of the taxing or tithing power to support churches has long been seen as a major form of religious establishment. As Justice Black recounted in *Everson,* 330 U.S. at 8-9, the "early settlers" of America had often been punished while they were still in Europe for "failure to pay taxes and tithes to support" established churches; many of them had emigrated to this country partly "to escape the bondage of [these] laws." See CLC Br. 14-15. Once in America, these settlers often formed their own established churches, and "dissenters were compelled to pay tithes and taxes to support [these] government-sponsored churches." *Everson,* 330 U.S. at 9-10. See CLC Br. 15. By 1727 to 1742, however, Massachusetts had passed a series of laws guaranteeing citizens the right to support only the churches of their choice. Thus, even though it retained a tax to support churches, Massachusetts had mitigated one of the most odious elements of an establishment for the colonists — compulsion to support a church of which one was not a member and whose beliefs one did not share. S. Cobb, The Rise of Religious Liberty in America 234-235 (1902).

This fear of being forced to contribute to a church in which one did not believe was central to the colonists' concerns during the Episcopacy Controversy. See n.8 supra. The colonists reasoned that "a Bishop must have a See," which would require "the Allotment of a large Tract of Land." Collinson letter, quoted in Bridenbaugh 232-233. In order "[t]o support all this . . . the Laity must be taxed," and eventually, there would be "Laws fram'd by" the Episcopate "in its own Spiritual court." Id. The colonists saw in this a horrible fate for those whose forefathers had "fled from their native Land to avoid a Persecution inflicted upon them by this kind of Church Power." Id.

It was precisely the use of the state's power to assist churches in collecting tithes that prompted the colonists to accuse Britain of "establishing" the Roman Catholic religion in Quebec, after the passage of the Quebec Act of 1774. See p. 10 supra. The attempts of the British to tax citizens to support churches to which they did not belong formed a central part of the "establishment of religion" that the First Amendment's Framers sought to prohibit to Congress and that the Fourteenth Amendment thus forebade to the states. See *Abington,* 370 U.S. at 254-59 (Brennan, J., concurring).

Section 16C, in creating a subtler and more sinister form of quasi-taxation for churches, patently violates this aspect of the Establishment Clause by enabling churches to exact sums of money from selected members of the community who have no reason (other than their desire to pursue a lawful occupation) to contribute to those churches and who may not even share those churches' beliefs. Furthermore, Section 16C places the manifestly highcost machinery of the state — including the liquor licensing boards and the state liquor commission — free of charge at the disposal of each church which raises an objection. At no time in the history of Massachusetts or the United States has an established church received any more.

bodies, State Br. 21, 56, 66, and that, "if the benefit furthers an evil proscribed by the Establishment Clause . . . [then] the program [itself] violates the Establishment Clause," id. 54-55, the argument could well end here. For, as appellee has shown, the practice it challenges is for several reasons an establishment of religion per se, not a mere "' foot in the door' or . . . 'nose of the camel in the tent' *leading to* an established church." *Walz v. Tax Commission*, 397 U.S. at 678 (emphasis added).

Appellee nonetheless proceeds to show that, *independent* of this fatal establishment clause objection, Section 16C's placement of public power in private hands offends the Due Process Clause of the Fourteenth Amendment (see Part II infra), and that no legitimate state interest could serve to justify *either* of Section 16C's departures from the Constitution's norms (see Part III infra).

II. By Subjecting Personal Liberty and Private Property to the Standardless and Unreviewable Control of Private Bodies Designated by the State, Section 16C Negates All that is Meant by "Due Process of Law."

Even if the Establishment Clause had never been adopted, the Due Process Clause of the Fourteenth Amendment would provide a separate and sufficient ground for upholding the decision of the court below that Section 16C is unconstitutional.[18]

---

18. There is no merit in the suggestion of the state appellants, State Br. 13 n.11, 23, 87 n.75, that the due process infirmities of Section 16C are not properly before this Court. The claim that Section 16C delegates public power to private bodies in violation of the Due Process Clause has been pressed by Grendel's at every stage of the proceedings below, was fully briefed and argued by both sides in both the district court and the court of appeals, was made a ground of decision by the district court, J.S.A. 122A, and was sympathetically treated in the en banc decision below, id. 13A-14A & n.5, even though that decision rested on grounds making resolution of the due process claim unnecessary. Id. 9A. As in Dandridge v. Williams, 397 U.S. 471, 476 n.6 (1970), the "issue having been fully argued both here and in the District Court, consideration of the . . . claim [here] is appropriate." Accord, New York City Transit Authority v. Beazer, 440 U.S. 568, 583 n.24 (1979). Moreover, in contrast with the two cases cited by the state appellants, State Br. 87 n.75, the instant case involves no unresolved statutory or factual issues which the courts below avoided, or as to which changed circumstances might furnish reasons for a remand. Finally, inasmuch as an appeal under 28 U.S.C. §1254(2) brings the entire case before this Court, see 17 C. Wright, A. Miller & E. Cooper, Federal Practice and Procedure 40 (1978), and inasmuch as the prevailing party is "entitled under [this Court's] precedents to urge any grounds which would lend support to the judgment below," Dayton Bd. of Education v. Brinkman, 433 U.S. 406, 419 (1977); R. Stern & E. Gressman, Supreme Court Practice 537 (5th ed., 1978), there is no basis whatever for treating the due process claim as not properly here, or for remanding that claim for initial disposition by the court of appeals en banc.

Whether Grendel's is "entitled" to a liquor license is irrelevant to the due process analysis: even if Grendel's is *not* "entitled" to serve liquor and its patrons are *not* "entitled" to consume it, the state is hardly free to dispense with the dictates of the Fourteenth Amendment in ruling on Grendel's application. See *Wisconsin v. Constantineau,* 400 U.S. 433, 436 (1971) (even "police power . . . over intoxicating liquors. . . ." must be exercised in accord with "rule by law," not "rule by fiat");[19] cf. *Perry v. Sindermann,* 408 U.S. 593, 597 (1972) (no entitlement is needed if denial of benefit involves "interference with constitutional rights").[20] And, while the state appellants insist on derogating appellee's interests in this case by resurrecting the long-discredited "right/privilege" distinction,[21] both "liberty" and "property" interests *are* in fact at stake here. For, in submitting the appellee's occupational liberty, see *Hampton v. Mow Sun Wong,* 426 U.S. 88, 102-103,

19. "It is firmly established, of course, that the state has the right to regulate or prohibit traffic in intoxicating liquor in the valid exercise of its police power . . . but this is something quite different from a right to act arbitrarily and capriciously. Merely calling a liquor license a privilege does not free the municipal authorities from the due process requirements in licensing and allow them to exercise an uncontrolled discretion." Hornsby v. Allen, 326 F.2d 605, 609 (5th Cir., 1964), cited with approval by this Court in Goldberg v. Kelly, 397 U.S. 254, 262-263 n.9 (1970) (specifically noting that *Hornsby* dealt with liquor licensing). Accord, Mayhue v. City of Plantation, Florida, 375 F.2d 447, 449 (5th Cir. 1967); *Raper v. Lucey,* 488 F.2d 748, 752 (1st Cir. 1973) (citing *Hornsby,* and holding driver's license application proceeding to be protected by due process); Bell v. Burson, 402 U.S. 535, 539 (1971) (license suspension proceeding governed by due process principles).

20. However narrow might be the category of interests triggering the *procedural* due process right to a trial-type hearing, a much broader category of interests is protected, to a greater or lesser degree, as a matter of *substantive* due process. The claim in this case, while in part an objection to the *process* (or absence thereof) by which Grendel's was denied a valued opportunity, is unmistakably grounded as well in the *substantive right* to be governed by laws, not by standardless, ad hoc private will. See Coates v. City of Cincinnati, 402 U.S. 611, 614-615 (1971) (law forbidding the "annoying" conduct of small sidewalk assemblies is void because it subjects people to policeman's whim, not rule of law); Lanzetta v. New Jersey, 306 U.S. 451, 457 (1939) (organized crime law so vague that court's ad hoc application of it to defendants subjected them to rule of judge, not that of law).

21. See State Br. 34 n.21, 89 n.77, 101 n.83. Appellants are presumably encouraged to repeat this argument because it found evident favor with two members of the original First Circuit panel. See J.S.A. 39A-40A n.4. Since the state appellants cite, State Br. 87, 89, 90, 91, 94, 102, 104, and even quote, id. 100-101, this opinion so often and largely neglect the en banc decision, it might be well to recall that appellants' very presence before this Court is a result of their appeal from that same en banc decision — which did, after all, vacate the first panel's judgment and opinion.

n.23 (1976), and the personal liberty of those who might wish to congregate and drink at appellee's restaurant, to the absolute veto of Holy Cross Church, Section 16C denies both of these liberties without due process of law and unconstitutionally deprives the appellee of property by permitting another private body to decide how Grendel's may use its restaurant.[22]

By leaving to the governing body of Holy Cross Church the unilateral authority to decide that granting Grendel's a liquor license is not in the public interest, Section 16C delegates a power that is inherently and indisputably governmental. See n.12 supra. Both the state appellants, State Br. 18, and the city appellants, CLC Br. 32-33, indeed stress that the balancing of interests required to make such a decision is exclusively a *legislative* function.[23] The delegation of such lawmaking power to politically unaccountable and judicially unreviewable private bodies is exactly analogous to, and indeed even worse than, the standardless delegation condemned by this Court in *Eubank* v. *City of Richmond*, 226 U.S. 137 (1912), which struck down a local zoning ordinance delegating to the owners of two-thirds of the property abutting an affected street the power to demand a building set-back line. In invalidating that ordinance, this Court stressed the decisive character of the delegation,[24] cf. *New Motor Vehicle Board* v. Fox, 439 U.S. 96,

---

22. The dual nature of Grendel's interest as one in *both* property *and* liberty is suggested by Moore v. City of East Cleveland, 431 U.S. 494 (1977). While the majority characterized Mrs. Moore's constitutional right to live with her son and two grandsons (who were cousins) in her home as a liberty interest, id. 499-502, Justice Stevens in his concurrence concluded that the city ordinance banning such living arrangements ran afoul of the Constitution by unjustifiably, and without just compensation, restricting the "appellant's right to use her own property as she sees fit." Id. 513.

23. Section 16C gives churches the inherently governmental role of restricting proposed land uses and preventing proposed uses of a purchased license altogether, cf. Jackson v. Metropolitan Edison Co., 419 U.S. at 353 (taking private property is a function "traditionally associated with sovereignty"); see also Youngstown Sheet & Tube Co. v. Sawyer, 343 U.S. 579, 587-88 (1952) (disposition of private property is a uniquely legislative function); id. 630-31 (Douglas J., concurring) (same).

24. "It leaves no discretion in the committee on streets as to whether the street line shall or shall not be established in a given case. The action of the committee is determined by two-thirds of the property owners. In other words, part of the property owners fronting on the block determine the extent of use that other owners shall make of their lots, and against the restriction they are impotent. This we emphasize. One set of owners determines not only the extent of use but the kind of use which another set of owners may make of their property." *Eubank,* 226 U.S. at 143.

108-109 (1978),[25] and the lack of any standards circumscribing the exercise of the unaccountable power thus delegated.[26] Both those features are present here. And both offer painful reminders of the eighteenth century English experience that was ended by the Beer Act of 1830 — an experience in which the "licensed victualler, alone among tradesmen, [was] 'subjected to the ruinous effects of petty tyranny . . . .'" Manchester Observer, Feb. 14, 1818, quoted in Webb, supra, at 108-09. Many "vehemently resented the fact that unrepresentative bodies, like the magistrates in Brewster Sessions, could, without appeal, deprive the working-man of his beer, the honest publican of his means of livelihood, and the brewer of his property, out of mere caprice, and not without grave suspicions of political partisanship and even pecuniary corruption." Id. 93-94. Such lawless subjugation is the very antithesis of due process of law — particularly where, as here, the power in question is delegated to a *private body* and not, as in *Eubank,* to a *community of neighbors* in which those subject to that power are included and may at least cast a vote. Cf. *City of Eastlake* v. *Forest City Enterprises, Inc.,* 426 U.S. 668, 678-679 (1976) (rezoning decision properly reserved to all voters of the affected community).

A. Recasting Section 16C as a Waivable Ban Cannot Save It From Condemnation Under *Eubank.*

Appellants seek to avoid the sting of this history and the authority of *Eubank* by conforming Section 16C post hoc to a licensing scheme like that upheld by this Court in *Cusack* v. *City of Chicago,* 242 U.S. 526 (1917). In the guise of following this Court's precedents, appellants in truth repudiate them. The challenged ordi-

25. In *New Motor,* the Court upheld the delegation, to private franchisees of new car dealerships, of a right to protest the establishment of new franchises, stressing that the private party's protest operated *not* as a *veto,* but only as a *trigger* which required a public agency to determine, based upon standards written into the law, whether to permit the establishment of the new franchise. See 439 U.S. at 107-109. The crucial distinction is that between a legislative scheme in which a private choice merely sets in motion a publicly accountable process of evaluation and decision by an agency of government, as in *New Motor,* and a legislative scheme in which a private choice brings about an injurious outcome for someone without any intervening process of government evaluation, as in Section 16C.

26. "The statute and ordinance, while conferring the power on some property holders to virtually control and dispose of the proper[ty] rights of others, creates no standard by which the power thus given is to be exercised; in other words, the property holders who desire and have the authority to establish the line may do so solely for their own interest or even capriciously." *Eubank,* 226 U.S. at 143-144.

nance in *Cusack* generally prohibited the construction of billboards in residential areas, but permitted *waiver* of that restriction by the affirmative consent of the owners of the majority of the property fronting on both sides of the affected street. *Cusack*, 242 U.S. at 527-528. The *Cusack* Court distinguished *Eubank* on the explicit ground that the *Cusack* ordinance "delegated" *no* "legislative power" to private owners in permitting them to *waive* or "remove a [billboard] restriction" otherwise *legislatively imposed*. Id. 531.[27]

While the district court carefully reviewed these precedents and correctly concluded that the settled test of a law's constitutionality under the *Eubank-Cusack* line of cases is "whether it incorporates a legislative policy subject to *waiver* or whether it actually licenses private persons to *impose* policy on the public," J.S.A. 113A (emphasis in original), the state appellants' brief persists in deliberately confusing a privately *waivable ban* enacted by a public body with a private *veto power* delegated by public law.[28] In *Eubank* the ordinance empowered property owners to *compel* a public body to *impose* a restriction; in *Cusack* the prohibition was established by law although the law's "reference to [the concerned] neighborhood," 242 U.S. at 530, enabled affected property owners to *waive* its application. In the instant case, like *Eubank* but unlike *Cusack,* Section 16C enacts *no general prohibition* on locating liquor licenses near churches or schools, but merely allows each such private institution to *veto* any *particular* application for such a license by a business situated anywhere within the nearly million-square-foot area surrounding the institution. The suggestion, see State Br. 93-94, that Section 16C resembles the *Cusack* ordinance rather than the *Eubank* provision is thus palpably frivolous and was properly rejected by the district court. J.S.A. 118A-122A. To accept that suggestion here would obliterate the very distinction that this Court treated as pivotal in *Cusack*. 242 U.S. at 530-531.[29]

27. The vitality of this distinction for due process purposes was assumed by this Court in *City of Eastlake,* supra, 426 U.S. at 677-678 n.12. Subsequent to *Cusack,* in Washington ex. rel. Seattle Title Trust Co. v. Roberge, 278 U.S. 116 (1928), this Court invalidated a scheme which operated like the one upheld in *Cusack.* See also *New Motor,* supra, 439 U.S. at 108-109.
28. See State Br. 18, 20, 23, 59, 90, 91. The distinction between these two categories may, of course, be immaterial to the establishment clause analysis of Part I supra.
29. The state appellants attempt to show by a review of Section 16C's legislative history that only the *form* of implementation has changed while the legislative *policy* has remained constant. State Br. 37-38, 102-104. But each of the changes in the law between 1954 and 1970, the date of the last relevant amendment, has gone distinctly beyond the merely technical. The texts of the various versions are set out in the Statutory Appendix to State Br. at 2a-9a.

B. Treating Section 16C's Veto Power as Subject to Public Scrutiny and Control Likewise Cannot Save It From *Eubank*.

The state appellants attempt to dismiss the potential for abuse inherent in Section 16C by assuring this Court that it need not fear

---

In 1954, as originally enacted, Section 16C flatly forbade the licensing of liquor outlets within 500 feet of a church or school. In 1968, the law was changed to permit licenses within the 500-foot zone of a *church* if the church's governing body consented in writing. It is important to note that, while the 1968 form of the statute is correctly set out in the State's Statutory Appendix at 7a-8a (this version corresponds exactly with that contained in the official State House Archives in Boston), the state appellants flatly misquote the statute at page 37 of their brief by saying that *both* schools and churches could waive the ban under the law as amended in 1968. (The Supreme Judicial Court of Massachusetts made the same slip in Arno v. Alcoholic Beverages Control Commission, J.S.A. 172A, on which the state appellants frequently rely in their brief. See, e.g., State Br. 34, 36, 38, 90.) In 1969, State Representative Ralph Sirianni introduced a bill (never enacted) that would have left intact the ban subject to waiver by churches, but would have put in place a permission subject to veto by schools. Proposed 1970 Mass. Acts & Statutes c. 192 (in State House Archives). In 1970, the Sirianni bill was amended to the law's present form, which permits licensing of liquor outlets within 500 feet of schools *and* churches absent the *affirmative objection* of the school's or church's governing body.

The upshot of this history is that the legislative policy has *not* remained constant as appellants maintain. Instead, the state's policy has shifted gradually from an *absolute ban,* to a ban subject to *church waiver,* to a policy of *legislative neutrality, see* district court opinion, J.S.A. 114A-115A, subject to an *absolute veto* by either schools *or* churches.

Appellants' attempt to avoid the thrust of *Eubank* by arguing that the legislative *purpose* of Section 16C remained the same from version to version is thus not only irrelevant (what counts in this area of the law is *what* the law does, not *why*), but also utterly implausible. Moreover, it flies in the face of Washington ex rel. Seattle Title Trust Co., supra. There, this Court plainly held that a "grant of permission for [a] use, although [literally framed as a prohibition] . . . subject to . . . consents, shows that the legislative body found [such use to be] in harmony with the public interest." Id. 121. Yet the state appellants insist on arguing, as did the vacated original First Circuit majority opinion, J.S.A. 55A-56A, that solely because a "grant of permission" subject to veto has in a *previous* version been framed as a prohibition subject to waiver — a circumstance at best bringing the case marginally closer to *Roberge* on the spectrum from legislative resolution to legislative abdication — the resulting scheme may be regarded as one in which the legislative body has found the use in question to be contrary to the public interest. State Br. 90-91, 103-104. Such convoluted word-play by appellants cannot change the fact that the *current* form of Section 16C delegates unguided discretion to churches.

Unlike the situation in *New Motor,* supra, the veto of Grendel's application for a liquor license by Father Luke and the Holy Cross Church was not merely the *initiation of a government decision process;* it was in itself *the decision.* The fact of the delegation of legislative authority cannot be changed by noting that, more than a decade ago, Section 16C did *not* provide Father Luke with veto power. Nor is that statute saved by treating as dispositive the fact that the veto power it *did* provide as of 1970 was delegated to private individuals by a well-considered, prior legislative choice. For such a legislative judgment is not the finale but the overture of any consideration of the resulting delegation's validity.

that a church will ever veto an application for invidious reasons inasmuch as the Cambridge License Commission may be able to "reject or ignore any objection under Section 16C which was made for discriminatory or otherwise illegal reasons." State Br. 85 n.74. That is simply false. As the state appellants concede six pages later, the official objection of a church or school has a *"guaranteed effect."* Id. 91 (emphasis added). The Cambridge License Commission likewise concedes that churches and schools have the *"right . . .* to *prevent* the issuance of liquor licenses within 500 feet." CLC Br. 39 (emphasis added). As these terms suggest, there is *no* review of *any* kind to assess the objecting institution's reasons for casting a veto. The church elders simply mail in their objection; the result is then assured. Indeed, the state appellants argue that it is just this "narrow relationship" which avoids excessive entanglement between church and state. State Br. 22. They note in their First Amendment argument the minimal contact between the clergy and the licensing commission which results from this "self-operating procedure," id. 83, and, on the very same page where this Court is told not to worry about possible abuse, the state appellants praise the *total absence* of "administrative assessment of a church's concerns." Id. 85. See also n.2 supra (state appellants, both directly and through the Attorney General, respond to Grendel's interrogatories by saying that the church's governing body need not state "any reason" for its veto).

The Supreme Judicial Court in *Arno,* supra, J.S.A. 161A, construed Section 16C as a "delegation . . . of a veto power," id. 175A, which the church may exercise "in its discretion," id. 179A, subject to a hearing only with respect to such relatively mechanical questions as "whether the objecting institution qualifies as a 'church' for the purpose of the statute, whether it is within the statutorily protected zone of 500 feet, and whether the written objection was duly authorized by the appropriate 'governing body' of the church." Id. 179A-180A. A *virtue* of this arrangement, according to the state appellants, is that the protected church or school, "as the party most knowledgeable about its own exposure to injury," is allowed to weigh for itself the advantages and disadvantages of a new liquor outlet nearby. State Br. 39. It is thus impossible to escape the conclusion of the district court that, "[s]imply put, under Section 16C a church or school may exercise its discretion to object for good reason, bad reason, or no reason at all." J.S.A. 116A n.8. Given what the ABCC itself called this "absolute veto" power, J.A. 25, wielded on the basis of undisclosed reasons by politically unaccountable and judicially unreviewable religious institutions, it is an utter mystery how the state appellants manage to conclude that an objection to a license application under Section 16C "is not the imposition of a private policy, but the implementation of a public policy enacted *and supervised* by the elected Legislature." State Br. 91 (emphasis added).[30]

C. *Eubank* Cannot Be Distinguished on "the Equities," for Equitable Considerations Especially Condemn Section 16C.

In one final effort to avoid the authority of *Eubank,* the state appellants argue that this case is distinguishable on "the equities inherent in [its] underlying facts." State Br. 95. Any such comparison with the statute challenged in this case, however, shows that Section 16C, not the ordinance in *Eubank,* creates by far the greater risk of inequitable results.

One of the vices noted by this Court in its review of the *Eubank* ordinance was its lack of uniformity: one side of a street might have a set-back line while the other did not; houses might be staggered back and forth on successive blocks; set-back lines might be set at greatly different distances. *Eubank,* 226 U.S. at 144. Yet, for all that, the *Eubank* ordinance at least had the virtue of being consistent for the group of property owners who compelled a set-back line's establishment and were thereby reciprocally bound, along with their neighbors, by the results of their action. For whenever the owners of two-thirds of the relevant property decided to impose a set-back, it was a single line, set by a public body and applicable uniformly to themselves and their neighbors. They could not establish one line for themselves and another for those they did not like, or one line for their friends and another for those who refused to make appropriate "contributions."

Section 16C is in this sense far *more* offensive, because it allows a church to target and veto particular license applicants on an ad hoc, non-uniform, and wholly non-reciprocal basis. It bears repeating that, in its answers to plaintiff's interrogatories, the Alcoholic Beverage Control Commission of Massachusetts admitted that Section 16C, as applied by the ABCC, "does not require the governing body of a church to state any reason for its objection to the issuance of a license." J.A. 35, 37-38. The ABCC is thus unable to dispute that a church might, without any fuss, deny a license to any establishment within 500 feet solely on the basis of the applicant's race, sex, religion, national origin, political affiliation, or shoe size. The elders of Holy Cross Church are free to wield their

---

30. Indeed, the concession of all appellants on the antitrust issue, see n.4 supra, itself shows that the private institutions exercising anti-competitively the power delegated by Section 16C are *not* acting in accord with legislatively dictated policy but are imposing a policy arrived at privately.

veto power so as to extort contributions to the church, visit punishment upon their personal enemies, or stultify the local commercial competitors of their parishioners who are in the restaurant and
liquor business. A more comprehensive list of motives offensive
both to the Bill of Rights and to common decency — and yet
unreviewable in any particular case — would be hard to imagine.[31]
No state interest could possibly justify this outrageous delegation
of unbridled governmental power — seemingly the worst such delegation ever to reach this Court.[32] As this Court recognized nearly a
century ago,

31. This is not a case where an otherwise valid law is being challenged because its
"legitimate objectives . . . may be subverted by conscious design or lax enforcement," Tilton v. Richardson, 403 U.S. 672, 679 (1971), but one in which
the evils derive from the statute's *inherent* and *inescapable* effects. Indeed, these
very evils were exposed in 1891 by Louis D. Brandeis, appearing before the
Massachusetts Legislature to testify against a law similar to Section 16C:

> You cannot with yard stick decide whether the location of the saloon would be an injury.
> It may or may not be. . . . But if you give power to every person within twenty five feet of
> every proposed liquor store to determine that question for himself, you put into his hands a
> great power which he is likely to abuse. It needs no evidence (although much evidence was
> introduced), to prove that such power will often be abused. To give a neighboring real
> estate owner an uncontrollable right to object may, under [certain] circumstances, be giving
> him the whip hand over the applicant for a license; and it will depend entirely upon the
> character of him who holds that whip, whether this instrument of castigation be used for
> the owner's protection or be applied in securing unjust booty . . . [W]hen you give the
> absolute right to object, you have put into the hands of men an irresistible weapon.

Argument of Louis D. Brandeis before the Joint Committee on Liquor Law of
the Massachusetts Legislature, Feb. 27, 1891, reprinted in 1 Hearings on the
Nomination of Louis D. Brandeis before a Subcommittee of the Senate Committee on the Judiciary 1057, 1065 (1916).

32. See Part III infra. In the course of its establishment clause argument, the Cambridge License Commission actually suggests that Section 16C's delegation of
veto power to churches is justifiable as a way of keeping provoked parishioners
from physically retaliating against nearby liquor licensees. CLC Br. 36. This is
tantamount to saying that, in order to prevent angry church elders from taking
the law into their own hands, we should *give* it to them. If the government were
to abandon its monopoly over coercive force, see Ogden v. Saunders, 25 U.S. (12
Wheat.) 213, 345, 346-47 (1827) (Marshall, C.J., dissenting), every time some
group threatened to take to the streets, legislative delegations of authority
would operate on a principle little nobler than that of a protection racket. To
accept the License Commission's quite astounding rationale for Section 16C's
delegation would be to turn back the clock to those primordial times — before
the state arose out of the morass of private protection agencies, see R. Nozick,
Anarchy, State and Utopia 16-17, 88-89 (1974) — when there was "neither
peace, nor rest nor a moment's safety" because men "knew no law but the law
of club and fang." J. London, The Call of The Wild 39 (1929). Precisely because
dispute resolution in our society is subject to the rule of law, not "the will of
strategically placed individuals," Boddie v. Connecticut, 401 U.S. 371, 374-375
(1971), we no longer live in a "state of nature." But were the government to
capitulate to the spectre of marauding mobs of angry churchmen or their
followers, we would once again inhabit a world where life would indeed be
"nasty, brutish and short," T. Hobbes, Leviathan 185 (1651) (Penguin ed.
1978), and the "law of the world . . . a winter law, and casual." J. Gardner,
Grendel 115 (1971).

the very idea that one . . . may be compelled to hold his life, or the means of living, or any material right essential to the enjoyment of life, at the mere will of another [is] intolerable in any country where freedom prevails.

Yick Wo v. Hopkins, 118 U.S. 356, 370 (1886).

III. No Legitimate State Interest Can Justify Section 16C's Establishment of Selected Private Institutions — Those "Dedicated to Divine Worship" — as Regulatory Arms of the State.

A. *Neither the Goal of Controlling Liquor Traffic, Nor that of Regulating Land Use to Preserve Tranquility, Nor That of Accommodating Religious Needs With Minimum Entanglement, Can Support Section 16C's Delegation of Coercive Power to Designated Religious Bodies.*

If this Court were ever to sustain a delegation of power as sweeping as Section 16C's, or a grant of privileged status as narrowly and unequally confined as Section 16C's to specific religious bodies, this would be the worst imaginable case in which to do so. For any legitimate secular goal to be served by preserving tranquility around institutions needing such protection (something Section 16C does not really do at all) could be served far better — without either delegating power to private parties *or* singling out particular religious bodies as favorites of the state, and certainly without hostility to religion, contra State Br. 71 n.64 — simply by directing the responsible public authorities to give due weight to the interests of each such institution, whether sua sponte or at the institution's behest, in appropriate proceedings, cf. *New Motor Vehicle Board,* 439 U.S. at 109[33] — as Massachusetts already *does,* independent of Section 16C. See State Br. 36 n.24.

Only two arguments have been advanced against the adequacy of this obvious and altogether traditional solution. *First,* it is said that letting churches and synagogues submit their objections to public licensing authorities on the same basis as everyone else would require unseemly governmental inquiry into these groups'

33. As Justice Brandeis observed when he testified before the Massachusetts Legislature against a provision similar to Section 16C, see n.31 supra, it is surely a "fallac[y]" to assume "[t]hat the Licensing Boards are so feeble or corrupt that they cannot be entrusted with the duty of determining whether the establishment of such a liquor store would be a nuisance in the particular case." Id.

religious concerns and practices, State Br. 22, 83, causing a degree of entanglement between church and state that delegating an absolute veto power can avoid. Id. 85. *Second,* it is said that only conferring an unquestioned *"right . . .* to prevent the issuance of liquor licenses within 500 feet," CLC Br. 39, could adequately avoid "actions so inherently inflammatory" — the city appellants are describing the act of having a glass of chablis with one's lunch within 500 feet of a church — "as to provoke the average person to retaliate, and, in protecting his church or his child's school, cause a breach of the peace of the commonwealth." Id. 36.

Unless such claims are being made in jest, the premise they reflect is a profoundly dangerous one. Not even Section 16C honors a supposed wish on the part of school or church leaders always to have their way, no questions asked, on threat of taking the law into their own hands. See n.32 supra. Even with Section 16C in force, church leaders who object to liquor being served or sold *over* 500 feet away, for example, must submit their views to the same governmental process as that available to all others in the community. See State Br. 36 n.24.[34] And if the state *were* to capitulate to such supposed desires for total disentanglement from others or total power over others, it is hard to see why such appeasement should start — or stop — with schools and churches. Are we to suppose that church leaders are more likely than homeowners to find unbearable the prospect of nearby drinking or the burdens of submitting their objections peacefully to public scrutiny? To state the claim is to explode it: *no* group in a democratic republic may commandeer "the machinery of the State to practice its beliefs," *Abington,* 374 U.S. at 226, by *coercing* rather than *persuading* the people and their representatives to accede to the group's will. To the degree that Section 16C rests on a contrary view, it is hopelessly incompatible with the form of government created by our Constitution.

B. *In Reserving Certain Spheres of Sovereign Power to the States, the Tenth and Twenty-first Amendments Free Neither the Exercise Nor the Delegation of Such Power From the Restraints of the First and Fourteenth Amendments.*

---

34. And church leaders or members who have misgivings about a liquor license *within* the 500-foot circle, but who are reluctant to exercise a veto, *cf.* J.S.A. 57A n.7, are likewise relegated to the same process as everyone else. State Br. 84 n.72. At all events, Section 16C itself plainly *creates* more entanglement problems than it *solves.* See n.15 supra.

Appellants' reliance on the Tenth and Twenty-first Amendments to add weight to the state interests supposedly served by Section 16C, *see* State Br. 25, 26-27; CLC Br. 11, 13, 38, is badly misplaced. The Tenth and Twenty-first Amendments reserve power to the *states* — not to *churches*. Moreover, to say that state power to ban a thing *completely* "necessarily" entails the power to ban it *in part*, State Br. 38-40, is to twist both law and logic by overlooking the basic proposition that a state's power to ban *any* activity, whether in whole *or* in part, remains fully subject to the strictures of the First and Fourteenth Amendments regardless of the affirmative source of *whatever* power the state purports to exercise. See *Craig v. Boren*, 429 U.S. 190, 206-209 (1976) (state law setting lower drinking age for females than for males violates equal protection notwithstanding Twenty-first Amendment); *Wisconsin v. Constantineau*, 400 U.S. 433 (1971) (state power to decide who may consume alcoholic beverages is subject to due process requirements); cf. *California Retail Liquor Dealers Assn. v. Midcal Aluminum, Inc.*, 445 U.S. 97, 109 (1980) (Twenty-first Amendment did not "repeal" even the Commerce Clause and must be reconciled with its negative implications).

Once the matter is seen in this light — with recognition that a supposed state power to ignore the Bill of Rights and the Fourteenth Amendment is in no sense a "lesser" included power — it should not seem at all surprising that these strictures often prevent the state from proscribing unevenly, and especially through too open-ended a delegation of authority to private parties, conduct that the state itself might constitutionally have forbidden altogether. A state that would be free completely to ban alcohol obviously could not, despite the Tenth and Twenty-first Amendments, limit social drinking to white males, to those who will forego political criticism while in a bar, to individuals approved as devout by designated church authorities, or to persons willing to pay sufficient tithes to such authorities. So too the state's ability to zone liquor entirely out of certain areas manifestly implies no subsumed ability *to confer upon churches or other private bodies* an unbridled power to decide *which* nearby establishments may sell liquor or serve it with the meals they sell, and which may not. In no sense is the state's ability to take this latter step a "lesser" included power — neither in terms of its economic impact upon the affected establishments as they compete with one another for patrons; nor in terms of the difference between dependence upon an agency legally and politically accountable for its acts and dependence upon the private will of another; nor in terms of the pressure to offer "donations" to a church or other private body as the price of making full use of one's liberty and property.[35]

It follows that neither the Tenth Amendment nor the Twenty-first does anything to alter the proper decision in this case, and that the court of appeal's holding to that effect, J.S.A. 24A n.11, was entirely correct.

Conclusion

The supreme importance of preserving the opportunity of all religious bodies and believers to invoke the Bill of Rights as a *shield* whether they retreat into private worship or venture into open public debate[36] must not obscure the equal significance of resisting all measures that would put into the hands of selected religious groups the *sword* of official public power — the power to make legally binding decisions about the liberty and property of others.

Far from advancing the ultimate cause of religion in a pluralistic society, any such delegation of civil authority to ecclesiastical officials would inevitably endanger the spiritual as well as the secular sphere. For legally sanctioned power in our system eventually

35. This analysis plainly does not conflict with this Court's decisions sustaining "the power of a State to prohibit topless dancing in an establishment licensed by the state to serve liquor." New York State Liquor Authority v. Bellanca, 101 S. Ct. 2599, 2600 (1981) (per curiam); California v. LaRue, 409 U.S. 109 (1972). For, even assuming that the state's "power to ban the sale of alcoholic beverages entirely includes the lesser power to ban the sale of liquor on premises where topless dancing occurs," *Bellanca,* 101 S. Ct. at 2601 (but see id. at 2602 & n.3 (Stevens, J., dissenting)), that conclusion reflects two special considerations, both absent here: *first,* that unique problems are "associated with mixing alcohol and nude dancing," 101 S. Ct. at 2601; and *second,* that zoning erotic activities away from places where alcohol is consumed may indeed be a "lesser" exercise of governmental power than banning either component of the mix — suggestive nudity *or* liquor — altogether. Cf. Schad v. Borough of Mount Ephraim, 101 S. Ct. 2176 (1981) (striking down community-wide ban on live entertainment); Young v. American Mini Theatres, Inc., 427 U.S. 50 (1976) (upholding municipal ordinance requiring at least 1,000 feet between adult book stores, adult movie theaters, liquor stores, pool halls, and the like). *Delegating* to churches the power to zone the sale of liquor out of the business district such churches occupy — and especially the power to do so *selectively,* banning whichever nearby liquor establishments the churches in question decide to veto — differs in both these crucial dimensions from the legislative actions upheld in *Bellanca* and *LaRue.*
36. See McDaniel v. Paty, 435 U.S. 618 (1978) (ministers cannot be excluded from legislative office); Walz v. Tax Commission, 397 U.S. 664, 670 (1970) (religious bodies have same right as secular bodies to "take strong positions on public issues") (dictum).

brings politically imposed responsibility in its wake.[37] Unless utter despotism is to prevail, churches that begin as unaccountable enclaves of coercion backed by law — the sort of coercion sanctioned on a discriminatory basis by Section 16C — will end as the servants of a theocratic state, themselves the subjects of the coercive power they undertake to wield. "It seems trite but necessary to say that the First Amendment to our Constitution was designed to avoid these ends by avoiding these beginnings." *West Virginia Board of Education* v. *Barnette*, 319 U.S. 624, 641 (1943). The religious establishment created by Section 16C, both because of what it *does* and because of what laws like it *threaten* to do, should be struck down by this Court, and the judgment of the court of appeals should accordingly be affirmed.

Respectfully submitted,
LAURENCE H. TRIBE,
1525 Massachusetts Avenue,
Cambridge, Massachusetts 02138.
(617) 495-4621
Counsel of Record.

IRA KARASICK,
206 Fifth Avenue,
New York, New York
DAVID ROSENBERG,
1525 Massachusetts Avenue,
Cambridge, Mass. 02138.
Counsel for Appellee.

April 12, 1982

---

37. See, e.g., the 1631 statute quoted in W. Hening, 1 Statutes at Large of Virginia 158 (1823):

Mynisters shall not give themselves to excess in drinkinge, or riott, spendinge their tyme idellye by day or night, playinge at dice, cards, or any other unlawful game; but at all tymes convenient they shall heare or reade somewhat of the holy scriptures, or shall occupie themselves with some other honest study or exercise, always doinge the thinges which shall apperteyne to honesty, and endeavour to profitt the church of God, always haveinge in mynd that they ought to excell all others in puritie of life, and should be examples to the people to live well and christianlie.

In the
Supreme Court of the United States

OCTOBER TERM, 1983

No. 83-2627

NATIONAL AUDUBON SOCIETY
Plaintiff-Petitioner

v.

WILLIAM P. CLARK,
Secretary of the Interior
Defendant-Respondent

No. 83-2653

WILLIAM P. CLARK,
Secretary of the Interior
Defendant-Petitioner

v.

NATIONAL AUDUBON SOCIETY
Plaintiff-Respondent

Opening Brief of
WILLIAM P. CLARK, Secretary of the Interior

Henryk Hiller
Duke University School of Law
Durham, NC 27706

Counsel for Defendant-Petitioner Clark

Table of Contents

Table of Authorities

CASES

In the
Supreme Court of the United States

OCTOBER TERM, 1983

No. 83-2627

NATIONAL AUDUBON SOCIETY

Plaintiff-Petitioner

v.

WILLIAM P. CLARK

Secretary of the Interior

Defendant-Respondent

No. 83-2653

WILLIAM P. CLARK,

Secretary of the Interior

Defendant-Petitioner

v.

NATIONAL AUDUBON SOCIETY

Plaintiff-Respondent

Opening Brief of
WILLIAM P. CLARK, Secretary of the Interior

Opinions Below

The opinions of the United States District Court for the District of Alaska and the United States Court of Appeals for the Ninth Circuit have not yet been reported; they are appended to this brief.

Jurisdiction

The Supreme Court has jurisdiction by writ of certiorari granted upon petition. 28 U.S.C. §1254(1) (1976). Defendant-petitioners timely applied for certiorari, which was granted January 12, 1984, thirty-eight days after the December 5, 1983 judgment of the Court of Appeals. See 28 U.S.C. §2101(c) (1976).

Questions Presented

I. Whether Congress, in enacting the compromise necessary to settle Native claims to federal lands, intended that the Secretary of the Interior have the discretion to specify narrow criteria for the conveyance of public lands as Native "historical places" under section 14(h)(1) of the Alaska Native Claims Settlement Act.

II. Whether, after all Alaska Native aboriginal land claims are extinguished by Congress to insure clear federal title to public lands, the First Amendment freedom of religious exercise clause requires that a tribe of Natives be given access to a site on federal land that is being conveyed to a private party.

Statutes and Regulations Involved

Defendant-petitioners seek reversal of the judgment of the United States Court of Appeals for the Ninth Circuit, which held that section 14(h) of the Alaska Native Claims Settlement Act (ANCSA) was intended to include solely religious sites as historical places to be conveyed to Native groups under that section.

The pertinent portion of section 14(h) reads as follows:

The Secretary is authorized to withdraw and convey 2 million acres of unreserved and unappropriated lands located outside the areas withdrawn by sections 1610 and 1615 of this title, and [sic] follows:

(1) The Secretary may withdraw and convey to the appropriate Regional Corporation fee title to existing cemetery sites and historical places.

43 U.S.C. §1613(h) (1976).

The regulations promulgated under ANCSA section 14(h)(1) set forth criteria for determining whether a selection site is a historical place. The pertinent part of section 2653.5(d) of Title 43 of the Code of Federal Regulations reads:

> For purposes of evaluating and determining the eligibility of properties as historical places, the quality of significance in Native history or culture shall be considered to be present in places that possess integrity of location, design, setting, materials, workmanship, feeling, and association, and:
> (1) That are associated with events that have made a significant contribution to the history of Alaskan Indians, Eskimos, or Aleuts, or
> (2) That are associated with the lives of persons significant in the past . . . or
> (3) That possess outstanding and demonstrably enduring symbolic value in the tradition and cultural beliefs and practices of Alaskan Indians. . . .

Alaska Native Selections, 43 C.F.R. §2653.5(d) (1976).

Defendant-petitioners also seek reversal of the appellate court holding that plaintiff-respondent Otterwauk Tribe is entitled to access to the St. Matthew Island site under the free exercise clause of the Constitution and the American Indian Religious Freedom Act. The pertinent part of the Act states: "[I]t shall be the policy of the United States to protect and preserve for American Indians their inherent right of freedom to believe, express, and exercise the traditional religions. . . . " 42 U.S.C. §1996 (Supp. V 1981).

Statement

In 1975, plaintiff-respondent Otterwauk Tribe (the Tribe), as a duly incorporated Alaska Native Corporation, applied to the Bureau of Land Management (BLM) to have a 40-acre federally-owned site on St. Matthew Island conveyed to them. District Court Opinion (D. Ct. Op.) 2. The Tribe applied for conveyance of the site as a Native selection under section 14(h)(1) of the Alaska Native Claims Settlement Act (ANCSA), 43 U.S.C. §1613(h)(1). Id. The site is one at which the Tribe has held a religious ceremony, although how many times the ceremony has occurred there is not known. Id.

BLM determined in 1981 that the Tribe's selection did not meet the criteria specified in the regulations promulgated under ANCSA section 14(h)(1), 43 C.F.R. §2653.5, for the conveyance of historical sites. Id. The site was solely religious in character, and thus could not be conveyed under section 14(h)(1) and its regulations.

Defendant-petitioner Secretary of the Interior (the Secretary) therefore denied the selection application. Id. This denial was affirmed on appeal by the Board of Land Appeals in July 1983.

In August 1983, the United States Department of the Interior (Interior) entered into a land exchange agreement with the defendant-petitioner Cook Inlet Region, Incorporated (CIRI), an Alaska Regional Corporation. In this agreement CIRI is to convey 14,000 acres of land to the United States, and the United States is to convey 4,092 acres on St. Matthew Island to CIRI in determinable fee. Id. at 3; Complaint of National Audubon Society (Comp. NAS) 6. All lands involved in the transaction are National Wildlife Refuge Lands, and authorization for the exchange was found in section 1302(h) of the Alaska National Interest Lands Conservation Act. Comp. NAS 3, 6. CIRI intends to lease the lands to Atlantic Richfield Company for use as a base for oil exploration in the Bering Sea. D. Ct. Op. 2. The site the Tribe sought to have conveyed to it is located within the lands that are to be conveyed to CIRI.

The Tribe brought an action in the United States District Court for the District of Alaska against defendant-petitioners the Secretary, the Deputy Undersecretary of the Interior (Alaska) and CIRI, requesting declaratory and injunctive relief. Complaint of Otterwauk Tribe (Comp. OT) 1. The Tribe requested that the district court declare that the denial of its selection application was invalid. The Tribe also requested an injunction against altering the site and an order that it be allowed continued access to the site. Id. at 3. The suit was consolidated with one brought by the National Audubon Society against defendant-petitioners, which requested: (1) a declaration that the land exchange agreement between CIRI and Interior is invalid; and (2) that its implementation be enjoined. Comp. NAS 11-12.

The District Court dismissed all claims against defendant-petitioners in September 1983. D. Ct. Op. 4. The United States Court of Appeals for the Ninth Circuit affirmed that part of the District Court's holding concerning the land exchange agreement, but reversed with regard to the Tribe's claims. Court of Appeals Opinion (Ct. Ap. Op.) 1-2. The Court of Appeals held that Congress did not intend sites that are solely religious to be excluded from ANCSA section 14(h)(1) conveyances. Id. at 2. The court also held that the free religious exercise clause of the United States Constitution, and the American Indian Religious Freedom Act (AIRFA), entitled the Tribe to access to the site on St. Matthew Island. Id. The holding of the Court of Appeals regarding the Tribe should be reversed. The regulations promulgated under ANCSA section 14(h)(1) are consistent with legislative intent, and the Tribe's free exercise claim is invalid.

Summary of the Argument

I. The first issue presented is whether the legislature intended the Secretary to have the discretion to narrowly define "historical places" to be conveyed under ANCSA section 14(h)(1), 43 U.S.C. §1613(h)(1). The regulations promulgated by the Secretary require "historical places" to be characterized by something human-made, and to be associated with particularly significant historical events, periods, figures, or symbolism. Alaska Native Selections, 43 C.F.R. §2653.5(d) (1976). The Tribe argues that solely religious sites should be included under the category of "historical places." ANCSA's legislative history does not provide the Secretary with specific criteria for determining which sites are "historical." However, an examination of the words employed by the legislature, their context, and the purposes of ANCSA clearly indicates that the legislature intended the Secretary to have the discretion to narrowly define "historical places," and thereby to exclude solely religious sites from being conveyed.

A comparison of the words employed in ANCSA with those in unenacted versions indicates that Congress differentiated historical sites from those of a cultural or economic character, as well as from abandoned villages and cemeteries. Each of these five categories appeared in the prior versions of ANCSA, but the enacted version provides only for conveying cemeteries and historical sites. There is no indication that Congress intended to broaden the category of historical sites. Sites of a religious character are cultural, and not intended to be conveyed as historical unless they also have the characteristics required of historical sites.

The discretion of the Secretary is consistent with the general purpose of ANCSA. Claims of Alaska Natives to federal and state-owned lands, based on aboriginal use and occupancy, had prevented the development of the Alaskan economy as well as impeding other major land use programs. ANCSA was enacted as a compromise among the interests at stake to extinguish all Native claims, provide Natives with legal title to certain lands, and thereby clear the title of the state and United States to the remainder of the public lands. Native groups received title to certain lands surrounding the villages. Section 14(h)(1) was to supplement these conveyances with exceptionally significant lands elsewhere in the state.

A broad construction of "historical" would render the Secretary unable to limit the location of section 14(h)(1) conveyances, since most of the state is associated with the Native past. Including solely religious sites under "historical places" would not allow for the necessary compromise, as it would greatly increase the number of sites the Secretary would be bound to convey. A narrow interpretation of "historical" allows for the conveyance of particularly significant sites while reducing the likelihood that sites of importance to the state and federal governments will be conveyed. The prior versions of ANCSA also provided mechanisms for limiting conveyances outside village areas.

II. The second issue is whether the Tribe's freedom of religious exercise would be unconstitutionally violated by a denial of access to the site on St. Matthew Island. A free exercise claim is valid only if the plaintiffs establish a burden on religious exercise and there is no government interest of sufficient magnitude to override that burden. The Tribe's claim does not satisfy either component of this test.

The Tribe has not demonstrated that a burden exists. It has not been shown that the Tribe annually conducts the rite at the St. Matthew site; there is therefore no evidence to indicate that a religious tenet compels annual worship at the site. Moreover, even if such a burden is established, the government interest in extinguishing all Native land claims is sufficiently important to override it. To allow the Tribe access to the site would be to honor a claim extinguished by ANCSA, and therefore create a wide exception to the settlement that ANCSA embodies. This would resurrect many, and perhaps all, Native claims, and once again prevent Alaskan energy resources and other land uses from being developed. Denying the Tribe access on the basis of such an overriding interest is consistent with the American Indian Religious Freedom Act, which was intended simply to assure Indian religions the constitutional guarantees accorded all religions.

Argument

I. THE LEGISLATIVE PURPOSE UNDERLYING THE ENACTMENT OF ANCSA AND THE SPECIFIC WORDING OF SECTION 14(h)(1) INDICATE THAT CONGRESS INTENDED THE SECRETARY TO EXERCISE DISCRETION IN NARROWLY DEFINING "HISTORICAL PLACES."

Section 14(h)(1) of the Alaska Native Claims Settlement Act (ANCSA) provides that the Secretary may convey to Native corporations fee title to cemetery sites and historical places. 43 U.S.C. §1613(h)(1) (1976 and Supp. V 1981). The regulations promulgated by the Secretary, under section 25 of ANCSA, 43 U.S.C. §1624 (1976), set forth the criteria for determining which Native selections are "historical" sites. See Alaska Native Selections, 43 C.F.R. §2653.5 (1976).

The regulations require that the site have a certain "quality of significance" beyond a simple association with the Native past. See id. §2653.5(d). This significance exists when two factors are present. First, the site must possess "integrity of location, design, setting, materials, workmanship, feeling and association." Id. Each of these seven characteristics must exist; the site is therefore to be characterized by something human-made. Second, the site must either be associated with particularly significant Native historical events, periods or figures, or possess "outstanding and demonstrably enduring symbolic value" in Native tradition and cultural beliefs. See id. This second factor must be present in addition to the first.[1]

It is this narrow use of "historical" that respondents have challenged in contending that Congress did not intend "historical places" to exclude solely religious sites. However, there is nothing in ANCSA's legislative history that explicitly provides criteria for the Secretary to use in determining what constitutes a "historical place." Indeed, the clear intent of the legislature was to provide the Secretary with the discretion to set narrow standards for historical sites, and thereby to further the objectives of ANCSA.

Legislative intent is to be garnered from the words used, their context, and the purposes of the law. See, e.g., *Kokoszka* v. *Belford*, 417 U.S. 642, 650 (1974), reh'g. denied, 419 U.S. 886 (1974); *Vermilya-Brown Co.* v. *Cornell*, 335 U.S. 377, 386 (1948), reh'g. denied, 336 U.S. 928 (1949). An examination of these factors clearly indicates that "historical" was not intended in its broad sense. The legislature left it to the Secretary to set forth precise criteria for determining the historical character of sites, with the intention that the term be interpreted narrowly.

A. *The Words Employed Require a Narrow Construction, as There Is No Indication That Congress Intended to Broaden the Meaning of "Historical" from Its Narrow Usage in the Senate Version of ANCSA.*

---

1. Subsection (e) expands upon these factors, and must therefore be read as incorporating them. 43 C.F.R. §2653.5(e) (1976).

There is nothing in ANCSA's legislative history that gives specific criteria for the Secretary to use in determining what constitutes a "historical place." Nor is there any explicit indication that solely religious sites are to be considered within the category of "historical places." Indeed, a comparison of the words employed in ANCSA with those employed in unenacted versions clearly indicates that Congress intended "historical" to be construed in such a narrow sense that it would exclude solely religious sites.

The first version of ANCSA to pass the Senate provided for certain conveyances "to provide protection for cemeteries, abandoned villages, and areas of historical and cultural significance." S. 1830, 91st Cong., 2d Sess. §18(b)(2), 116 Cong. Rec. 24,203 (1970). No bill was passed by the House during that session. The second version to pass the Senate (the version that went to the conference committee) provided for Natives to select one of two conveyance plans. In the first plan the language of the prior bill was repeated. See S. 35, 92d Cong., 1st Sess. §19(a)(2)(B), 117 Cong. Rec. 38,305 (1971). In the second plan, a new category was added: areas of "economic significance" to Natives. See id. §19(b)(2)(C). Historical sites were thus specifically differentiated from those of strictly cultural or economic significance, as well as from cemeteries and abandoned village sites. Historical sites were to be characterized by more than just a general association with past Native activity, whether that activity was of a social, cultural, or economic character.

The reduction in explicit categories for conveyance in ANCSA is left unexplained by Congress. In the absence of any indication that "historical" was to be broadened to include the omitted categories, we must conclude that Congress intended the differentiation to remain. This is supported by the retention of the category of "cemetery sites." If "historical" was to become the multipurpose category, there was no need to retain "cemeteries" as a separate category, since such sites are clearly within the broad meaning of historical.

The regulations promulgated by the Secretary require a historical site to be characterized by something human-made and particularly important in the group's past. This narrow construction is consistent with the way in which "historical" is employed by the legislature. Sites of a religious character are best characterized as cultural, unless they also incorporate the elements required for historical sites. Land characterized solely by its religious value is unarguably cultural, and therefore differentiated from sites of a historical character.

B. *The Discretion of the Secretary Is Consistent with the General Purpose of ANCSA, Which Is to Effect a Compromise Among the Interests of the Natives, the State, and the Federal Government.*

  1. ANCSA's compromise requires limiting the conveyance to Natives of lands outside village selection areas in order to protect state and federal government interests.

ANCSA was enacted to give the Natives legal title to specific lands, and, by extinguishing Native claims based on aboriginal use or occupancy, to give the state and federal governments clear title to the remainder of the public lands in the state. To deny the Secretary discretion in conveying section 14(h)(1) lands would defeat the general intent of Congress with regard to the land claims settlement.

The status of Native claims had remained unresolved since the passage of the Organic Act in 1884. See Act of May 17, 1884, 23 Stat. 24. In this and subsequent acts, Congress provided that the Natives were to remain undisturbed in the possession of lands that they used, occupied, or claimed. S. Rep. No. 925, 91st Cong., 2d Sess. 69, 70 (1970). Congress retained sole power to determine the extent of the Natives' title. Id.

The Statehood Act of 1958 granted Alaska the right to select over 103 million acres of federally-owned and unappropriated public lands. 48 U.S.C. §21 (1976). The Natives, reacting to the first wave of state selections, filed official protests over these selections, claiming much of the available land as their own. S. Rep. No. 925, supra, at 77. The state was unable to complete its Statehood Act selections or fully develop its natural resources. Id. at 66.

The unresolved status of Native claims delayed the opening of federal lands for oil and gas exploration, and in 1969 a general freeze on all appropriation of public lands went into effect. Id. at 78, 79. The removal of this land freeze was of primary importance to the legislature. Id. at 66.

Congress recognized that resolving the outstanding Native claims required balancing these three interests: "a just and equitable settlement can be constructed around the long-term land needs of the Natives, the United States, and the State of Alaska." Id. at 78; see also Conf. Rep. No. 746, 92d Cong., 1st Sess. 34, reprinted in 1971 Code Cong. & Ad. News 2247.

The compromise in ANCSA provides that all Native land claims based on aboriginal use or occupancy be legally extinguished. See 43 U.S.C. §1603 (1976). As compensation, the Natives receive:

1) title to a prescribed amount of land surrounding their villages, as well as to specifically designated additional lands; 2) a collective payment of $962.5 million; and 3) participation in a program of revenue sharing of the proceeds from federal mineral leasing. See 43 U.S.C. §§1605, 1606, 1613. The extinguishment of Native claims allows the federal and state governments to pursue development and conservation programs on the remaining public lands.

Congress did not intend Native groups to have a free hand in selecting unappropriated public lands under section 14(h)(1). The interests of both the state and federal government in the use of public lands for development and conservation (interests protected by ANCSA in its compromise) are to be honored in any plan for conveyance under that section. Congress therefore intended that the Secretary limit these conveyances to provide this protection.

Binding the Secretary to convey on the basis of the history of a given Native group would make him unable to limit Native selections of mineral-rich (or any other) lands.[2] Most of the lands in Alaska are generally associated with the past of one or another Native group. See e.g., H.R. Rep. No. 523, 92d Cong., 1st Sess. 4, reprinted in 1971 U.S. Code Cong. & Ad. News 2192, 2194. A narrow construction of "historical places" allows for conveying particularly significant sites only. Strict criteria minimize the likelihood that lands that are particularly important to the government will be conveyed. These criteria reduce the likelihood that meritorious selection sites will be located on those lands.

The authority of the Secretary to convey sites would be significantly weakened if solely religious sites were included in "historical places." Since the belief systems of Native groups are likely to define large numbers of sites as "religious" in character, such a construction of "historical" would vastly increase the number of sites that the Secretary would be bound to convey.[3] This would also increase the opportunity and incentive for Native groups to select "religious sites" on the basis of the land's economic value. The Secretary would be unable to distinguish such selections. The

---

2. Once a regulatory scheme is promulgated, the Secretary would be bound to honor selections that meet its criteria; thus, any general discretion to deny selections provided in section 14(h)(1) would be lost. See Wisenak, Inc. v. Andrus, 471 F. Supp. 1004, 1009 (D. Alaska 1979).

3. Eskimos, for example, believe the visible world to be ruled by supernatural powers, called "inua": "strictly speaking, scarcely any object existing either in a physical or spiritual point of view may not be conceived to have its inua." 5 Encyclopaedia of Religion and Ethics 394 (Hastings ed. 1912).

result would be a conveyance scheme tilted strongly in favor of Native interests.

The regulations that the Secretary promulgated properly balance the interests of all concerned. Requiring that the historical site be characterized by something human-made allows the validity of a selection to be objectively verified while limiting the number of sites available. In this way, particularly significant sites are conveyed while minimizing the threat to the interests of the state and federal governments.

> 2. In order to protect the interests of state and federal government, prior versions of ANCSA provided mechanisms limiting conveyances to Natives of lands outside village selection areas.

The Senate and House versions of ANCSA provide mechanisms to insure that conveyances outside Native village areas do not deny legitimate federal or state interests.

The Senate version provided for Native Village Corporations to select a prescribed amount of land surrounding the villages. See S. 35, supra, §14. In addition, a statewide Native organization (the Services Corporation) was to apply for conveying public lands in order to, among other things, "provide protection for cemeteries, abandoned villages, and areas of historical and cultural significance to Natives." Id. §19(a)(2)(B); see also id. §19(b)(2)(C). The Services Corporation was to apply to the Alaska Native Commission, and this Commission was to have minority Native participation. Id. §6(a). The Commission's assessment of the merits of each selection was to be final and unreviewable. Id. §19(a)(2)(B). When the Commission terminated after seven years, all Commission functions, including this discretionary task of certifying applications, were to vest in the Secretary. Id. §6(m).

In the House version of ANCSA, the Natives selected land in two stages. In the first stage, 18 million acres of land surrounding the villages were to be conveyed to the Native Village Corporations. H.R. Rep. No. 523, supra, at 6. In the second stage, 22 million acres were to be conveyed, with the land in each of 11 regions being selected by and conveyed to a Native Regional Corporation. H.R. 10367, 92d Cong., 1st Sess. 12(j), 117 Cong. Rec. 37,067. It was to be in this second stage that lands similar to those in section 14(h) would be selected. However, between the two stages the state would be entitled to select all lands in accordance with the Statehood Act, and the federal government could reserve any additional lands for its own needs. H.R. Rep. No. 523, supra.

The balance would be achieved by insuring that Native selections beyond the village areas did not conflict with those of the state and United States.

These mechanisms for limiting Native selections outside village areas were abandoned in conference. Both the Services Corporation and the Commission were eliminated, and a one-stage selection process was adopted. In this one-stage selection process, Congress gave the Secretary discretion to specify narrow criteria for meritorious conveyances, under section 14(h)(1), thereby allowing Native groups to receive exceptional historical places while minimizing the threat to government interests in the rest of the state.

> 3. The conveyance of fee title to lands under section 14(h)(1) indicates that Congress intended the Secretary to limit the conveyance of historical sites by promulgating strict criteria.

Section 14(h)(1) of ANCSA provides that the Secretary may convey to Natives title in fee to selections of any unreserved and unappropriated public lands. 43 U.S.C. §1613(h)(1) (1976 and Supp. V 1981). The Natives would therefore receive title to the subsurface estate of selected lands, and to any minerals in those lands.

As indicated in point I(B)(2), it is in the interest of the United States and the State of Alaska to avoid having Natives select lands outside village areas on the basis of economic value. The compromise embodied in ANCSA provides for Native control of minerals in village selection areas, as well as for royalty payments on minerals procured by state or federal efforts elsewhere in the state. See e.g., S. Rep. No. 925, supra, at 47.

A broad use of "historical" would allow Native groups to select virtually any area not yet appropriated, and would thereby threaten future Alaskan development and conservation programs. This would be inconsistent with the prior versions of ANCSA, which limited Native selections outside the villages.

Both versions of ANCSA that passed the Senate limited the conveyance of historical and cultural sites, cemeteries, and abandoned villages to the surface estate alone. See S.35, supra, §§19(a)(2)(B), 19(b)(2)(C); S. 1830, supra, §18(b)(2). In this way, Natives were discouraged from selecting lands for subsurface qualities. Indeed, the state and federal governments were assured title to all subsurface lands outside village selection areas.

The two-stage selection process in the House version of ANCSA accomplished the same objective. See H.R. 10367, supra, §11. The state and federal governments would be able to make any land reservations before Natives selected outside village selection areas.

These mechanisms for limiting Natives' selection of lands outside village selection areas were not incorporated into the final version of ANCSA, which provided for a one-stage selection process and full fee title to historical sites. A narrow construction of "historical" is the necessary mechanism of limitation in the enacted version. It achieves the compromise of ANCSA by insuring that exceptional Native claims are honored while protecting the interests of the federal and state governments.

II. THE TRIBE'S FREE EXERCISE CLAIM MUST FAIL. NO BURDEN HAS BEEN ESTABLISHED, THE GOVERNMENT INTEREST INVOLVED IS OF THE HIGHEST IMPORTANCE, AND DENYING ACCESS WOULD NOT CONFLICT WITH THE AMERICAN INDIAN RELIGIOUS FREEDOM ACT.

A. *The Tribe's Free Exercise Claim Lacks Validity, Since No Burden on Religious Practice Has Been Established and the Interests of the Governments Are of Sufficient Magnitude to Override a Burden if It Does Exist.*

The Tribe does not have a First Amendment right of continued access to the St. Matthew Island site after it was conveyed from Interior to CIRI. The appellate court holding that the Tribe be allowed this access under the free exercise of religion clause should be reversed.

There are two steps in the process of determining the validity of a free exercise claim. The party asserting the infringement must first demonstrate that the statute or government action in question imposes a burden on the exercise of religion. E.g., *Sherbert* v. *Verner*, 374 U.S. 398, 403 (1963). If such a burden is established, the court then determines whether there is a government interest "of sufficient magnitude to override the interest claiming protection under the free exercise clause." *Wisconsin* v. *Yoder*, 406 U.S. 205, 214 (1972); see also *Sherbert*, 374 U.S. at 406. Applying this test to the present case clearly leads to the conclusion that no valid infringement claim exists. The Tribe has failed to demonstrate the necessary burden, and even if a burden could be established, sufficiently important national interests exist to overcome it.

1. The Tribe has failed to sustain the evidentiary burden of demonstrating that the proposed denial of access improperly restricts the Tribe's free exercise of religion.

A law or government act is unduly restrictive if its objective or effect is "to impede the observance of one or all religions." *Braunfeld* v. *Brown,* 366 U.S. 599, 607 (1961). However, the impediment to religious observance is held to exist only when the statute or government act either prohibits a religious tenet from being followed, or strongly compels that the tenet be abandoned. See *Thomas* v. *Review Board of Indiana Employment Security Division,* 450 U.S. 707, 717 (1981) (unemployment statute required abandoning religious tenet to qualify for benefits); *Yoder,* 406 U.S. at 618 (compulsory school statute denied exercise of central Amish tenet of integrating children into lifestyle); *Sherbert,* 374 U.S. at 404 (unemployment statute required abandoning religious tenet to qualify for benefits). The instant case can be distinguished, since the alleged interference is geographic rather than substantive.[4]

The Tribe has not adequately demonstrated that a denial of access to St. Matthew will force the Tribe to abandon a tenet of the Tribe's religion. It is not clear that the Tribe is required by a religious tenet to worship at the island site each year. The District Court found that "there is no indication that the ceremonies have always occurred on St. Matthew Island." D. Ct. Op. 2. The testimony of the eldest tribe member indicated only that she had attended the ceremony for many years but did not specify the location. See id. Similarly, the Tribe's Chief, in response to a question of whether the tribe had ever held the ceremony elsewhere, testified to the events in one particular year, without indicating whether that was the only year the site was not used. See District Court Transcript at 291.

There is no suggestion that denial of access to the site would result in the Tribe's abandoning the whale ceremony or the worship of the gods. The Tribe has failed to establish that its religious tenets include a yearly pilgrimage to this particular site.

Prohibiting a nonreligious event associated with but not requisite to a religious observance does not constitute a burden on the free exercise of religion. There is therefore no basis for concluding that the Tribe's religious exercise would be impeded by denying it access to St. Matthew.

---

4. Freedom of expression was not considered by the appellate court. The burden/overriding interest test also applies to free expression claims. See, e.g., Hudgens v. NLRB, 424 U.S. 507, 520 (1976); Konigsberg v. State Bar of California, 366 U.S. 36, 49-51 (1961). The District Court held that no burden existed. D. Ct. Op. 1. This is clearly correct. Denial of access does not prohibit or compel that the speech elements of the ceremony be abandoned; it is the religious elements that are at issue.

2. Even if a burden exists, extinguishing all Native claims is a government interest of sufficient importance to the state and federal governments to override the free exercise claim.

Even if it is concluded that denying access constitutes a burden on the free exercise of the Tribe's religion, the government interest that would be impaired by allowing access is of sufficient magnitude to override that burden and deny the claim. The government interest here meets the requisite standard as an interest of the highest order, which cannot otherwise be served without burdening the Tribe's free exercise rights. See *Yoder,* 406 U.S. at 215; *Sherbert,* 374 U.S. at 406, 407.

In determining whether the government interest is sufficiently compelling, the general policy behind the statute or administrative order is to be considered. See, e.g., *Thomas,* 450 U.S. at 718 (purpose of unemployment scheme considered to determine government interest in denying benefits); *Yoder,* 406 U.S. at 218 (purpose of compulsory education statute considered). In the present case, a denial of access is consistent with the provisions and objectives of ANCSA. To allow access would be to defeat those objectives.

As discussed in point I(B)(1), the legislative purpose in enacting ANCSA was two-fold: to provide Natives with clear legal title to certain lands, and to facilitate the general development of the rest of the state. The second of these objectives was to be achieved by removing the cloud on state and federal title to Alaskan public lands. This cloud was a result of the claims to the lands made by Natives on the basis of aboriginal use or occupancy. The key element in the settlement was the legal extinguishment of these claims. See, e.g., S. Rep. No. 925, supra, at 46. Extinguishing the claims was the concession the Natives made in exchange for the land, money, and revenue sharing received under ANCSA. E.g., id. at 47.

Thus, the first finding and declaration in ANCSA states: "there is an immediate need for a fair and just settlement of all claims by Natives and Native groups. . . . " 43 U.S.C. §1601(a) (1976). The pertinent part of the declaration of settlement states: "[A]ll aboriginal titles, if any, and claims of aboriginal title in Alaska based on use and occupancy . . . are hereby extinguished." 43 U.S.C. §1603(b) (1976); see also Conf. Rep. No. 746, supra, at 40.

The extinguishment of all claims was explicitly accepted by the Alaska Federation of Natives, which claims to represent "virtually all Alaska Natives." See Alaska Native Land Claims: Hearings on S. 1830 Before the Senate Comm. on Interior and Insular Affairs, 91st

Cong., 1st Sess. 111 (1969). The Federation submitted its own version of ANCSA, which contained a section extinguishing all claims, and stated that this section was to ease the concern of "the State and a number of oil companies that, even after legislation to settle land claims was enacted the Natives would be free to challenge the rights of any land holder other than the Federal Government." Id. at 586. The challenge to the federal government was simply the exercise of selection rights.

To allow the Tribe access to the site on St. Matthew Island would be to honor a claim extinguished by ANCSA. The consequences of such an action would be tremendous. It would, in effect, nullify section 4 of ANCSA, which had extinguished all claims. Native groups would once again be able to challenge public and private title to land anywhere in the state. (As discussed in point I(B)(1), a large amount of land may be subject to religious claims.) Sites yet to be leased by the government for oil or mineral exploration could lose their value, since land alterations and operations may not be possible if the lessor must provide access to the tribes. Moreover, operations already underway may be required to shut down to honor tribal needs. The cloud on all titles would be resurrected, and the land-freeze necessarily reimposed. The development of the state would again be hindered. See, e.g., S. Rep. No. 925, supra, at 56. Moreover, the threat to energy resources that are crucial to the United States would again arise.

It is also possible that ANCSA could not withstand such a wide exception to the settlement it prescribes. There would surely be challenges to the Native groups receiving the land, cash, and revenue-sharing aspects of the settlement while they were only partially fulfilling their side of the compromise. If the settlement were to fall apart, all Native land claims would be resurrected.

There is no practical alternative for assuring that the federal and state governments would have clear title to public lands while also honoring all Native religious claims in the state. The cloud would be inescapable, and the objectives of ANCSA necessarily frustrated.

It is clear that the importance of providing the federal and state governments with clear title to Alaskan public lands overrides the Tribe's claim to free exercise. *Braunfeld* held that free exercise could be overridden by the domestic tranquility interest of a state in declaring a single day of rest from work. 366 U.S. at 608; *Sherbert*, 374 U.S. at 408 (stating Braunfeld holding). The economic interests at stake in the instant case are surely of higher importance. Compare *Badoni v. Higginson*, 638 F.2d 172 (10th Cir. 1980) (maintenance of multi-state water storage and power generation project overrides Indian claim of free exercise).

B. *Denial of the Free Exercise Claim Is Consistent with the American Indian Religious Freedom Act, Which Was Intended Solely to Emphasize First Amendment Protection of Indian Religion.*

Denying the Tribe access to the site on St. Matthew Island will not violate the American Indian Religious Freedom Act (AIRFA). 42 U.S.C. §1996 (Supp. V 1981). The pertinent part of that act states: "it shall be the policy of the United States to protect and preserve for American Indians their inherent right of freedom to believe, express, and exercise the traditional religions of the American Indian, Eskimo, Aleut, and Native Hawaiians." Id. The legislative intent underlying the enactment of AIRFA was not to deny the federal government the right to interfere with Indian religions when an overriding national interest requires it. See *Wilson* v. *Block,* 708 F.2d 735, 745-47 (D.C. Cir. 1983).

AIRFA was enacted in response to discriminatory practices of federal officials, such as the physical denial of access to sites and the disruption of rites. See H.R. Rep. No. 1308, 85th Cong., 2d Sess. 2-3, reprinted in 1978 U.S. Code Cong. & Ad. News 1262, 1263-4; S. Rep. No. 709, 85th Cong., 2d Sess. 2-4. The intent of the legislature was to combat these abuses by asserting that Indian religions were protected, as any other religion, by First Amendment guarantees. See H.R. Rep. No. 1308, supra, at 1; S. Rep. No. 709, supra, at 6. Therefore, a sufficiently important national interest may still override the free exercise of an Indian religion. See 124 Cong. Rec. 21,445 (1978) (statement of Rep. Udall).

Wilson held that AIRFA requires federal agencies to consider the views of Indian leaders (though not necessarily to defer to them), and to avoid unnecessary interference with religious practices. 708 F.2d at 747. This standard was met by Congress while considering ANCSA. As noted in point II(A)(2), the Alaska Federation of Natives submitted its own settlement bill (accepting the extinguishment of claims), and it repeatedly submitted statements on various other versions. See, e.g., Alaska Native Land Claims: Hearings on H.R. 3100 and Related Bills Before the House Comm. on Interior and Insular Affairs, 92d Cong., 1st Sess. 343 (1971). Moreover, other Native representatives also submitted statements. See, e.g., id. at 350. As discussed in points I(B)(1) and II(A)(2), extinguishing all claims was an essential feature of the compromise among the interests of the Natives, the State of Alaska, and the United States.

Conclusion

For the foregoing reasons, defendant-petitioners pray that the Court enter judgment reversing the judgment of the Court of Appeals, deny plaintiff-respondents declaratory and injunctive relief, and award defendant-petitioners the costs of the suit.

Respectfully submitted,

HENRYK HILLER
Attorney for Defendant-Petitioners

Appendix:
An Overview
of English
Sentence
Structure

A Patterns of Necessary Elements

Law professors, judges, and other educated readers expect documents to be correct. When they see errors, these readers may make negative inferences about the writer's attitude and ability. One way to minimize the danger of being considered incompetent as a writer (and as a lawyer) is to eliminate errors. However, not all errors are equally easy to identify and correct. To correct spelling, you only need motivation and access to a dictionary; to correct typographical errors, you only need to plan well enough to allow time for proofreading. But to correct other problems, such as incomplete or garbled sentences, you need to understand sentence structure well enough to determine what, if anything, is wrong with sentences or phrases that don't "sound quite right" to you.

To understand how English sentences work, you need to master the concepts of **elements** and of **patterns.** Most English sentences include both *necessary elements* (revealing the *who* and *what* of the sentence) and *optional elements* (revealing *when, where, why, how, to what extent,* etc.). To be a necessary element, an element must fall into one of four categories: subject, verb, object, or complement. Necessary elements can only appear in certain patterns, i.e., in specific combinations and sequences; optional elements can appear almost anywhere.

The purpose of this section is to give you practice in separating necessary elements from optional ones and in identifying the functions that necessary elements serve. Because necessary elements do appear in patterns, reviewing the most common sentence patterns is the most efficient way to improve your understanding of sentence structure.

1. Who or What Is Who or What

This pattern for English sentences consists of three necessary elements: a subject, a linking verb, and a complement.

1. The *subject* (S) of the sentence tells who or what is being described.
2. The *linking verb* (LV) of the sentence describes a state of being and connects the subject to its complement; it is the verbal equivalent of an equal sign. It is often some form of the verb *to be* (is, were, are, will be, etc.).
3. The *complement* (C) of the sentence describes the subject by answering the question "the subject is who or what?"

Here is one way to represent this pattern:

$$S = LV = C$$

In this example, you can see how the linking verb acts as an equal sign and how the whole pattern creates a verbal equation (This = That).

> The cases are distinguishable.

> The cases are distinguishable.
>   S   LV   C

A sentence may include other words that give more information about the subject or the complement. The parts of the basic $S = LV = C$ pattern make up the *core* of the sentence. The other words are *modifiers*. In the next two examples, you can see how the core follows the $S = LV = C$ pattern.

> The appellant is Sammie Lynn Puett, a commissioner of the Tennessee Department of Human Services.

> The appellant is Sammie Lynn Puett.
>   S   LV   C

> The court was correct in granting plaintiff Clark's motion for a preliminary injunction.

> The court was correct.
>   S   LV   C

From these examples, you can see that in an $S = LV = C$ pattern

1. The subject (S) tells *who* or *what* the sentence is about.

2. The complement (C) describes the subject by answering the questions who? or what?

the cases are *what?*   distinguishable

the appellant is *who?*   Sammie Lynn Puett

the court was *what?*   correct

3. The verb only connects or links the subject to the complement. It does not tell about any action.

The modifiers (the words and word groups that are *not* part of the core or basic pattern) usually answer other questions, such as:

when?	what kind?
where?	which one?
why?	in what way?
how?	to what extent?

If the first example read

The cases are thus distinguishable

it would have a modifier (*thus*) between the verb and the complement. This sentence might be represented as

S = LV-mod = C

In the second and third examples, the modifiers, which happen to be word groups, appear at the end of the sentence. In example 2, for instance, "a Commissioner of the Tennessee Department of Human Services" modifies or gives details about the complement, "Sammie Lynn Puett." So examples 2 and 3 could both be represented like this:

S = LV = C-mod

Modifiers can also appear in other positions, but no matter where they appear, modifiers do not change the basic pattern or core (S = LV = C).

EXERCISES

1. In each of these sentences, the core is indicated for you. The subject and complement appear in all capital letters and the linking verb is italicized. Your task is to represent each sentence two ways: (1) by symbols that

indicate the pattern and the position of modifiers; and (2) by words (who is what).

Example:

> THE COURT *was* CORRECT in granting plaintiff Clark's motion for a preliminary injunction.
>
> Symbolic representation: $S = LV = C$-mod
>
> Verbal translation: What was what

a. THE PRIVATE INTEREST to be protected in this case *is* THE LIFESTYLE of the appellee, Jessie Clark.

b. For this reason, THE TERMINATION of this statutory entitlement *would be* A SIGNIFICANT DEPRIVATION of an important right.

c. THE PRETERMINATION NOTICE sent by the state to recipients of homemaker services *was* therefore INADEQUATE.

d. In June of 1980, COMMISSIONER PUETT *was* RESPONSIBLE for administering and enforcing Title XX of the Social Security Act within the state of Tennessee.

2. List the positions where modifiers can appear in a sentence that has the $S = LV = C$ pattern.

3. In each of these sentences, indicate the core by

circling the subject   ◯

underlining the verb   ———

underlining the complement twice   ═══

Example:

> (The private interest) to be protected in this case <u>is</u> the <u>lifestyle</u> of the appellee, Jessie Clark.
>
> OR
>
> The private (interest) to be protected in this case <u>is</u> the <u>lifestyle</u> of the appellee, Jessie Clark.

a. The effect of this statute is the same on Reverend Farewell.

b. Farewell's interest in his driver's license is more vital than the average person's interest.

c. The procedural safeguards were sufficient to protect the recipient's interests.

d. In *Mathews,* the third factor considered by the court was the governmental interest involved, including any fiscal and administrative burdens resulting from additional requirements.

e. Therefore, the notice requirements in *Benton* are not applicable in the case of Ms. Clark.

f. Because of the language of the lease, our client would probably be unsuccessful in getting a second renewal.

g. With only a 30 percent reduction in funding, the agency was still able to offer these services to some recipients.

h. According to the *Procedures* manual, staff members in county and local offices are responsible for providing assistance to recipients wishing to make an appeal.

2. There Exists Who or What

This second pattern, like the first, also consists of three necessary elements. They are the word *there*, a linking verb, and a subject. The core of a sentence with this pattern always begins with the word *there*. This pattern is easy to recognize even when other words come before the core in the sentence.

In sentences following this pattern the word *there* has no meaning. It does not indicate a particular place or area as it does, for example, when it is used to distinguish *there* from *here*. It simply fills the place the subject usually has in a sentence so that you can put the subject after the verb. Normally, the subject comes before the verb, but you might want to put the subject after the verb because you want to add modifiers to it. We will represent this pattern this way:

$$Th = LV = S$$

Study these examples to see how the word *there* simply serves as a filler in what is normally the subject's position in a sentence.

There must, however, be an opportunity for a fair hearing before suspension of a driver's license.

<u>There</u> must be <u>an opportunity</u>.
 Th   LV   S

In fact, there seems to be no way for Farewell to ever get his property back.

<u>There</u> seems to be <u>no way</u>.
 Th   LV   S

In this case, however, there is no compelling state or public interest.

<u>There</u> is <u>no compelling state or public interest</u>.
 Th LV   S

There was not any attempt by the Department to determine the severity of the injuries or the amount of the damages allegedly caused by Reverend Farewell.

<u>There</u> was not <u>any attempt</u>.
 Th   LV   S

From these examples, you can see

1. That the core of this pattern simply asserts that something (the subject) does or does not exist (the linking verb):
an opportunity must exist
no way exists
no state or public interest exists
no attempt existed
2. That modifiers can appear before, after, or in the middle of the core just as they could with the $S = LV = C$ pattern
3. That linking verbs can be several words long (must be, seems to be)
4. That when the negative is the word *not,* it can be considered part of the verb; when the negative word *no* precedes the subject, it can be considered part of the subject

Only a few verbs are linking verbs, but they can be combined in many ways. **Table A-1** will help you see how basic linking verbs can be combined to form multiple-word linking verbs. The past tense forms appear in parentheses.

In addition to the basic linking verbs in **Table A-1,** a few other verbs can serve as linking verbs. These verbs sometimes serve as linking verbs and sometimes as action verbs, as shown in **Table A-2.**

TABLE A-1

Basic Linking Verbs	Examples of Combined Forms
to be	should have been
am (was)	was to have been
is (was)	could have become
are (were)	will become
to become (became)	ought to have become
to seem (seemed)	seemed to be
to have to be (been)	seems to have been
has to have been (had to have been)	
have to have been (had to have been)	may have seemed
other verb + *be*	had to be
can be (could be)	will have to be
will be (would be)	
shall be (should be)	
may be (might be)	
must be	
ought to be	

TABLE A-2

Verb	as Linking Verb	as Action Verb
appear (appeared)	when it means *is, was, seem(ed) to be*: She appeared anxious.	when it means *was present*: She appeared as a witness. when it means *enter(ed)* or *walk(ed)* into: She appeared on the stage.
look (looked)	when it means *is, was*, or *seem(ed) to be*: The chances of winning looked bleak.	when it means *positioning the eyes to see*: He looked at the jury. when it means *examine(d)*: He carefully looked through the records.
feel (felt)	when it means *is, was*, or *seem(ed)*: He feels optimistic about the outcome.	when it means *touch(ed)*: He felt the child's forehead. when it means *sense(d)* or *recognize(d)*: I feel the breeze.
sound (sounded)	when it means *is, was*, or *seem(ed)*: Her argument sounded logical.	when it means *made a noise*: The alarm sounded when the window broke. when it means *attempt to discover another's opinion* or position (always occurs with the word *out*): She had *sounded out* the plaintiff's attorney before drawing up the settlement.
smell (smelled)	when it means *is, was*, or *seem(ed)*: The room smells musty.	when it means *recognize an odor*: He smelled the smoke.
taste (tasted)	when it means *is, was*, or *seem(ed) to be*: The bread tasted fresh.	when it means *recognize a flavor*: She tasted the curry in the rice. when it means *test by placing in the mouth*: I'll taste the sauce.

EXERCISES

1. In each of these sentences, indicate the core by
   underlining the word *there* twice ⸺⸺⸺
   underlining the complete linking verb once ⸺⸺⸺
   circling the subject ◯

   Example:

   Furthermore, <u><u>there</u></u> <u>is</u> (conflicting evidence) regarding the status
   of homemaker services as mandatory or optional.

   OR

   Furthermore, <u><u>there</u></u> <u>is</u> conflicting (evidence) regarding the status
   of homemaker services as mandatory or optional.

   a. In summation, there would be very little chance of convincing a
      judge to allow our client to renew the lease a second time.
   b. This way there will be no direct conflict with public policy.
   c. There seems to be no need to discuss the element of consideration.
   d. Clearly, then, there are many policy arguments both for and against
      enforcement of the contract.
   e. In jurisdictions adopting an invasion of privacy tort, there has been a
      clouding of the distinctions of existing tort laws.

2. Review of the first two patterns.
   Some of these sentences fit the $S = LV = C$ pattern and some the
   $Th = LV = S$ pattern. Underline the words that form the core (the
   necessary elements). Indicate which pattern the sentence fits.

   Example:

   In this case, however, <u>there is no compelling state or public
   interest</u> indicated by the facts. $\mathbf{Th = LV = S}$

   OR

   In this case, however, <u>there is no compelling state or public
   interest</u> indicated by the facts. $\mathbf{Th = LV = S}$

   a. With *in personam* jurisdiction readily available, there is no need for
      the state to suspend Reverend Farewell's driver's license.
   b. In this case, the timeliness of the hearing was merely coincidental.
   c. Under Georgia law, this unverified report is sufficient to trigger the
      process for suspending Reverend Farewell's driver's license.
   d. There is no evidence within the report to substantiate this claim.
   e. Suspension of an individual's driver's license is a provisional remedy
      depriving the person of important property.

   f. Any evidence of an oral statement contradicting the terms of the lease would probably not be admissible as evidence.

   g. There is little or no indication of the intent of the parties to create a perpetual right to renewal in the lease.

   h. In that case, as here, there was no stipulation regarding the amount of rent to be paid for renewal.

   i. For these reasons, the *Andrews* decision is applicable in this case.

3. Who or What Is Acting

Unlike the first two patterns, this pattern requires only two elements: a subject and an action verb.

1. The *subject* (S) of the sentence tells who or what is being described.
2. The *verb* (V) of the sentence tells what the action is.

The subject may either do the action (be the *actor*) or be acted upon (be the *receiver* of the action). Because the subject can be either actor or receiver of the action, the pattern can be represented two ways.

> When the subject is the *actor*   S → V
> (called active voice)
> When the subject is the *receiver*   S ← V
> (called passive voice)

Here are three examples of subject as actor (S → V) and three of subject as receiver (S ← V).

Subject as actor

This appeal follows.

This appeal   follows
    S   →   V

She could appeal to the Tennessee Department of Human Services for a hearing.

She   could appeal
 S →   V

In effect, the suspension of his driver's license acted to decrease his ability to pay the damages.

The suspension   acted
    S   → V

Subject as receiver

Ms. Clark is represented by Barbara Burns, acting as court appointed counsel for Appellee.

Ms. Clark   is represented
   S   ←   V

In November 1979, a statewide review of the Tennessee Social Service program was conducted.

A statewide review   was conducted
    S   ←   V

The notice requirements of *Goldberg* were further defined in *Vargas* v. *Trainor,* 508 F.2d 485 (1974).

The notice requirements   were defined
    S   ←   V

From these examples, you can see that this pattern tells about an action and

1. That the subject can be either the actor or receiver
2. That modifiers can appear before the core, between the two elements, within one of the elements, or after the core

When the subject is being acted upon (**S** ← **V**), the verb must include *at least two words*: The verb must have at least one word to direct the action toward the subject (making the sentence structure passive). This word must be some form of the verb *to be* (see **Table A-3**). The verb must also include the *past participle* of an action verb (see **Table A-4**).

TABLE A-3

Forms of the Verb *To Be*

am	was	be	*(be, being,* and *been* only
is	were	being	work when the entire
are		been	verb includes 3 words
			or more)

TABLE A-4

	Present	Past	Past Participle
REGULAR VERBS			
add -d	determine	determined	determined
	recognize	recognized	recognized
add -ed	act	acted	acted
	interpret	interpreted	interpreted
IRREGULAR VERBS			
past and past participle the same	hold	held	held
	find	found	found
	has *or* have	had	had
present and past participle the same	become	became	become
	come	came	come
all 3 forms the same	put	put	put
	hit	hit	hit
all three forms different	begin	began	begun
	do	did	done
	drink	drank	drunk
	go	went	gone
	drive	drove	driven
	speak	spoke	spoken
	show	showed	shown

EXERCISES

1. For each of these sentences, circle the subject. Indicate whether the pattern is S → V (subject as actor, active voice) or S ← V (subject as receiver, passive voice). The complete verbs appear in capital letters.
   a. Under the standards of *Vargas,* these reasons MUST BE PLACED on the notice in order to satisfy the due process requirements.
   b. The homemaker services of appellee Jesse Clark ARE PROVIDED by the State under Title XX of the Social Security Act.
   c. The Georgia suspension procedures FAIL to reflect a balance of Reverend Farewell's interests with the interests of the state and the private party.
   d. Again the Louisiana system HAS SOUGHT to minimize the risk of error.
   e. To meet the standards of *Vargas,* the recipients of benefits MUST

BE fully and adequately NOTIFIED of the reasons for the termination or reduction of their benefits.

   f. Within ten days of receiving the notice, Mrs. Clark COMPLIED by
having Ms. Burns contact the local agencies.

2. In these sentences, circle the subject and underline the complete verb
once. Indicate whether the sentence is $S \rightarrow V$ or $S \leftarrow V$.

   a. The fundamental rights of due process were set forth by the Supreme
Court in *Fuentes* v. *Shevin,* 407 U.S. 67 (1972).

   b. The appellant has been seriously harmed by the suspension of his
license.

   c. The Georgia Department of Public Safety further erred in acting as
a trial court, a violation of the Supreme Court's ruling in *Mitchell.*

   d. Outright seizure of property by a state has only been allowed under
special circumstances.

   e. Because of the nature of the fixtures, damage to the realty and to the
plumbing and heating equipment might result if they are removed.

   f. In *Warrington,* great weight is placed on the intention of the party to
permanently affix the articles to the property.

   g. In order to convert the first floor to a men's clothing shop and the
second floor to an apartment, several alterations were made to the
premises by Brooks.

   h. In all probability, our client will not prevail on the issue of renewal of
the lease.

   i. This liberal treatment of trade fixtures has not been confined to
Maryland.

4. Who or What Is Acting on What or Whom

This pattern also involves action, but it requires three elements: a subject, an
action verb, and an object.

1. The *subject* (S) of the sentence tells who or what is acting (actor).
2. The *verb* (V) of the sentence reveals what the action is.
3. The *object* (O) of the sentence tells who or what is receiving the action
(receiver).

We will represent this pattern as:

    S - V - O

Here are several examples. Note that modifiers can appear before the core,
within the core, or after the core.

On July 20, 1980, Commissioner Puett filed an appeal with this court.

Commissioner Puett filed an appeal
          S   V   O

The pretermination notice sent to recipients did not provide adequate notice of the reasons for termination.

The pretermination notice did not provide adequate notice
        S   V   O

In *Mathews* v. *Eldridge,* a case dealing with Social Security disability benefits, the Supreme Court provided a balancing test for determining the process due in a particular case.

The Supreme Court provided a balancing test
        S   V   O

In this case, Ms. Burns is representing Mrs. Clark as court appointed counsel for Appellee.

Ms. Burns is representing Mrs. Clark
    S   V   O

To determine if a particular word is the object of the sentence, repeat the subject and action verb followed by the question *what?* or *whom?* For example:

> Puett filed *what?*   an appeal
> The notice did not provide *what?*   adequate notice
> The Supreme Court provided *what?*   a balancing test
> Ms. Burns is representing *whom?*   Mrs. Clark

If the verb is an action verb, the answer to your *what?* or *whom?* will be a person or thing that serves as the object of the sentence. Remember that if the verb is a linking verb, you have a *complement,* not an object. Remember that *answers to other questions* (e.g., how? in what way? why? when? where? to what extent?) are *modifiers,* not objects.

EXERCISES

All of these sentences have action verbs in the core. Some have objects (**S-V-O**) and some do not (**S** → **V** or **S** ← **V**). For each, circle the subject and underline the complete verb. If the sentence contains an object, underline the object twice. Then note the pattern (S $\rightarrow$ V or S $\leftarrow$ V or S-V-O).

a. In *Mathews,* the state agency received medical reports from the recipient, from his physician, and from a psychiatric consultant.
b. The statute is not narrowly drawn to meet conditions such as intoxication.
c. In response to the review, Puett initiated several reforms within the social services system, including the termination of several services provided by county offices and local agencies.
d. From these decisions certain characteristics of property interests protected by due process emerge.
e. Therefore, the interests of Mrs. Clark were not sufficiently protected by the procedural safeguards.
f. To provide adequate notice, the notice of termination of services must include the reasons for the intended agency action.
g. The homemaker services program of Senior Citizens, Inc. only received a 30 percent reduction in funding.
h. The manual (Procedure for Complaints, Appeals and Fair Hearings, Volume 4) was sent to all regional, county, and area offices of the Tennessee Department of Human Services.
i. Property interests may take many forms in addition to the traditional concept of property as real estate, chattels, and money.

a. *Passive Sentences with the* S-V-O *Pattern*

Because the verb in the S-V-O pattern involves action, the subject can be acted upon just as it can in the S-V pattern. The form of the verb (the passive structure of *to be* plus the past participle) directs the action toward the subject.

> In this case, the recipients *were paid* monthly benefits under the Federal Aid to Families with Dependent Children program.

> The recipients were paid monthly benefits
> S   V   O

The passive form of the verb (were paid) directs the action toward the subject. When the verb is passive, the object still answers the question *what?*

> Recipients were paid *what?*   monthly benefits

Here are other examples where the passive form of the verb (*to be* plus the past participle) directs the action toward the subject (S $\leftarrow$ V $\leftarrow$ O).

Recipients of optional benefits are not given a constitutional right to the perpetual continuance of their benefits.

Recipients are not given a constitutional right
   S   V   O

In the instant case, Reverend Farewell was not granted a fair hearing by the Georgia Department of Public Safety.

Reverend Farewell was not granted a fair hearing
   S   V   O

In *Sniadach*, default on a loan was not considered an extraordinary situation requiring special protection.

Default was not considered an extraordinary situation
   S   V   O

EXERCISES

All of these sentences have action verbs and objects. For each, circle the subject, underline the complete verb once, and underline the object twice. Indicate the pattern as $S \rightarrow V \rightarrow O$ or $S \leftarrow V \leftarrow O$. Only use the $S \leftarrow V \leftarrow O$ representation when the form of the verb (*to be* plus the past participle) directs the action towards the subject (passive structure).

a. With an action for breach of contract, our client might be awarded damages under the doctrine of reliance.

b. When applying for insurance from All-Risk, the appellant did not authorize an investigation into his past medical history.

c. The leading Supreme Court case on point, *Winslow* v. *Baltimore*, follows the same reasoning as *Lewis*.

d. The manner of attaching a fixture has been considered an important factor in determining a tenant's right to remove the fixture at the end of a lease.

e. The Court should not usurp the legislature's power by creating a tort action for invasion of privacy.

f. The removal of these articles would, no doubt, seriously damage the realty.

g. The Michigan Supreme Court, in the more recent *Beaumont* proceeding, modified its earlier publicity requirements.

h. In *Warrington*, the Delaware court followed this doctrine of maintaining the original condition of the lessor's property.

i. Unlike the recipient in *Mathews* Mrs. Clark was not given a meaningful chance to respond to the termination of her benefits.

j. Brandon was denied insurance from All-Risk because of his hospitalization over 18 years ago.

b. *Active Sentences with Direct and Indirect Objects*

So far the examples have been sentences that have one object that answers either *what?* or *whom?* However, sentences often have more than one object. A common situation involves two objects. One object, sometimes called a *direct object* (**D.O.**) answers *what?* and the other object, sometimes called an *indirect object* (**I.O.**), answers *to or for whom?* To have both objects, the verb must be active, not passive.

PASSIVE   Recipients of optional benefits *are not given* a constitutional right to the perpetual continuance of their benefits.

Recipients are not given [*what?*] a constitutional right
    S   V   O

The U.S. Constitution *does not give* recipients of optional benefits a right to the perpetual continuance of their benefits.

The U.S. Constitution does not give [*to whom?*] recipients
        S   V   I.O.

[*what?*] a right
    D.O.

PASSIVE   In the instant case, Reverend Farewell *was not granted* a fair hearing by the Georgia Department of Public Safety.

Reverend Farewell was not granted [*what?*] a fair hearing
    S   V   O

ACTIVE   In the instant case, the Georgia Department of Public Safety *did not grant* Reverend Farewell a fair hearing.

The Department did not grant [*to whom?*] Reverend Farewell
    S   V   I.O.

[*what?*] a fair hearing
    D.O.

From these examples you can see how placing the actor in the subject position can lead to two objects, one answering *to or for whom?* and one answering *what?* When the two appear without any prepositions (to, for), the indirect object, answering *to or for whom?*, usually appears first. When the indirect object follows a preposition, it usually appears after the direct object.

The Department did not grant <u>Reverend Farewell</u> a <u>fair hearing</u>.
                                    I.O.   **D.O.**

The state paid <u>recipients</u> <u>monthly benefits</u>.
                    I.O.   **D.O.**

The Department did not grant a <u>fair hearing</u> to <u>Reverend Farewell</u>.
                                      D.O.   **I.O.**

The state paid <u>monthly benefits</u> to <u>recipients</u>.
                      D.O.   **I.O.**

c. *Active Sentences with Object and Complement*

In some cases, when you place the actor in the subject position (by changing a passive verb to active), you do not create two objects, one answering *to or for whom?* and one answering *what?* Instead, you get one object (answering either *whom?* or *what?*) and a complement (a description of the object, answering the question *to be what?*).

PASSIVE In *Sniadach*, default on a loan was not considered an extraordinary situation requiring special protection.

Default was not considered an extraordinary situation
  S   V   C

Default was not considered *to be what?*   an extraordinary situation

ACTIVE In *Sniadach*, the court did not consider default on a loan an extraordinary situation requiring special protection.

The court did not consider default an extraordinary situation
  S   V   O   C

The court did not consider *what?*   default
The court did not consider default *to be what?*   an extraordinary situation

PASSIVE In *Sullivan*, the physician was held liable for breach of contract.

The physician was held liable
  S   V   C

The physician was held *to be what?*   liable

ACTIVE In *Sullivan*, the court held the physician liable for breach of contract.

The court held the physician liable
  S   V   O   C

The court held *whom?*   the physician
The court held the physician *to be what?*   liable

In the passive form, the *Sullivan* and *Sniadach* examples appear to be like the earlier examples of **S** ← **V** ← **O**. However, when the actor (the court) is put in the subject position, you can see that they are really **S** ← **V** ← **C** sentences. What appeared to be an object is a description of the receiver of the action.

EXERCISES

Each of these sentences has an action verb. Some have objects and some do not. For each, circle the subject and underline the verb once. Then, if the sentence includes objects, underline the objects twice. You do not need to distinguish between direct and indirect objects. If an object has a complement, underline the complement twice and draw an arrow from it to the word it describes.

Examples:

    In *Goldberg,* the (state) paid recipients monthly benefits under the Federal Aid to Families with Dependent Children program.
    In *Sullivan,* the (court) held the physician liable for breach of contract.

a. In the hearing, Farewell could not introduce evidence on the issue of his liability for the accident.

b. Given the language of the lease, the court will probably not grant Brooks another renewal.

c. As a result, a Maryland court would probably consider the relationship between Pat and Tracy adulterous.

d. On appeal, the *Miller* court, in light of the uncertain construction of the lease, did not grant the lessee a right to perpetual renewals.

e. In *Hartberg,* a provision in the lease gave the landlord the right to all temporary and permanent improvements by the lessee.

f. The need for a tort protecting privacy interests was first espoused in 1890, in an article by Samuel Warren and Louis Brandeis.

g. In *Della Corp.* v. *Diamond,* the Delaware Supreme Court denied a tenant restaurant operator the right to remove a custom-cut carpet.

h. The Restatement (Second) of Torts, §652B, does not make this physical aspect of intrusion a requirement.

i. A similar line of reasoning has been used in numerous cases, including *Tureen* v. *Equifax, Inc.*

j. The Fair Credit Reporting Act directly addresses the central problem of the case presently before this court.

5. Summary

1. Most English sentences include necessary elements and optional elements.
2. Necessary elements form the *core* of the sentence (reveal the basic who and what).
3. Optional elements, *modifiers,* provide additional information and answer questions like:

when?	what kind?
where?	in what way?
why?	to what extent?
how?	under what conditions?

4. Optional elements can appear almost anywhere in a sentence:
   - before the core
   - between any two elements of the core
   - within an element of the core
   - after the core
5. Necessary elements appear in patterns. Two common patterns simply tell who or what exists:

$$S = LV = C$$
$$Th = V = S$$

Two other common patterns focus on action. They reveal who or what is acting or being acted upon:

$$S \rightarrow V \text{ or } S \leftarrow V$$
$$S \rightarrow V \rightarrow O \text{ or } S \leftarrow V \leftarrow O$$

REVIEW EXERCISES

Here are two passages from student papers. For each sentence, circle the subject and underline the verb once. If a sentence contains other necessary elements (the word *there* in $Th = V = S$ or any object or complement), underline those elements twice. Indicate whether the pattern is $S = LV = C$ or $Th = V = S$ or S-V or S-V-O.

a. First Passage

(1) The Georgia procedures for suspension of an individual's driver's license do not reflect a proper balance of the interests of the licensee, the

state, and the private party initiating the suspension. (2) Further, the Georgia procedures fail to mandate a fair hearing on the issue of suspension in a timely and meaningful manner. (3) The Georgia procedures for driver's license suspension are unconstitutional. (4) The Georgia procedures violate the Fourteenth Amendment's safeguards against deprivation of property by the state without due process of law. (5) The decision of the Georgia Department of Public Safety to suspend Reverend Farewell's license pursuant to state procedures should be reversed.

b. Second Passage

(1) In *Pearson,* the plaintiff's own employees had removed confidential files from the plaintiff's office without authorization. (2) The employees, in turn, gave the defendants the confidential files. (3) The information from the files was used by the defendants to write several newspaper columns about the plaintiff. (4) The court found the conduct of the plaintiff's employees to be an improper intrusion. (5) However, the court did not hold the defendants liable for receiving the information. (6) Here the case is much the same. (7) Metro Data Services, Inc., in providing a necessary service to its client, has made certain inquiries in a reasonable manner — no bullying, no threats, no physical intrusion, no force. (8) The investigators simply received the information by listening. (9) There has been no improper intrusion on the part of Metro Data Services, Inc.

B How Word Groups Function Within Patterns

If you have worked through section A, you should be able to distinguish between necessary and optional elements in English sentences. You should also be able to recognize four common patterns of necessary elements.

Many of the sentences you produce for legal documents will not be as simple as those you worked with in section A. In fact, the sentences that you are likely to have the most trouble with will probably be relatively complex. To be able to analyze more complex sentences well enough so that you can identify and solve structural problems, you need to understand three concepts.

1. Groups of words can function as a unit. These units can fill the slot of either a necessary element or an optional element.
2. A word group that functions as a single element (either necessary or optional) may have its own subject and verb.
3. A sentence may contain two or more core patterns. These core patterns may be alike (for example, **S-V-O** and **S-V-O**) or different (for example, **S-V-O** and **S-V**).

1. Groups of Words Can Function as Units

a. *Compound Structures Serving as Necessary Elements*

The subject, object, or complement of a sentence may consist of more than one word. Here are a few examples. The words that join the compound subject, object, or complement are in italics. Compound structures appear in capital letters.

Compound Subject

> *The heating system* AND *the plumbing fixtures,* being replacements, cannot be removed by our client. (S ← V)

> *The intention* of the parties AND *the ease* of removal of the fixtures are two important factors in determining a tenant's right to fixtures. (S = LV = C)

> NEITHER *the carpet* NOR *the air conditioner* poses this problem of altering or injuring Finn's building. (S → V → O)

Compound Object

> The tenant can probably remove BOTH *the carpet* AND *the frame.* (S → V → O)

> Brooks installed *a window air conditioner* to cool the first floor AND *an electric heat pump* with a forced hot-air duct system to warm the whole building. (S → V → O)

Compound Complement

> Reverend Farewell's hearing was NEITHER *fair* NOR *meaningful* in terms of the standards set forth by the Court in *Fuentes.* (S = LV = C)

> Given recent decisions, your chances of recovering damages in a Massachusetts court are *good* BUT NOT *definite.* (S = LV = C)

Verbs, too, can be compound. Because verbs may have objects or complements, compound verbs can appear in different ways.

Compound Verb

1. The two verbs forming the compound may share an object or complement:

> Our client *purchased* AND *installed* a window *air conditioner.* (S → V + V → O)

Because of policy issues, many courts *have been* AND *are* still *reluctant* about upholding implied contracts in family-like relationships. (S = LV + LV = C)

2. Each verb may have its own object or complement:

The Minnesota courts *should follow* the current *trend* of jurisprudence AND *recognize* an *action* for tortious invasion of privacy. (S → V → O + V → O)

In *Lynch,* the contract between the parties *was considered independent* of their meretricious relationship AND *was held* to be *enforceable.* (S = LV = C + LV = C)

A challenge to the lessor's termination of the lease *would be costly* AND *would* probably *yield* an unfavorable *result.* (S = LV = C + V → O)

3. One of the verbs may have an object or complement and the other may not:

In *Mathews,* the recipient *was adequately informed* of the reason for the agency's action and *was provided* procedural *safeguards.* (S ← V + V → O)

At the end of the investigation, the defendant's report on the plaintiff *was marked* "*confidential*" and *submitted* only to All-Risk, the defendant's client. (S = LV = C + ← V)

4. Both verbs may be action verbs that are not followed by an object or complement:

In *Hartberg,* the carpet *was attached* to wooden strips and *could be removed* with no damage to the floor. (S ← V + ← V)

From the examples, you can see

1. That compound structures can appear in any pattern (S = LV = C, Th = V = S, S-V, or S-V-O) and
2. That compound structures are formed when items are joined by a connector. The connectors *and, or, nor, but, for, so,* and *yet* are often called coordinating conjunctions.

EXERCISES

Some of the necessary elements in these sentences are compound structures. Analyze each sentence by following these steps:

1. Circle the subject. Underline the verb once.
2. If a sentence contains other necessary elements (the word *there* in **Th = V = S** or any object or complement), underline those elements twice.
3. Indicate whether the pattern is **S = LV = C** or **Th = V = S** or **S-V** or **S-V-O**.
4. Circle the symbol in the pattern for the compound element (e.g., if the subject in an **S-V-O** were compound, you would have (S)-V-O).
    a. To be binding, an offer to enter into a contract in the future must specify all of the material terms and leave nothing to be agreed upon in future negotiations.
    b. Her pregnancy and the subsequent delivery of her third child are clear indications of the operation's failure.
    c. The Minnesota legislature has considered the issue of privacy and has enacted legislation protecting specific classes of people.
    d. As part of the application process for insurance, an investigation of the applicant's background may occur and is often required.
    e. The ex-wife and the neighbor had some knowledge of the appellee's mental illness.
    f. Contrary to the defendant's contention, to be eligible the recipient of homemaker services must show both physical need and financial eligibility.
    g. As a result of this invasion of his privacy, the appellant has suffered injury to his reputation and mental and emotional distress.
    h. This information was compiled without the appellant's knowledge or consent and was sent to All-Risk on January 7, 1981.

b. *Entire Phrases as Subjects, Objects, or Complements*

The same sentence can be written in many different ways. Look at these versions of the sentence about Reverend Farewell's license:

1. The Georgia Department of Public Safety *suspended* Reverend Farewell's *driver's license.* S → V → O
    This *reduced his ability* to pay the damages. S → V → O
2. In effect, the suspension of Reverend Farewell's driver's license *reduced his ability* to pay the damages. S → V → O

3. The effect of the suspension of Reverend Farewell's driver's license *was a reduction* in his ability to pay the damages. **S = LV = C**
4. In effect, suspending Reverend Farewell's driver's license *reduced his ability* to pay the damages. **S → V → O**
5. In effect, the suspension of Reverend Farewell's driver's license *meant reducing his ability* to pay the damages. **S → V → O**
6. In effect, suspending Reverend Farewell's driver's license *meant reducing his ability* to pay the damages. **S → V → O**

The first three examples look like the sentences you have already worked with. Example 1 has two simple verbs: *suspended, reduced*. The verb of the first sentence in Example 1 has become a noun and the subject of the sentence in Example 2: *the suspension*. The subject in Example 3 is *the effect*. The idea of the verb in Example 1 (*reduced*) has become part of the modifier (*reduction*) in Example 3. The other word groups before the verb in Examples 2 and 3 (*of Reverend Farewell's driver's license*) are also modifiers. They answer questions like *which? what kind?*

In Example 4, however, the subject is the entire word group *suspending Reverend Farewell's driver's license*. The ideas that were in the modifiers have become part of the subject.

In Example 3, the verb from the second part of Example 2 (*reduced*) has become a noun (*reduction*). It is now the complement of the sentence, *a reduction*. The rest of the sentence after the word *reduction* modifies the complement. It answers the question *what kind of reduction?* In Examples 5 and 6, the entire word group *reducing his ability* is the object of the verb *meant*.

We can make entire word groups into subjects or objects or complements when the key word of the subject, object, or complement can have a verb form using -*ing* (suspending, reducing) or *to* (to suspend, to reduce).

Here you see that

verb	can become	*noun*	or	-*ing* form	or	*to* form
suspend		suspension		suspending		to suspend
reduce		reduction		reducing		to reduce

The important point is that -*ing* word groups and *to* word groups can function as single units within a sentence. The examples above show -*ing* word groups as subject and object.

The *to* form of a word that can be a verb (like *suspend* or *reduce*) creates the same effect — it can make modifiers into necessary elements.

Original	The effect of the suspension of Reverend Farewell's driver's license *was a reduction* in his ability to pay the damages. (S = LV = C)
With *to* phrase as complement	The effect of the suspension of Reverend Farewell's driver's license *was to reduce his ability to pay the damages.* (S = LV = C)
With *to* phrase as subject and complement	In effect, *to suspend* Reverend Farewell's driver's license *was to reduce his ability to pay the damages.* (S = LV = C)

From these examples you can see

1. That *to* phrases, as well as *-ing* phrases, can serve as necessary elements (as subjects, objects, or complements) answering the question *what?*
2. That when a *to* phrase appears as a necessary element, the entire word group functions as a single unit.

A reminder. To be a necessary element, an *-ing* or *to* phrase must answer the question *who?* or *what?* Not all *-ing* and *to* phrases are subjects, objects, or complements. In fact, most are just modifiers or parts of modifiers and answer modifier questions like these:

when?	which one?
where?	what kind?
why?	in what way?
how?	to what extent?

For instance, both the *-ing* phrase and the *to* phrase are modifiers in this sentence:

The effect of *suspending Reverend Farewell's driver's license* is a reduction in his ability *to pay the damages.* (SV = LV + C)

The *-ing* phrase is part of the modifier that begins with *of* and answers the question *which effect?* The *to* phrase is a modifier by itself that answers the question *what kind of ability?*

EXERCISES

Some of these sentences have subjects, objects, or complements that are *-ing* phrases or *to* phrases. Analyze each sentence by following these steps:

1. Circle the subject and underline the verb once.
2. If a sentence contains other necessary elements (the word *there* in Th = V = S or any object or complement), underline those elements twice.
3. Indicate whether the pattern is S = LV = C or Th = V = S or S-V or S-V-O.
4. If a necessary element is an *-ing* or *to* phrase, circle the symbol for that element.

Examples:

In effect, suspending (Reverend Farewell's driver's license) reduced his ability to pay the damages. (S)-V-O

In effect, (to suspend Reverend Farewell's driver's license) was to reduce his ability to pay the damages. (S)= LV = (C)

a. Gathering certain types of information was recognized in *Tureen* v. *Equifax, Inc.*, 571 F.2d 411 (8th Cir. 1978), as a legitimate business need.

b. *Benton* involved an across-the-board cut in specific types of optional services, including dental services and cosmetherapy.

c. The purpose of the agency's action may have been to ensure a better quality of services for recipients.

d. Accepting the *Marvin* rule would seem to be going against state policy by encouraging cohabitation and common law marriages.

e. We will attempt to support our contention by supplying the court with evidence from conversations between you and Doctor Cooper.

f. Since the *Warrington* court's decision, determining a tenant's right to fixtures has centered on two important factors — the lessee's intention and the ease of removal.

g. The notice did not actually require Mrs. Clark or her representative either to go to the local agency or to write a letter.

h. To convince one medical doctor to testify against another doctor is difficult.

i. According to the appellant, terminating homemaker services was a matter of state policy.

j. In *Warrington,* the Delaware Court also promoted this doctrine of maintaining the original condition of the lessor's property.

2. A Word Group Can Have Its Own Subject and Verb

a. *Clauses Serving as Necessary Elements*

So far in this section you have worked with the first of three new concepts: Groups of words can function as units and be either a necessary element or an optional element. The word groups you have been reviewing are compound structures, -*ing* phrases, and *to* phrases. Now you will work with the second new concept: A word group that functions as a single element (either necessary or optional) can have its own subject and verb.

Essentially a clause is a word group that has its own subject and verb. Each sentence pattern that you have reviewed contains a subject and some kind of verb.

$$S = LV = C \qquad \text{S-V}$$
$$Th = LV = S \qquad \text{S-V-O}$$

So each pattern represents an *independent clause*.

The term *independent clause* is just a more technical term for what we have been calling basic sentence patterns. The word *clause* indicates that the word group contains a subject and verb, and the word *independent* indicates that the word group is a complete sentence.

A second kind of clause is a *dependent clause*. Here the word *clause* also indicates that the word group contains a subject and verb; however, the word *dependent* indicates that the word group is *not* a complete sentence. These pairs show the difference between independent and dependent clauses.

Independent Clause	Dependent Clause
The termination of a statutory entitlement would be a deprivation of an important right. (S = LV = C)	why the termination of a statutory entitlement would be a deprivation of an important right
There must be an opportunity for a fair hearing before the suspension of a driver's license. (Th = V = S)	whether there must be an opportunity for a fair hearing before the suspension of a driver's license
Our client would not prevail on the issue of renewal of the lease. (S → V)	that our client would not prevail on the issue of renewal of the lease
The courts in Massachusetts have awarded damages in cases similar to yours. (S → V → O)	how the courts in Massachusetts have awarded damages in cases similar to yours

From the examples you can see that in each pair, one word (*why, whether, that, how*) makes the difference between the independent clause in the left column and the dependent clause in the right column.

The word added in the right column transforms what was an independent clause into a dependent one. In each case, the added word functions as a *connector*. When a connector (sometimes called a *conjunction* or *relative pronoun*) transforms an independent clause into a dependent clause, the dependent clause must become part of — that is, be connected to — an independent clause.

A dependent clause can become either a necessary or an optional element within an independent clause. For now we will only look at dependent clauses serving as necessary elements within an independent clause. These examples will show you how dependent clauses can serve as subjects, complements, and objects.

Dependent Clauses as Subjects

Why the termination of a statutory entitlement would be a deprivation has been explained in Goldberg. (S ← V)

How the courts in Massachusetts have awarded damages in cases similar to yours has varied from court to court. (S → V)

Whether there must be an opportunity for a fair hearing before the suspension of a driver's license is another due process issue. (S = LV = C)

Dependent Clauses as Complements

Another issue to be resolved is *why the termination of a statutory entitlement would be a deprivation of an important right.* (S = LV = C)

The most likely outcome is *that our client would not prevail on the issue of an additional renewal of the lease.* (S = LV = C)

Dependent Clauses as Objects

Counsel must explain *why the termination of a statutory entitlement would be a deprivation of an important right.* (S → V → O)

You must understand *how the courts in Massachusetts have awarded damages in cases similar to yours.* (S → V → O)

From these examples, you can see that a dependent clause can function as a unit, as a necessary element in a sentence. Here are the connectors that most often create dependent clauses that function as subjects, objects, or complements in sentences:

what	whatever	why
when	whenever	how
where	wherever	whether
that (the most common connector)		

EXERCISE

Some of the subjects, objects, and complements in these sentences are dependent clauses. Analyze each sentence by following these steps:

1. Circle the subject and underline the verb once.
2. If a sentence contains other necessary elements (the word *there* in Th = V = S or any object or complement), underline those elements twice.
3. Indicate whether the pattern is S = LV = C or Th = V = S or S-V or S-V-O.
4. If a necessary element is a dependent clause, circle the symbol for that element.

Examples:

Whether there must be an opportunity for a fair hearing before the suspension of driver's license is a due process issue. S = LV = C

You must understand how the courts in Massachusetts have awarded damages in cases similar to yours. S-V-O

a. In the same way, only the aggressive recipients of the notice would learn that their services were terminated on the basis of need.
b. The question to ask is whether the method of gathering data would be objectionable to a reasonable person.
c. A jury should determine if the publicity requirement was met.
d. The reason for the court's insistence on proof is that patients often transform doctors' statements of opinion into firm promises.
e. On the basis of these reports, the state agency determined that the recipient was no longer disabled.
f. The issue at hand is whether the terms of the lease are sufficient to justify a second five-year renewal.
g. The court found that these procedural safeguards were sufficient to protect the recipient's interests.
h. That you did give birth to a third child is clear proof of a breach of the doctor's promise.
i. Appellee does not consider what information would be appropriate for the party requesting the investigation.
j. What the appellants fail to consider is the impact on existing law of the adoption of this tort.

b. *Clauses Serving as Modifiers*

Dependent clauses can also serve as modifiers within independent clauses. Dependent clauses that modify can be formed in the same way as dependent clauses that serve as necessary elements. As these examples illustrate, one word makes the difference between the independent clause in the left column and the dependent clause in the right column.

Independent Clauses	Dependent Clauses
Our client moved into Funn's building in January 1980. (S-V)	when our client moved into Funn's building in January 1980
He had the right to have his case reconsidered. (S-V-O)	because he had the right to have his case reconsidered
There is an assessment of need involved in the termination of benefits. (Th = V = SO)	if there is an assessment of need involved in the termination of benefits
A determination of eligibility was made on an individual basis. (S ← V)	that a determination of eligibility was made on an individual basis

To understand how these dependent clauses serve as modifiers, which are optional elements, you must see them within complete sentences. Here are the four dependent clauses functioning as single units within complete sentences.

When our client moved into Funn's building in January 1980, he converted the first floor into a men's clothing store (dependent clause answering the question *when?*).

The recipient in *Mathews* was afforded adequate procedural protection *because he had the right to have his case reconsidered* (dependent clause answering the question *why?* or *in what way?*).

Because of the possibility of error, a more detailed notice is necessary *if there is an assessment of need in the termination of benefits* (dependent clause answering the question *under what circumstances?*).

In the present case, however, the record provides evidence *that a determination of eligibility was made on an individual basis* (dependent clause answering the question *what kind?*).

From these examples, you can see

1. That dependent clauses can serve as modifiers and

2. That some of the connectors that create dependent clauses (for instance, *when* and *that*) can create either modifiers or necessary elements.

Here is a list of connectors that create dependent clauses that can function as modifiers:

although	even though	that	while
after	if	than	when
as (or as if)	in order that	though	where
because	so that	until	whereas
before	since	unless	

A sentence may have more than one dependent clause serving as a modifier. Here are two examples. The modifiers that are dependent clauses are in italics.

why?   *Since the recipients did not have a property interest in home-*
when?   *maker services,* they were not entitled to due process *before the services were terminated.*
when?   *When the lease ended,* the tenant removed the toilet *that he had*
which?   *installed for his own use* and replaced it with the original, broken toilet.

EXERCISES

Some of these sentences contain modifiers that are dependent clauses, and some do not. Analyze each sentence by following these steps:

1. Underline every necessary element once (i.e., the core of the sentence).
2. Indicate whether the pattern of the core is S = LV = C or Th = V = S or S-V or S-V-O.
3. If any modifier is a dependent clause, underline that modifier twice. (Some sentences contain no dependent clauses; some contain one, and some contain two.)

Example:
Because of the possibility of error, <u>a more detailed notice is necessary</u> <u><u>if there is a need assessment involved in the termination of benefits.</u></u> S = LV = C

NOTE: The first word group beginning with the word *because* is a modifier answering *why?* However, it is *not* a dependent clause because it does not have its own subject and verb.

a. Although Maryland courts have never decided this issue, there is substantial authority from other jurisdictions to support the contention that contracts between cohabiting parties are enforceable.

b. Since none of the recipients filed a timely appeal, the state is not required to continue their benefits.

c. The appellant has been employed as a police officer for the City of Wabash since 1970.

d. If the court follows the canon law interpretation, then Smith would be guilty of adultery unless the adultery statute is declared unconstitutional.

e. Before a provider agency may participate in a Social Security program, it must establish a plan to provide recipients with an opportunity for a fair hearing whenever their benefits are terminated.

f. The notice requirements in *Benton* are not applicable in the case of Mrs. Clark because the termination of her homemaker services involved both an assessment of need and a complete denial of all homemaker services.

g. Without this requirement, recipients would not have any protection against errors in calculating the amount of their grants.

h. An intrusion is "physical" when it is an intrusion into a place where the plaintiff has secluded himself.

i. One of the lessor's contentions is that carpeting is realty if it has been custom cut to fit the building's contours.

j. In *Lewis* the court blocked an attempt to renew a lease a second time even though the lease provided for renewal of all the lease provisions.

c. *Relative Clauses Serving as Modifiers*

Relative clauses are like the dependent clauses you have just studied in every way but one — relative clauses do not have their own subjects. In the following examples, the clause is italicized and the word that the clause modifies is in bold lettering.

Example 1

Dependent clause

In the present case, however, the record provides **evidence** *that a determination of eligibility was made on an individual basis* (dependent clause answering the question *what kind?*).

The verb within the dependent clause (*was made*) has its own subject (*determination*).

Relative clause

> The *Mathews* Court considered the fiscal and administrative **burdens** *that would result from additional requirements to protect procedural safeguards* (relative clause answering the question *what kind?*).

The verb within the relative clause (*would result*) is directly related to the word that the clause is modifying (*burdens*).

Example 2

Dependent clause

> In addition, the *Marvin* rule gives people incentives to avoid marriage, an **institution** *that the State wants to protect* (dependent clause answering the question *what kind?*).

Relative clause

> In Maryland, adultery is not a criminal offense, perhaps indicating a **public policy** *that would favor the enforcement of the contract between Pat and Mary* (relative clause answering the question *what kind?*).

Relative clauses answer the questions *which one?* or *what kind?* The verb of the relative clause always *relates* directly to the word that the clause modifies and that is why the clause is called a *relative* clause. Only three words can create relative clauses:

> who (or whom)
> which
> that

Here are examples of each of these words as connectors for relative clauses.

WHO   Our client, *who lived in an arguably adulterous relationship,* may have some difficulty in enforcing the oral promise.

The State is required to continue providing Title XX benefits to any recipient *who files an appeal within ten days.*

WHICH   The State of Massachusetts recognizes an alternative form of compensation, *which is more appropriate in your case.*

The social service agencies, *which deal directly with recipients,* are in the best position to determine eligibility.

THAT   The only Maryland case *that speaks to this problem* is *Delash-mut* v. *Thomas*, 45 Md. 140 (1876).

Marvin was a highly publicized case *that set a precedent for other jurisdictions.*

EXERCISES

Analyze each sentence in this passage by following these steps:

1. Underline every necessary element once (i.e., the core of the sentence). Remember that a necessary element may be a single word, a compound structure, or a word group (a *to* phrase or *-ing* phrase or a dependent clause).
2. Indicate whether the pattern of the core is **S = LV = C** or **Th = V = S** or **S-V** or **S-V-O**.
3. If any modifier is a dependent clause, underline that modifier twice.
4. If any modifier is a relative clause, circle it.

(a) There are several cases that deal with enforcing contracts between nonmarried partners. (b) In *Tyranski* v. *Piggins*, 44 Mich. App. 570, 205 N.W.2d 595 (1973), Mrs. Tyranski was a married woman who had lived with Piggins for approximately four years. (c) When Piggins died, she brought an action against the ancillary administrator of Piggins's estate. (d) She sought title to the house that they had lived in together. (e) The title was held in Piggins's name. (f) The court of appeals held that their illicit cohabitation did not render all agreements between them illegal.

3. A Sentence Can Contain More Than One Core

A sentence can contain two independent clauses. The two independent clauses can have the same core pattern, or the two can have different core patterns. When any two core patterns are combined into one sentence, they are joined by one of seven connectors:

and	or	so
but	for	yet
	nor	

The connector between the core patterns is usually preceded by a comma. Here are a few examples to illustrate how core patterns can be combined.

Combinations of Like Patterns

The language in Brooks's lease is more specific, *but* the outcome will probably be very similar. (S = LV = C, *but* S = LV = C)

Along with her financial contributions, Tracy gave Pat emotional support, *and* she performed all of the homemaking functions throughout the nine-year period. (mod, S-V-O, *and* S-V-O mod)

The record is not clear on this point, *but* it appears that Senior Citizens Services, Inc., suffered a reduction in Title XX funding because of deficiencies in its performance. (S = LV = C mod, *but* S = LV = C — the second complement is a dependent clause followed by a modifier)

Combinations of Different Patterns

A lease is a contract, *and* the general rules of contract law apply. (S = LV = C, *and* S-V)

The law has never interpreted this type of language to mean more than one renewal, *and* it is doubtful that we can convince a Maryland court to go against the tide of one hundred years of influential precedents. (S → V → O mod, *and* S = LV = C mod clause)

The lease was originally negotiated by phone, with Mr. Funn in California and Mr. Brooks in Baltimore, *and* there is disagreement concerning what was said during those negotiations. (S ← V mod, *and* Th = V = S mod)

From these examples, you can see

1. That each core can include modifiers,
2. That the patterns of the cores may be the same or different, and
3. That the individual cores can be either short and simple or long and complex (e.g., have several modifiers or have word groups functioning as subjects, objects, or complements).

4. Summary

1. Groups of words can function as units. These units can be either necessary or optional elements.
   - The subject, verb, object, or complement of a sentence can be a compound structure.
   - Compound structures can appear in any sentence pattern.

- Compound structures are connected by coordinating conjunctions:

and	for
or	so
nor	yet
but	

- An entire phrase can function as a subject, object, or complement if the verb is an *-ing* or *to* form.

2. A word group can have its own subject and verb (dependent clause) or just its own verb (relative clause).

- A dependent clause can be either a necessary element or a modifier.
- Relative clauses serve as modifiers.

3. A sentence can have more than one core, joined by a coordinating conjunction.

REVIEW EXERCISES

Analyze each sentence in the two passages below by following these steps:

1. Underline every necessary element once (i.e., the core of the sentence). Remember that a sentence may have more than one core pattern.

2. Indicate the pattern of each core (e.g., **S** = **LV** = **C** or **S-V-O** *but* **S-V**).

a. First Passage

(1) This is a case of first impression in Maryland, and as such, it is impossible to give a definite prediction of the outcome. (2) While cases dealing with similar issues seem to point toward the possibility that *this* contract will be enforced, the courts may be reluctant to adopt a general rule permitting recovery in all cohabitation cases. (3) To the extent that the court relies on the generally applicable rules stated in earlier cases, there is a greater likelihood of recovery. (4) Several recent decisions in other jurisdictions have upheld contracts between cohabiting couples, but there have been two recent decisions denying recovery. (5) The public policy and contractual agreements that are contained within this memorandum suggest some possible justifications for the court to enforce contracts between cohabiting couples.

b. Second Passage

(1) In summary, the courts will not enforce a promise when the consideration given is merely cohabitation. (2) The courts are split on the sufficiency of homemaking duties, some allowing *quantum meruit* recovery. (3) In our case, Tracy provided lawful consideration in return for a promise, i.e., financial support in the form of payment of rent, food, etc. (4) Since the promise was

based on lawful consideration and did not arise expressly from Pat and Tracy's illicit relationship, the promise is enforceable despite the illicit relationship, and recovery should be allowed. (5) As long as the adequate consideration is independent of the illicit nature of the relationship, the courts have not barred the parties from making enforceable promises.

C Correcting Serious Errors

This section focuses on three errors in professional writing.

- Problems with subject-verb agreement
- Incomplete sentences
- Garbled sentences

The information in this section builds on the material that we presented in the previous sections. Specifically, it assumes that you already know

- What a subject is
- What a verb is
- What a modifier is
- What an independent clause is
- What a dependent clause is

If you do not know these terms, you will need to work through sections A through C.

1. Subject-Verb Agreement

The verb in every sentence must match its subject in number. If the subject is singular, the verb must be singular; if the subject is plural, the verb must be plural.

You know the basic subject-verb agreement rule: Add an -s or -es to present tense verbs whenever

1. The subject of the verb is singular and
2. That subject is any word other than the words *I* or *you* (I *go*, he *goes*).

Only the verbs *to be* and *to have* are exceptions. These two verbs have special forms in the present tense (see **Table A-5**). Compare them to the verb *to claim*, which follows the usual pattern: Add an -s (or -es) to the verb when the subject is a singular word other than *I* or *you*. The verb *to have* is different from the usual pattern in one way: Instead of adding an -s, you change the spelling to *has*. The verb *to be* is different from the usual pattern in two ways. First, the correct forms are not based on *be* (they are not I be, you be, the plaintiff bees, we be, etc.). Second, there are three present tense forms (am, is, are), not just two as with other verbs (claim, claims, or have, has).

The verb *to be* is different from the usual pattern in the past tense as well as in the present tense. *To be* is the only English verb that changes between singular and plural in the past tense as well as in the present tense.

Most errors in subject-verb agreement in legal writing occur in these situations.

1. The subject and its verb are separated. The writer pairs the verb with the wrong noun.

TABLE A-5

PRESENT TENSE

Type of Subject	Typical Verb	to have	to be
SINGULAR SUBJECTS:			
I	claim	have	am
you	claim	have	are
he, she, it	claims	has	is
(or any singular subject other than I or *you*)			
ANY PLURAL SUBJECT:			
(we, you, the plaintiffs)	claim	have	are

PAST TENSE

SINGULAR SUBJECTS:			
I	claimed	had	was
you	claimed	had	were
he, she, it	claimed	had	was
(or any singular subject other than I or *you*)			
ANY PLURAL SUBJECT:			
(we, you, the plaintiffs)	claimed	had	were

2. The number of the subject is unclear. The writer treats it as a plural when it is actually a singular or as a singular when it is actually a plural.

a. *Problems Created When the Subject and Verb Are Separated*

Subjects and verbs should appear next to one another in both complex sentences and simple sentences. The following sentence, for instance, contains four subject-verb pairs — one in the main clause and three in dependent clauses. Yet in each pair the subject and verb appear next to one another.

> This *language suggests* first that *it is* well-recognized that *abuses do occur* within the consumer reporting industry and second that the appellant's *claim is not based* upon an isolated incident.

However, the word just before a verb may not always be its subject. Instead, the nearest word may be part of a modifier that separates the subject and verb. Here are two examples.

> The *language* of various state statutes *suggests* first . . .
> The *provisions* of the Fair Credit Reporting Act *suggest* . . .

In sentences like these, you must ignore the words in the modifier and make your verb agree with the subject, not with the nearest word.

The agreement errors that arise when subjects and verbs are separated are easy to make and difficult to detect. Cognitive psychologists have demonstrated that our short term memory span is limited to seven items, plus or minus two. So people can only hold five to nine items in short term memory at one time. Then they either recode the items ("chunk" them into fewer items) or forget them. If many words separate the subject and verb, you are likely to "lose" the subject before you get to the verb. The real subject may be dropped from short term memory or it may be transformed in the recoding process.

Try to keep verbs near their subjects, and check each verb to be sure it agrees with its subject.

EXERCISES

Some of these sentences contain incorrect verb forms and some do not. If there is an incorrect verb form, correct the form of that verb. Then circle the subject you have made the verb agree with. If every verb in a sentence is correct, place a C (for *correct*) in front of the letter.

a. The trend of recent decisions in other jurisdictions has been to enforce agreements when the agreements are not based solely on sexual services.
b. If the relationship between two contracting parties include illegal behavior, courts are inclined to declare the promises between the parties unenforceable.
c. In *Winslow*, a new lease containing the same terms and covenants were executed every five years from 1872 through 1892.
d. Most of the cases involving this tort action have required the physical invasion to be somewhat analogous to what is required for trespass.
e. Our second claim is that the contract interest of persons are not subordinate to an unenforced policy consideration.
f. The rules governing fixtures in a vendor-vendee relationship is stricter than those governing landlord-tenant relationships.
g. When the terms of renewal in a lease is ambiguous, the lease will be construed as granting the lessee the right to one renewal.
h. Fixtures annexed to realty are generally held to have become part of the realty and as such are inseverable from it.

b. *Problems Created When the Number of the Subject Is Unclear*

Most of the time it is easy to tell whether a subject is singular or plural. There are two ways to judge. You can judge by the meaning (*she* is singular because it means "one female"; the word *several* is plural because it means "more than one"). Another way to judge is by the form. Most plural words end in -s or -es (clients, laws, cases, statutes). In some situations, however, neither the meaning nor the form clearly indicates the number of the subject.

1. When the plural form of the subject does not end in -s or -es
2. When the subject is a collective noun or an indefinite pronoun (we will define these terms in the next few pages)
3. When the subject is a compound structure

1. The plural form of the subject does not end in -s or -es. There are some exceptions to the rule that plural subjects end in -s or -es. Some nouns form their plurals by a change in spelling. Most of these exceptions do not create problems because they are common words (men, children). You know the meaning is plural and you immediately recognize the alternate spelling as the plural form. A few are less common in everyday speech, but common in professional writing.

Singular	*Plural*
criterion	criteria
datum	data
phenomenon	phenomena
alumnus	alumni
formula	formulae or formulas

Many of the words that once had unusual plural forms, e.g., formul*ae* as the plural for formula, are becoming "regularized" so that formul*as* is now an acceptable plural. The best advice we can give you is to check a recent dictionary whenever you have doubts about the plural form of a word.

2. The subject is a collective noun or indefinite pronoun. *Collective nouns* are labels that transform a group of individuals into a single unit (jury, legislature, team, staff, committee). In American English we focus on the idea of the single unit and treat these words as singular subjects even though the meaning is, in some sense, plural. Here are several short sentences with collective nouns as subjects. Note that the verb in each case is singular.

The *jury has* reached a verdict.
In the past two years, the *legislature has* convened for six special sessions.
When the judge called the recess, the defense *team was* relieved.
The editorial *staff is* being sued.
The *committee believes* that the projections are not realistic.

Indefinite pronouns are a small group of frequently used pronouns. Most of the pronouns in this group are singular; only two are plural.

Indefinite Pronouns that Are Singular

one	anyone	anybody	anything
each	someone	somebody	something
either	everyone	everybody	everything
neither	no one	nobody	nothing

Indefinite Pronouns that Are Plural

few several

These indefinite pronouns do not cause problems when they appear next to their verbs. Despite a sense of their plural meanings, you would not write "everybody are" or "everything are." Problems arise when indefinite pronouns are separated from their verbs. And, because indefinite pronouns are vague, they are often followed by phrases that clarify their meaning — so they are often separated from their verbs.

	indefinite pronoun	phrase to clarify the meaning	verb
	SINGULAR		
INCORRECT:	Each	of the facts	have been discussed.
CORRECT:	*Each*	of the facts	*has* been discussed.
INCORRECT:	Neither	of these cases	deal with adultery.
CORRECT:	*Neither*	of these cases	*deals* with adultery.
	PLURAL		
INCORRECT:	Several	of the facts	needs clarification.
CORRECT:	*Several*	of the facts	*need* clarification.

A few indefinite pronouns can be either singular or plural depending on the meaning of the noun or pronoun they refer to. Only four words belong in this group — *some, none, any,* and *all* (see **Table A-6**).

3. The subject is a compound structure. Compound subjects are those connected by *and, or,* or *nor.* When you join two subjects with the word *and,* you create a new plural subject. The idea of the *and* compound is "more than one" or X *plus* Y. When you join two subjects with the word *or* or *nor,* nothing changes because the idea is choice, not addition. So, when you use *or* or *nor* to join two subjects, you do not create a new plural. Instead, you just make it clear that you have two possible subjects. The problem then is to determine which of the two subjects joined by *or* or *nor* should govern the verb. The answer is to make your verb agree with the second subject, the one nearer the verb. Here are several examples of compound subjects followed by correct verbs.

Compound subjects joined by *and* (verb agrees with subject, which is plural):

Homemaking duties and financial support have been widely recognized as a valid legal consideration.

Reverend Farewell is charging that *the Director and the State have* violated his constitutional right to due process.

TABLE A-6

Correct Examples	Meaning
Some	
SINGULAR	
Some of the responsibility is ours.	a portion of; a noncountable
Some of the food seems to be spoiled.	quantity, an amount of
PLURAL	
Some of the courts have decided favorably.	a few, several, a number of, etc.
None	
SINGULAR	
None of the courts has ruled on this.	not a single one; not a single portion of
None of the information was available.	
PLURAL	
Of all the opinions, none are as clear as this one.	not all of them taken together
Any	
SINGULAR	
If any of the elements is missing the action will be unsuccessful.	any single one; any single portion of
If any of the responsibility lies with the corporation, it must accept it.	
PLURAL	
Submit your recommendations; if any are reasonable, I will consider them.	however many fall into the group
All	
SINGULAR	
All of the tape has been erased.	the whole or total
All of the money is in the trust account.	
PLURAL	
All of the issues have been identified.	each one counted separately
All of the depositions are ready.	

Compound subjects joined by *or* or *nor* (verb agrees with second subject):

Neither the State nor the child's parents have made any showing of the need for financial assistance.

Neither the child's parents nor the State has made any showing of the need for financial assistance.

Even if the court finds that *either the household services or the emotional support is* sufficient, it will probably find that the financial support is adequate consideration.

Even if the court finds that *either the emotional support or the household services are* sufficient, it will probably find that the financial support is adequate consideration.

Sometimes modifiers follow one or both elements of a compound subject. These modifiers do not affect the compound structure — *and* compounds still convey the idea of addition and take plural verbs; *or* or *nor* compounds still convey the idea of choice and the verb agrees with the second element of the compound structure. Here are some examples with modifiers added.

Compound subjects that are modified and joined by *and* (plural verb):

The risk of erroneous deprivation through miscalculations *and the probable value* of additional procedures *are* slight in this case.

Reverend Farewell is charging that *the Director* of the Department of Public Safety *and the State* of Georgia *have* violated his constitutional right to due process.

Compound subjects that are modified and joined by *or* or *nor* (verb agrees with the second subject):

Neither the State of Georgia nor the *parents* of the injured child *have* made any showing of the need for financial assistance.

Neither the parents of the injured child nor the *State* of Georgia *has* made any showing of the need for financial assistance.

Be careful not to confuse a compound modifier with a compound subject.

Simple subject followed by compound modifier	A *deprivation* of any length and severity *is* subject to close scrutiny.
Compound subject followed by modifier	The *length and severity* of the deprivation *were* not considered excessive.

EXERCISES

One verb in each of these sentences is incorrect. Write the correct form of the verb and circle the subject that you have made the verb agree with. Some of the errors occur because the subject and verb are separated and some because the number of the subject is unclear (unusual plural form, collective noun, indefinite pronoun, or compound subject).

a. There is no question that the parents of the minor has a valid cause of action if it can be shown that the doctrine of attractive nuisance applies.

b. Each of the cases cited above have held that the touching must be objectionable to the reasonable person.

c. A jury of the plaintiff's peers need to decide whether the method used by Metro Data Services was objectionable and whether the disclosure violated his right to privacy.

d. In addition, neither the Maryland Court of Appeals nor the Maryland Court of Special Appeals have ever construed the statute.

e. Thus, the appreciation of the value of privacy and the public excitement over the issue has dulled the senses of legislators who have made invasion of privacy a tort action in their states.

f. In Maryland, neither of these activities are considered criminal, perhaps indicating a public policy that would favor enforcement of the contract between Pat and Tracy.

g. The requirements for and the definition of "public disclosure" has been given extensive treatment by authors of legal treatises and by the courts.

h. From case law, Prosser, and the Restatement (Second) of Torts, criteria has been developed to use in determining whether or not there has been a public disclosure of private facts.

c. *More Complex Problems with Separated Subjects and Verbs*

Now that we have discussed special subjects (collective nouns, indefinite pronouns, and compound subjects) and subjects and verbs separated by rather short phrases, we will look at two more complex variations of separated subjects and verbs.

The verb is in a dependent clause but the word it must agree with is not. Many dependent clauses contain their own subject-verb pairs. Within those clauses, the subject and verb may appear next to one another or they may be separated by modifiers.

S-V in independent (main) clause	This *language suggests* first
S-V pair in dependent clause	that *it is* well-recognized
separated S-V pair in dependent clause	that *abuses* within the consumer reporting industry *do occur*
S-V pair in dependent clause	and second, that the Appellant's *claim is not based* upon an isolated incident.

One kind of dependent clause — the relative clause — is different. It may contain a verb but no subject. The verb in the relative clause must agree with the word that the clause modifies. Here are a few examples with the entire relative clause italicized. The verb in the clause and the word it must agree with are in boldface type.

Who clauses:

SINGULAR   The appellant is not the only **one** *who has* **had** his *privacy invaded.*

PLURAL   The exact number of **people** *who* **have** *already* **seen** *the report* is unknown, and the potential number of people receiving copies is unlimited.

Which clauses:

PLURAL   In addition to these two **cases,** *which clearly* **state** *the rule of replacements,* there is a binding **case** in

SINGULAR   Maryland *that* **bars** *removal of the forced air system and the upstairs plumbing fixtures.*

That clauses:

SINGULAR   Georgia is the only other **jurisdiction** *that* **has preferred** *to follow the majority in enforcing express agreements between cohabitants.*

PLURAL   Michigan is one of the **jurisdictions** *that* **recognize** *a tort action for invasion of privacy.*

The verb in these examples is separated from its subject by several short phrases or by a long clause. We have looked at subjects and verbs separated by no more than six words. In some sentences, however, the subject and verb may be more than six words apart. Look at these examples of incorrect sentences. The subjects and verbs are italicized.

A *change* in policy to prevent hardship and injuries caused by the enforcement of statutes against "meretricious and illicit" relationships *have been upheld* in several jurisdictions where the conflict has arisen.

The *fact* that the legislature has begun to regulate these various businesses *establish* the concern over the possible misuse of private information gathered for "legitimate" business purposes.

However, the *rules* that govern fixtures for a mortgagor-mortgagee relationship or a vendor-vendee relationship *is* stricter than those that govern landlord-tenant relationships.

Changing the verb form will make sentences like these grammatically correct, but it will not make them effective sentences. To produce better sentences *and* avoid the errors that can be caused by separated subjects and verbs, you need to follow the guidelines presented in Chapter 5. Here are sample revisions of these sentences. Revision of sentence 1 avoids the separated subject-verb problem by using the active voice, Revision of sentence 2 by eliminating unnecessary words, and Revision of sentence 3 by putting the parts of the sentence into logical order.

REVISION OF 1   Several jurisdictions have upheld a change in policy to prevent hardship and injustice caused by enforcing statutes against "meretricious and illicit" relationships.

REVISION OF 2   The legislature has begun to regulate various businesses because of its concern over the possible misuse of private information gathered for "legitimate" business purposes.

REVISION OF 3   The rules that govern fixtures are stricter for mortgagor-mortgagee and vendor-vendee relationships than for landlord-tenant relationships.

EXERCISES

1. Identifying and Correcting Errors
    Each sentence contains at least one error in subject-verb agreement. Find and correct the incorrect verb forms. For each incorrect verb, circle the subject (either a word or compound structure) it is supposed to agree with and draw a line from that circled word to your corrected verb. Some of the errors appear because the subject and verb are separated and some because the number of the subject is unclear (unusual plural form, collective noun, indefinite pronoun, or compound subject).

a. Furthermore, the regulations for implementing the program also imposes a duty on the state to provide adequate and timely notice and to provide an opportunity for a fair hearing in accordance with the standards of due process set forth in *Goldberg* v. *Kelly.*

b. Appellee Clark contends that because her friend who telephoned the various agencies was not told how to perfect an appeal, Clark's opportunity for a fair hearing and her chance to have her services continued pending that hearing was not adequate.

c. If the court interprets the adultery statute in terms of changing social attitudes toward cohabitation, as have other jurisdictions, and show more interest in prevention of hardship and injustice, then Tracy's chances of recovery becomes better.

d. Any damage incurred by plaintiffs in such a suit are seen to be offset by the benefits one receives from the companionship and potential of the child.

e. The doctor is liable to you for any consequences that has arisen or will arise from his breach of contract.

f. In 1937, the Maryland Court of Appeals established that it would not enforce contracts that are based on the consideration of past or future intercourse or that in any manner promotes or furnishes opportunity for unlawful cohabitation.

g. The legislature recognized the need of society and business for the gathering of information and have expressed that recognition in Minn. Stat. §65B.20 (1980).

h. The Minnesota legislature, by enacting the Minnesota Data Privacy Act, Minn. Stat. Ann. §15.162.169 (West 1976), and the Privacy of Communications Act, Minn. Stat. Ann. §625A.01-23 (West 1976), have established Minnesota as a leader on the issue of privacy.

2. Rewriting Sentences
   Now rewrite sentences a, c, f, g, and h. Your goal should be to improve the sentences. As you rewrite, try to reduce the distance between the subjects and their verbs.

2. Incomplete Sentences

Incomplete sentences are often called sentence fragments. The most common causes of fragments are:

- Leaving a necessary element out of the main (independent) clause
- Letting a dependent clause stand alone
- Only putting part of a verb in the main (independent) clause

a. *Leaving Out Necessary Elements*

The simplest fragments are incomplete because they are missing necessary elements, i.e., missing a verb or missing both the subject and verb. Here are two examples followed by correct versions of each of them. The fragments are underlined. If you need to review necessary elements, see section A.

Missing subject and verb

INCORRECT   The procedures established by the state for perfecting an appeal for a fair hearing were in compliance with federal regulations. *Providing Ms. Clark with a practical and reasonable opportunity to communicate her desire to obtain a fair hearing and to have her services continued pending the outcome of that hearing.*

CORRECT   The procedures established by the state for perfecting an appeal for a fair hearing were in compliance with federal regulations. The *procedures provided* Ms. Clark with a practical and reasonable opportunity to communicate her desire to obtain a fair hearing and to have her services continued pending the outcome of that hearing.

Missing subject and part of a verb

INCORRECT   The facts and details of his illness and hospitalization were not well known. *Until recently, not even known by his employer, coworkers, or friends.*

CORRECT   The facts and details of his illness and hospitalization were not well known. Until recently, the *details were* not even known by his employer, coworkers, or friends.
                                        or
             The facts and details of his illness and hospitalization were not well known — until recently, not even known by his employer, coworkers, or friends.

Notice the two possible ways to correct fragments. We've used each in one of the two correct versions of the second example. *To correct some fragments, you must add words,* i.e., add the missing necessary element or elements. In the first example, both a subject and a verb had to be added because the original fragment contained neither. In the first correction of the second example, a subject and part of a verb (*were*) had to be added for the sentence to make sense.

To correct other fragments, you only need to change the punctuation. This method of correcting fragments works only when the fragment (or sentence piece) is short and really belongs with another sentence — either the already complete sentence that precedes the fragment or the one that immediately follows it.

Because these simple fragments will make sense and seem complete in context, they are not always easy to identify. To identify them, read "bottom up" — read the last sentence of a paragraph, then the second-to-last sentence, and so on. As suggested in the proofreading section of Chapter 7, reading from the bottom to the top slows you down and makes you judge sentences as individual units. You will be less likely to supply the missing noun or verb in your head if you read from bottom to top.

EXERCISES

If there is a fragment in the groups of sentences below, underline it and then correct it either by changing the punctuation or by rewriting it as a complete sentence. If every sentence in the group is a complete sentence, place a C (for *correct*) in front of the letter.

   a. Recent case law has established that doctors can never guarantee a particular result of an operation. They can only inform the patient of the expected result of the operation. Therefore, we do not have sufficient evidence to support a cause of action in negligence.
   b. Thus we will sue for the difference between your promised condition (sterility) and your present condition. The damages will include the cost of your child's care until he reaches an age of self support. The out-of-pocket expenses for the operation by Dr. Cooper and the cost for another tubal ligation. We will also sue for any physical pain and mental anguish you have suffered as a result of Dr. Cooper's breach of contract.

b. *Letting a Dependent Clause Stand Alone*

The following examples should remind you of the common and correct uses of dependent clauses. In these examples, each dependent clause is italicized. (If you need more information on dependent clauses, see pages 313 to 318.)

Examples of dependent clauses as necessary elements

as subject	*What Mel said to Bill about options to renew* is insignificant because Bill subsequently signed a lease.
as object	Dr. Cooper told his patient *that the operation would result in sterility.*

as complement | The precise question is *whether the lease creates a right to perpetual renewal.*

Examples of dependent clauses as modifiers

explaining
when? | The State acted within its discretion *when it reduced the amount of Title XX funds allocated to homemaker services.*

explaining
under what conditions | A notice is timely *if it is mailed at least ten days before the date of the intended action.*

explaining
why? | *Since homemaker services are an optional Title XX benefit,* the recipients are not statutorily entitled to these services.

When dependent clauses are used correctly, they are attached to independent clauses. If a dependent clause is not connected to an independent clause, the dependent clause is considered a sentence fragment. Here are passages with incorrectly used dependent clauses followed by correct versions of the same passages.

Fragment that is one dependent clause

INCORRECT The *Moore* court based its decision on contractual theories. *Although the underlying principle condemning misappropriation of a person's name or picture has been recognized by other jurisdictions as being within the realm of privacy interests.*

CORRECT The *Moore* court based its decision on contractual theories, although the underlying principle condemning misappropriation of a person's name or picture has been recognized by other jurisdictions as being within the realm of privacy interests.

or

The *Moore* court based its decision on contractual theories. However, the underlying principle condemning misappropriation of a person's name or picture has been recognized by other jurisdictions as being within the realm of privacy interests.

Fragment that is two dependent clauses

INCORRECT There is no need to discuss the element of consideration or even special consideration. *Because, in this state, words of reassurance are not recognized as promises, which are required to complete the bargained-for exchange.*

CORRECT There is no need to discuss the element of consideration or even special consideration because, in this state, words of reassurance are not recognized as promises, which are required to complete the bargained-for exchange.

Changing the punctuation is the most common way to correct fragments that are dependent clauses. By changing the punctuation, you attach the dependent clause to the sentence it belongs with. Another way to correct a dependent clause fragment is to delete the word that makes the clause dependent. If you use this method, be certain that the relationships of your ideas remain clear (see the second correction of the *Moore* example, where the word *however* is added to keep the idea of contrast when the word *although* is deleted).

EXERCISES

Some of the groups of sentences below include sentence fragments, and some do not. If there is a fragment, underline it and then correct it. Some of the fragments are simple fragments and some are dependent clauses.

a. The statute itself can be attacked as archaic and nonfunctional. No person has ever been charged with adultery for the 285 years that the statute has been in effect. Even though ample opportunity has existed for the state to prosecute admitted adulterers after divorce proceedings. In addition, the fact that the legislature has allowed the $10 fine to remain as the prescribed punishment indicates that the state does not take the statute seriously.

b. Courts are, in fact, going beyond enforcing only express contracts. Many states are finding that a party may recover in other ways. For example, by implied-in-fact contracts, which look at the intent of the parties, or by implied-in-law contracts, which courts sometimes rely on to prevent unjust enrichment. There is no reason to believe that Maryland, in 1980, will not follow the trend.

c. If the court declares Reston's promise unenforceable due to the nature of his relationship with Miller, Reston will retain all the possessions that he accumulated during their cohabitation. A house in Roland Park, two Mercedes Benz automobiles, a 60-foot yacht, a condominium at Hilton Head and one at Aspen, and 10 percent of Roberto Duran, all in his name only. Even though Miller provided the financial and domestic support that allowed Reston to pursue the medical career that enabled him to acquire these possessions. This would create an injustice far outweighing the court's interest in protecting the sanctity of marriage.

d. However, most courts are willing to enforce express agreements if part of the consideration is some kind of financial contribution. For example, in

Tyranski, the court was persuaded by evidence that the plaintiff had contributed $10,000 toward the house that they agreed the defendant would convey to her. Similarly, the plaintiff in *McHenry* contributed her income, personal property, savings, and unemployment benefits.

e. If the courts in Maryland follow the majority of the states that so far have been faced with this issue, Tracy should be able to recover her share of the jointly accumulated property. Maryland cases have established grounds for such recovery. By espousing the doctrine of recovery as long as the contract is not based solely on the grounds of the meretricious relationship. The courts may separate the sexual agreement from the property agreement, and there is no legislation that would bar recovery.

c. *Putting Only Part of a Verb in the Main Clause*

Sentences with partial verbs are also fragments. Here are two examples.

Example 1

INCORRECT   The invasion of the appellant's right to privacy *based* upon the theory that the appellee's acts were an unreasonable intrusion into the appellant's private affairs and that the dissemination of this information to All-Risk Insurance Company constituted public disclosure of private facts.

CORRECT   The invasion of the appellant's right to privacy *is based* upon the theory that the appellee's acts were an unreasonable intrusion into the appellant's private affairs and that the dissemination of this information to All-Risk Insurance Company constituted public disclosure of private facts.

Example 2

INCORRECT   The *Kalicki* court *adhering* to the doctrine of disfavoring perpetuities when it held that the tenant would only be allowed one renewal because the language in the lease did not clearly indicate an intention to create a perpetuity.

CORRECT   The *Kalicki* court *was adhering* to the doctrine of disfavoring perpetuities when it held that the tenant would only be allowed one renewal because the language in the lease did not clearly indicate an intention to create a perpetuity.

or

The *Kalicki* court *adhered* to the doctrine of disfavoring perpetuities when it held that the tenant would only be allowed one renewal because the language in the lease did not clearly indicate an intention to create a perpetuity.

Both of these examples contain dependent clauses, but the dependent clauses are not problems because they are not standing alone. The problem in both examples is that the verb of the core (the independent clause) is incomplete.

In the first example, the verb is passive but the word that directs the action back to the subject is missing. You must add the word (*is*) that directs the action back to the subject. (For additional information on passives, see pages 300 to 301.)

The second example involves an *-ing* verb form instead of a passive structure, but the principle is the same. An *-ing* verb form cannot stand alone as the verb in an independent clause. You must also have a form of the verb *to be* (is, are, was, were). This sentence is incomplete:

> A woman trying to recover unpaid wages from her deceased employer's estate.

This sentence is complete:

> A woman was trying to recover unpaid wages from her deceased employer's estate.

Fragments caused by partial verbs are likely to appear in legal writing because it is complex writing that often uses the passive voice and other multi-word verb forms such as the *-ing* verb form (which is called the progressive). The most common way to correct these fragments is either to add the words that are missing from the verb (*is, was*) or to change the form of the verb (*adhering* to *adhered* or *being* to *is* or *was*).

A second way to correct fragments caused by partial verbs is to add information onto the sentence.

> FRAGMENT: The woman locked in the closet.
> CORRECTED: The woman locked in the closet *was a judge.*

Only use this method, however, when the fragment is short and you have new information to add.

EXERCISES

Some of the groups of sentences below include sentence fragments, and some do not. When you see a fragment, underline it and then correct it either by changing the punctuation or by rewriting it as a complete sentence. If every sentence in the group is a complete sentence, place a C (for *correct*) in front of the letter.

a. The doctor was negligent in that he subjected you to an unreasonable risk of harm. The doctor assured you that the operation would work, but it did not. Therefore, subjecting you to the unreasonable risk of having a third child that you had specifically told the doctor you did not want.

b. Your conversation with Dr. Cooper did not create an enforceable agreement. There is no need to discuss the element of consideration or even special consideration. Because, in this state, words of reassurance are not recognized as promises, which are required to complete the bargained-for exchange.

c. It could be argued that the attractive nuisance doctrine does not apply because the homeowner was in compliance with the local building code requirements for maintaining an artificial structure in his backyard. That the homeowner is released from liability for injuries caused to trespassing minors because he had taken all necessary precautionary measures by erecting a six-foot fence.

d. The general rule is in our favor. While the parents of the child appear to have a valid cause of action. It is important to take into consideration the fact that their case depends on the application of the doctrine of attractive nuisance. This doctrine reflects the traditional social interest in the safety and welfare of children.

e. In *Vargas,* the recipients were at least notified that their case workers would explain the reasons for the reduction or termination of benefits. In the present case, those receiving notice believed that they knew the reason that their benefits had been terminated when, in fact, they knew only part of the reason. The "reduction of funding" reason may indeed have misled many recipients.

f. The argument against this interpretation based on the recent Equal Rights Amendment, Md. Const. Declar. of Rights Art. 46 (1972) (hereafter ERA), which states that "Equality of rights under the law shall not be abridged or denied because of sex." Because of this law, both parents are responsible for child support.

g. The contract in *McCall,* though, can be distinguished from the contract between Pat and Tracy. In the *McCall* case, Frampton requested that McCall leave her husband and her employment and live with him. In *McCall,* then, part of the actual consideration was to commit adultery.

3. Garbled Sentences

When the meaning of a sentence is unclear because the structure of the sentence is unclear, the sentence is garbled. We distinguish garbled sentences from sentence fragments in this way: A sentence fragment is missing a necessary element; it is incomplete. In a garbled sentence, all the parts are there, but they do not form a coherent whole. We distinguish garbled sentences from problems with subject/verb agreement in this way: To correct a problem in subject/verb agreement, you usually only need to adjust the verb. To correct a garbled sentence, you probably need to rewrite, or rethink, the entire sentence.

Sentences can become garbled in many ways, but this section will only deal with two of the more common ways:

1. When there are tangled lists and misplaced modifiers (sentences that become garbled or contain certain illogical structures because the writer tries to put too much into the sentence too quickly).
2. When there are mismatched beginnings and endings (sentences that become garbled because the writer begins the sentence with one kind of structure and ends it with another).

a. *Problems with Tangled Lists and Misplaced Modifiers*

The writer of the following sentence has lost control of it in the process of adding items to the list.

> His conviction that he can successfully perform the operation, his understanding of what you wanted, and your understanding of his understanding, its implications and results are very clear.

The result is a garbled sentence that makes little sense. What, for example, is supposed to be "very clear"? his conviction? his understanding? its implications? implications of what?

Here, using a little more information, are two possible rewrites of the garbled sentence.

REWRITE A   It is clear that the doctor believed he could successfully perform the operation, that he understood you wanted to be sterile, and that you knew he understood what you wanted. The implications and results of this situation are also clear.

REWRITE B   Three facts are clear: (1) the doctor was convinced that he could successfully perform the operation, (2) he understood that you wanted to be sterile, and (3) you knew that he understood what you wanted.

In both rewrites, the original main verb and complement (*is clear*) have been

moved to the front of the sentence. Each sentence now begins with the core
($S = LV = C$). Beginning with the core has two advantages:

1. It provides the reader with a context for the details that follow and
2. It keeps the subject and verb together.

Both rewrites also signal the beginning of each item in the list. Rewrite A uses
the word *that* to signal a new item and Rewrite B uses numbers. In Rewrite A
we have made the confusing last part of the original sentence into a separate
sentence. Doing so shows that it is an empty sentence. What does it mean? In
Rewrite B we have dropped this part of the original sentence entirely.

    Here is another example of a garbled sentence. In this case, however, only
part of the sentence is garbled (the dependent *if* clause):

> If the birth of this child aggravated the condition substantially and the
> pregnancy was the direct result of the breach coupled with the ability
> to document and measure either in days lost from work or a new
> injury, the court may grant you compensation.

The writer of this sentence has also lost control in the process of adding items
to a list. The items in this case are conditions. Here are three possible rewrites
of this sentence. The first two are longer than the original and the last one is
slightly shorter than the original.

REWRITE A   The court may grant you compensation *if you can prove
that* the pregnancy was the direct result of the breach, *that*
the birth of this child substantially aggravated your back
condition, *and that* you either lost days from work or developed a new injury as a result of the pregnancy and birth.

REWRITE B   The court may grant you compensation for your back injury *if* the pregnancy was the direct result of the breach *and
if* the birth of this child substantially aggravated your back
condition. *However,* you must be able to document and
measure your losses either in terms of days you lost from
work or in terms of the new injury you developed.

REWRITE C   *If* the pregnancy was the direct result of the breach *and if*
the birth of this child substantially aggravated your back
condition, *then* the court may grant you compensation, *but*
you must be able to document and measure your losses.

Because the meaning was unclear in the original, each rewrite is based on a
slightly different interpretation of the original. Although the meaning varies

from rewrite to rewrite, each version has a clear, untangled structure. In Rewrite A, we provided structure by

1. Putting the main clause first
2. Putting the core of the dependent (if) clause at the beginning of the clause
3. Making the three conditions modifiers to the dependent (if) clause
4. Giving the three conditions parallel structures, introduced by *that*

In Rewrite B, we provided structure by

1. Putting the main clause first
2. Giving even more context (modifying the main clause with the phrase "for your back injury")
3. Putting the two main conditions in parallel clauses, introduced by *if*
4. Breaking the long sentence into two sentences
5. Signaling the relationships between the sentences by using *however*

In Rewrite C, we provided structure by

1. Making the sentence an *if, then* sentence
2. Putting the two main conditions in parallel clauses introduced by *if*
3. Signaling the relationships among the ideas in the sentence by using *then, but*

Any one of these rewrites is better than the original. Reading the original, you cannot immediately tell that the clause beginning *the pregnancy* is a second *if* clause, because the *if* is not stated. The phrase beginning *coupled with* is unclear because you don't immediately know what it modifies. The word *either* is ambiguous because the two choices are not written with parallel structures. Because the main idea comes at the very end of the sentence, you don't have any context to help you understand the *if* clauses. You may have asked yourself, "What is this all about?" And then, after reading the end of the sentence, you may have had to go back to the beginning to reread the first part.

Here is a third example of a garbled sentence. In this sentence, the problem is that the last phrase is in the wrong place.

> I have rejected the idea of bringing a third cause of action in negligence since this must be established by showing departure from a recognized standard practice *by medical testimony.*

The reader tries to link *by medical testimony* to *a recognized standard practice.* But that's not where the phrase fits, so the reader gets confused. The easiest way to correct this problem is to move the phrase.

REWRITE A   I have rejected the idea of bringing a third cause of action in negligence since this must be established *by medical testimony* showing departure from a recognized standard practice.

Moving the phrase so that it is next to the word it modifies (*established*) does correct the problem of ending the sentence illogically. However, the sentence can be improved if other changes are made.

REWRITE B   I have rejected the idea of bringing a third cause of action in negligence since *negligence* must be established by medical testimony *that shows the doctor departed* from a recognized standard *of* practice.

This version is longer than version A because this improved version includes words that make the relationship among the pieces clearer.

EXERCISES

Each of these sentences is difficult to understand because the writer lost control in adding information. Rewrite each sentence so that your interpretation of its meaning is clear. You may move parts of a sentence around, add words, repeat words to mark the beginning of each item in a series, change nouns to verbs, divide the sentence into two or more sentences, and make other changes.

a. In the past judges have dismissed such "past conversations" as evidence on the ground of hearsay.
b. In light of this factor, we must pursue your case by establishing that an express contract was made between you and Doctor Cooper in that Doctor Cooper promised you the desired result of infertility to the effect that, without such a promise, you would never have consented to the operation in the first place in return for any consideration (or payment) to him therefor.
c. Also the plaintiff should recover a substantial amount of money for the support of the child based on the doctrine of reliance.
d. This standard of care is higher than that of the reasonable, prudent person and it requires doctors to use the presumed skill and knowledge that is possessed by the profession and a standard of good practice in the community.
e. The harm caused was not limited to physical and mental suffering but also the incurring of financial responsibilities that you were unable to afford, and the doctor knew of when he promised certain results.

f. The doctrine of reliance applies in this instance which states that the courts can award damages to the plaintiff for the purpose of undoing the harm which his reliance on the defendants caused him.

g. One who engages in a business, occupation, or profession must exercise the requisite degree of learning, skill, and ability of that calling with reasonable and ordinary care.

h. As a result of our conversation of November 5, 1982, concerning the feasibility of commencing a lawsuit against Dr. Cooper for your recovery of damages sustained from his failure to perform a successful sterilization operation as requested and expected by you on January 30, 1978, which resulted in the unanticipated birth of your third child, I have compiled and incorporated in this letter both background information related to decisions of cases similar to your situation and have charted a basis for action to recover as a result of Dr. Cooper's failure to successfully perform your requested surgical operation.

b. *Problems with Mismatched Beginnings and Endings*

The second common way that a sentence becomes garbled is when a writer begins a sentence with one structure and ends it with another. Here is one example.

> Also considering your fear of another pregnancy because of back problems aggravated by the delivery of your second child, puts the statements by the doctor firmly into the category of a warranty of the successful performance of a tubal ligation.

The front half of the sentence is a participial phrase (*considering* . . .). If you begin a sentence with a participial phrase (a type of dependent clause), the subject of the core must be the same as the subject of the participial phrase. The last half of the sentence (*puts the statement* . . .) assumes a subject that is not present. The core is incomplete. One way to rewrite this garbled sentence is to complete each half.

REWRITE A   Also considering your fear of another pregnancy because of back problems aggravated by the delivery of your second child, *you would have insisted on assurances that the operation would be successful. Your insistence and the doctor's responses* put his statements firmly into the category of a warranty of the successful performance of a tubal ligation.

Although this rewrite solves the problem of the mismatched parts, it is not as clear as it could be. A better solution would be to rewrite the sentence as the story it, in fact, tells.

REWRITE B   Because of back problems aggravated by the delivery of your second child, *you feared another pregnancy.* Given this fear, *you insisted on assurances* that the tubal ligation would be successful. The doctor's *responses,* which led you to agree to surgery, *constituted a warranty* of his successful performance of a tubal ligation.

Dividing a garbled sentence into two or more sentences is often an effective solution.

Sometimes, the only indication of a problem in a sentence is that the writer has repeated the subject unnecessarily. In this example, the italicized *it* is incorrect.

As in *Adams* and in *Benton,* this broad reason, while it may not allow Mrs. Clark to decide conclusively whether she should appeal for a fair hearing, *it* does serve its limited constitutional purpose by providing her with notice of the advance claim against her and by affording her an opportunity to present her objections at an evidentiary hearing.

This sentence has the structure of the sentence

My sister she came yesterday.

This sentence could be corrected just by dropping the second subject (*it*):

REWRITE A   As in *Adams* and in *Benton,* this *broad reason,* while it may not allow Mrs. Clark to decide conclusively whether she should appeal for a fair hearing, *does serve its* limited constitutional *purpose* by providing her with notice of the advance claim against her and by affording her an opportunity to present her objections at an evidentiary hearing.

However, this change still leaves one very long sentence. Dividing the information into two sentences would make the point clearer.

REWRITE B   The *broad reason* given in this case, as in *Adams* and in *Benton, may not allow Mrs. Clark* to decide conclusively whether she should appeal for a fair hearing. The *broad reason does,* however, *serve its* limited constitutional *purpose* by providing her with notice of the advance claim against her and by affording her an opportunity to present her objections at an evidentiary hearing.

In this rewrite the second half of the sentence is almost unchanged, but it is a separate sentence. The only changes are (1) the added word *however* to signal the relationship between the two sentences and (2) the use of the noun (*broad reason*) in place of the pronoun *it*.

The sentence can also be improved even if you want to keep it as one sentence. Rewrite C illustrates the positive effect of keeping the necessary elements of the core together, choosing an appropriate word (*although*) to introduce the modifier, and dropping the reference to other cases.

REWRITE C   Although the broad reason may not allow Mrs. Clark to decide conclusively whether she should appeal for a fair hearing, the *broad reason does serve its* limited constitutional *purpose* by providing her with notice of the advance claim against her and by affording her an opportunity to present her objections at an evidentiary hearing.

From these sample rewrites, you can see that garbled sentences with mismatched halves can be rewritten in many ways. Some methods simply correct the error (Rewrite A), and some make the sentences more comprehensible (Rewrites B and C).

Here is a shorter sentence that has mismatched halves.

If given the appropriate information you may have chosen another avenue to solve your problem, but you were denied this choice by Dr. Cooper.

Because of errors in punctuation in the first half of the sentence, the reader expects all of the *if* clause to modify the second part. In fact, the second half is a second independent clause. The sentence should read

REWRITE A   If given the appropriate information, you may have chosen another avenue to solve your problem; but you were denied this choice by Dr. Cooper.

The mismatched second half is really a second sentence.

REWRITE B   If given the appropriate information, you may have chosen another avenue to solve your problem. However, you were denied this choice by Dr. Cooper.

The first sentence in Rewrite B is still difficult to understand. The combination of words, *if given,* is unclear. The reader does not know who the subject of *given* is.

REWRITE C   If you had been given the appropriate information, you might have chosen another avenue to solve your problem. However, you were denied this choice by Dr. Cooper.

You could make the sentences even clearer (as either one or two sentences) by using the active voice.

REWRITE D   If Dr. Cooper had given you the appropriate information, *you might have chosen* another *method* of solving your problem, but *he denied you this choice.*

Rewrite D improves the sentence by using the active voice (*Dr. Cooper had given* and *he denied you*) to emphasize the doctor's responsibility. Substituting the word *method* for *avenue* also improves the sentence. (*Avenue* is a metaphor for *method* and therefore harder to understand.)

Just as the halves of the entire sentence can be mismatched, so the halves of a dependent clause can be mismatched. Here is an example.

> The *Steffes* court evaluated the equities involved and determined that in allowing the defendant to prevail would be allowing him to be unjustly enriched.

The overall structure of this sentence is sound.

court	evaluated	*equities*	and	determined	*that*
S	V	O		V	O

The problem is that the halves within the dependent clause (the *that* clause) are mismatched.

> in allowing . . .   would be allowing . . .

This mismatch can be corrected by either changing the first half of the clause or changing the last half.

REWRITE A   The *Steffes* court evaluated the equities involved and determined that *allowing* the defendant to prevail *would be allowing* him to be unjustly enriched.

REWRITE B   The *Steffes* court evaluated the equities involved and determined that *in allowing* the defendant to prevail, *it would be allowing him* to be unjustly enriched.

EXERCISES

Each of these passages contains at least one garbled sentence. Some sentences have only one kind of problem and some have several. The problems include mismatched beginnings and illogical structures. Rewrite each garbled sentence so that your interpretation of its meaning is clear. You may move parts of the sentence around, add words, delete words, repeat words, change nouns to verbs, divide the sentence into two or more sentences, and make other changes.

a. If our client should care to raise a contention that the "option to renew" which he was granted in the pre-1980 telephone conversation can be offered as parol evidence to allow him to renew once more would almost definitely be ineffective.

b. Remembering that fixture law is interpreted in favor of the tenant in landlord-tenant situations, this should help our argument of the carpet remaining the personal property of Brooks.

c. Maryland law provides no precedent to guide the courts in deciding this issue. But in other jurisdictions, cases presenting the question of determining what renewals will be allowed when a lease presents options or covenants for renewal, and no specific number of renewals is expressed, as in the Brooks lease, it has been held that provisions or covenants of renewal will allow only one renewal in addition to the original term.

d. In the 1978 case under discussion, that no matter how firmly attached to the realty an object is, if it was placed on the property by the tenant for the purpose of his business, it is a trade fixture and remains the property of the tenant.

e. The notice requirements of *Goldberg* were further defined in *Vargas v. Trainor,* 508 F.2d 485 (7th Cir. 1974). Where the court held that the reasons for termination must be placed in the notice itself and the notice, which required a recipient to meet with a case worker in order to discover the reasons for termination and to decide whether to appeal, was not adequate.

f. Whether homemaker services were terminated solely due to a reduction in funding or whether it was also determined that some recipients were less needy than others, the social service agencies that deal with these recipients directly are in the best position to make these decisions.

g. Furthermore, based on your telephone conversation with Dr. Cooper in July, during which he further assured you that you could not be pregnant gives rise to an action of malpractice because if he had properly treated and cared for you, a duty which he owed you, your unwanted pregnancy could have been terminated by alternative means in sufficient time.

h. This letter is intended to give you some information about how the courts in Massachusetts generally decide on cases similar to yours and that your chances of recovering damages to this extent are good but not definite.

i. As far as any information obtained by Metro from neighbors and Brandon's ex-wife, it would seem that as a matter of general knowledge by the public, although the facts regarding Brandon's illness are not something common to everyday conversation, they were not matters that were considered private and under the exclusive control of Brandon so as to be protected from reasonable inquiry and disclosure in the manner in which they were disclosed.

4. Summary

1. The verb must match the subject in number. Problems are created by:
   - Subject and verb being separated
   - The number of the subject being unclear
2. Sentences must be complete:
   - Include all necessary elements
   - Don't let a dependent clause stand alone
   - Be sure the verb is complete
3. Be sure sentences are clear. Garbled sentences are caused by:
   - Problems with tangled lists and misplaced modifiers
   - Problems with mismatched beginnings and endings

Index